McGill-Queen's/Beaverbrook Canadian Foundation Studies in Art History

MARTHA LANGFORD AND SANDRA PAIKOWSKY, series editors

Recognizing the need for a better understanding of Canada's artistic culture both at home and abroad, the Beaverbrook Canadian Foundation, through its generous support, makes possible the publication of innovative books that advance our understanding of Canadian art and Canada's visual and material culture. This series supports and stimulates such scholarship through the publication of original and rigorous peer-reviewed books that make significant contributions to the subject. We welcome submissions from Canadian and international scholars for book-length projects on historical and contemporary Canadian art and visual and material culture, including Native and Inuit art, architecture, photography, craft, design, and museum studies. Studies by Canadian scholars on non-Canadian themes will also be considered.

The Practice of Her Profession
Florence Carlyle, Canadian Painter in the Age of Impressionism
Susan Butlin

Bringing Art to Life
A Biography of Alan Jarvis
Andrew Horrall

Picturing the Land
Narrating Territories in Canadian Landscape Art, 1500 to 1950
Marylin J. McKay

The Cultural Work of Photography in Canada
Edited by Carol Payne and Andrea Kunard

Newfoundland Modern
Architecture in the Smallwood Years, 1949–1972
Robert Mellin

The *Codex Canadensis* and the Writings of Louis Nicolas
The Natural History of the New World, Histoire Naturelle des Indes Occidentales
Edited and with an introduction by François-Marc Gagnon, translation by Nancy Senior, modernization by Réal Ouellet

Museum Pieces
Toward the Indigenization of Canadian Museums
Ruth B. Phillips

The Allied Arts
Architecture and Craft in Postwar Canada
Sandra Alfoldy

THE ALLIEDARTS

ARCHITECTURE AND CRAFT IN POSTWAR CANADA

SANDRA ALFOLDY

McGILL-QUEEN'S UNIVERSITY PRESS

Montreal & Kingston • London • Ithaca

© McGill-Queen's University Press 2012

ISBN 978-0-7735-3960-0 (cloth)
ISBN 978-0-7735-4003-3 (paper)

Legal deposit first quarter 2012
Bibliothèque nationale du Québec

Printed in Canada on acid-free paper

This book has been published with the help of a grant from the Canadian Federation for the Humanities and Social Sciences, through the Aid to Scholarly Publications Program, using funds provided by the Social Sciences and Humanities Research Council of Canada.

McGill-Queen's University Press acknowledges the support of the Canada Council for the Arts for our publishing program. We also acknowledge the financial support of the Government of Canada through the Canada Book Fund for our publishing activities.

Library and Archives Canada Cataloguing in Publication

Alfoldy, Sandra, 1969–
The allied arts : architecture and craft in postwar Canada / Sandra Alfoldy.

(McGill-Queen's/Beaverbrook Canadian Foundation Studies in art history)
Includes bibliographical references and index.

ISBN 978-0-7735-3960-0 (bound)
ISBN 978-0-7735-4003-3 (pbk)

1. Architecture–Canada–History–20th century.
2. Handicraft–Canada–History–20th century.
3. Decorative arts–Canada–History–20th century.
I. Title. II. Series: McGill-Queen's/Beaverbrook Canadian Foundation studies in art history

NA745.A44 2012
720.971
C2011-907181-9

This book was designed and typeset by studio oneonone in Sabon 10/14.5

Frontispiece
Helen Frances Gregor, "Lifescape No. 1: John Deutsch," wool, 1976.

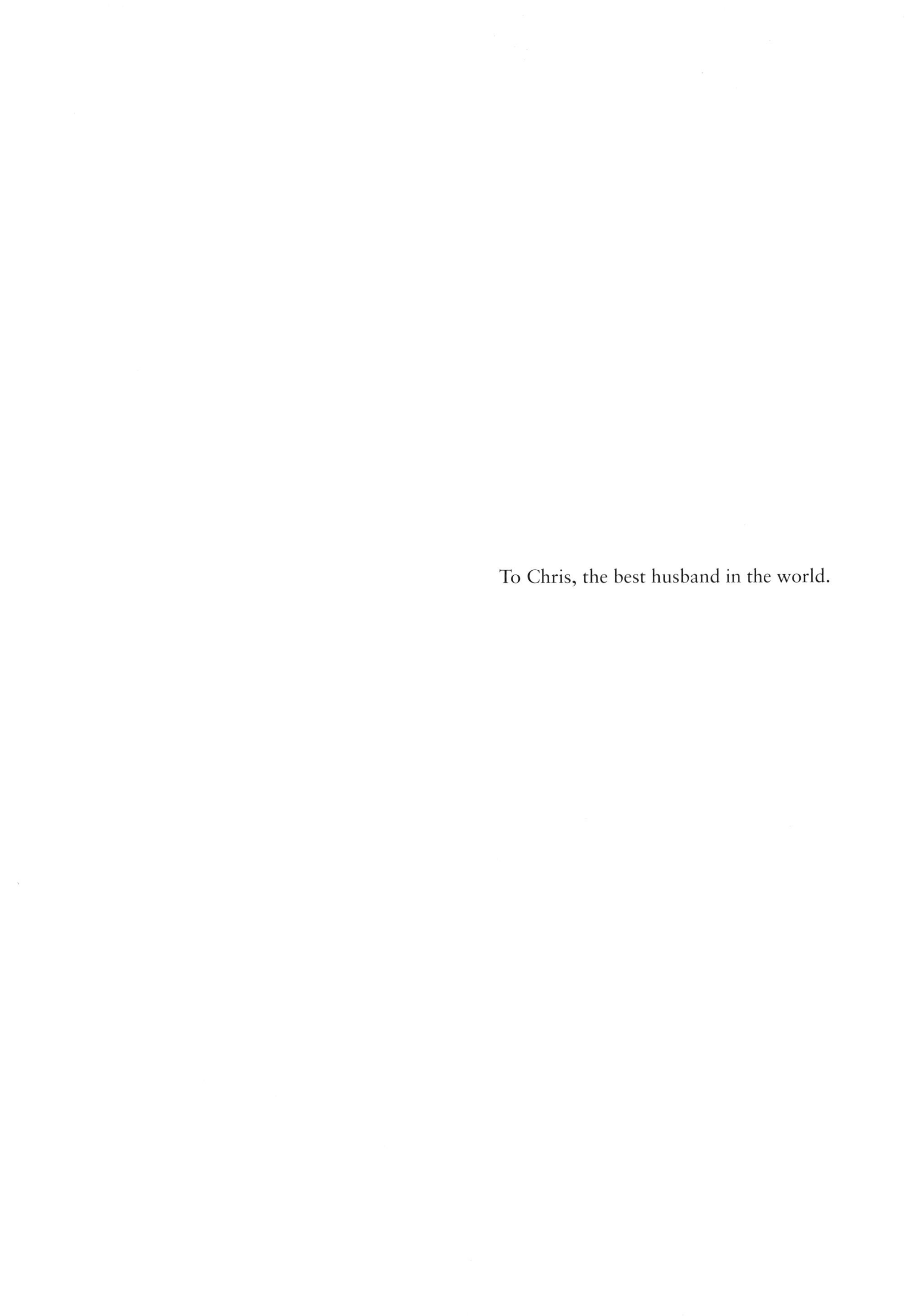

To Chris, the best husband in the world.

Plate 1
Installation of Thor Hansen's "Canadiana," interior design, 1954.

CONTENTS

Plate 2
Greg Payce, "SSSSSSSSSSSSSSSS," bronze, 2003.

The research for this book required the efforts of many individuals, from my husband and sons and mom and dad, all of whom patiently drove back and forth across the country while I tracked down artworks, to my graduate students who helped me compile and record my findings. Thank you to my wonderful husband, Christopher, my inspiring mom and dad, Elaine and Andy Alfoldy, and my precious angels, Viktor and Nicholas. I could not have written *The Allied Arts* without the help of my remarkable graduate students and research assistants: Marlene Guenther, who worked tirelessly securing permissions for the images, as well as MacKenzie Frere, Dorrie Millerson, Stephanie Rozene, Krista Bennett, Catherine Allan, and Veronika Horlik.

The generosity of the artists I met through my research must be acknowledged, as they shared so much with me and helped to shape the book. The Royal Architectural Institute of Canada has been an invaluable resource, and I am indebted to them for being so generous in providing me with primary research materials. I am also thankful to my colleagues at NSCAD University for supporting my research, in particular Dr Kenn Honeychurch, who during his tenure as vice-president academic made research a priority. Thanks to Jonathan Crago, who has been a patient and insightful editor. Finally, I am deeply grateful to the Social Sciences and Humanities Research Council of Canada, which made this all possible.

Plate 3
Luke Lindoe, "Petroglyph Mural," etched concrete, 1966–67.

PLATES

Frontispiece: Helen Frances Gregor, "Lifescape No. 1: John Deutsch," wool, 1976. John Deutsch University Centre, Queen's University, Kingston, Ontario. Photo courtesy of the author.

1 Installation of Thor Hansen's "Canadiana," interior design, 1954. British-American Oil Company head office, Bay Street, Toronto. Photo courtesy of the Government of Ontario Art Collection, Archives of Ontario.

2 Greg Payce, "SSSSSSSSSSSSSSSS," bronze, 2003. Calgary International Airport. Photo courtesy of the author.

3 Luke Lindoe, "Petroglyph Mural," etched concrete, 1966–67. Royal Alberta Museum (Provincial Museum of Alberta), Edmonton. Photo courtesy of the author.

4 Jordi Bonet, "The End of Time," ceramic mural, 1968. Commissioned by the Government of Ontario for the MacDonald Block, Toronto. Photo courtesy of the Government of Ontario Art Collection, Archives of Ontario.

5 The Sturdy Stone Centre, Saskatoon, with exterior scaffolding and completed Jack Sures mural, 1979. Photo courtesy of Jack Sures.

6 Worker installing the Sturdy Stone Centre mural, 1979. Photo courtesy of Jack Sures.

7 Finishing a single stoneware tile (unfired) for the Sturdy Stone Centre, 1977–79. Photo courtesy of Jack Sures.

8 Arthur Erickson, interior, Museum of Anthropology, 1976. University of British Columbia, Vancouver. Photo by Goh Iromoto, courtesy of the UBC Museum of Anthropology, Vancouver.

Plate 4
Jordi Bonet, "The End of Time,"
ceramic mural, 1968.

Plate 5
The Sturdy Stone Centre, Saskatoon, with exterior
scaffolding and completed Jack Sures mural, 1979.

Plate 6
Worker installing the Sturdy
Stone Centre mural, 1979.

Plate 7
Finishing a single stoneware
tile (unfired) for the Sturdy
Stone Centre, 1977–79.

Plate 8
Arthur Erickson, interior, Museum of Anthropology,
1976. University of British Columbia, Vancouver.

Plate 9
R. Eleanor Milne, "Set 1: The First Inhabitants of the North American
Continent," History of Canada Frieze, detail, high-relief carved Indiana
limestone. House of Commons Lobby, Parliament Buildings, Ottawa.

Plate 10
Rory MacDonald, "Curbworks," curb patch, glazed earthenware, 2003.

Plate 11
Barbara Peterson, "Famous Five," detail of tea cup with rubbed handle, 1999.

THE ALLIEDARTS

1 THE ALLIED ARTS

We have much to give each other in the mutual enrichment of our various professions through working projects. What is of the utmost importance is that the architect and artist "find" each other in every sense.
Anita Aarons[1]

The Allied Arts, as referred to here, represent the intersection of architecture and craft. As the term suggests, rather than being considered wholly separate fields (architecture a profession or a fine art, and craft an occupation or creation of a lower order), architecture and craft are ideally closely linked as Allied Arts in the interior spaces and exterior construction of many buildings. In this chapter I briefly trace the relationship between architecture and craft, from the Greek vision of *architekton* to the enduring Arts and Crafts philosophies of integrated art and architecture. At the same time, I highlight important Canadian moments that have reflected the reality of the schisms and the parallels between the fields, and draw attention to the efforts of the Royal Architectural Institute of Canada (RAIC) to unite the Allied Arts, the professionalization of interior design, and Quebec's leading role in craft education. Together, these examples illustrate the reasons for which architecture and craft may today still be viewed as Allied Arts.

Research for this book began with the idea of architectural craft, a term referring to any large-scale public artwork that was created specifically for use inside or outside a building and employing traditional craft materials. It soon became clear that not only were there a vast number of examples of monumental craft objects present in the public arena but there were no neat and tidy boundaries that defined craft within architecture. The usual parameters of ceramics, glass, textiles, wood, and metal simply did not apply to many artworks that fluidly crossed material boundaries. Instead, the concept of the Allied Arts was better suited to this project, as it allowed for an understanding of the interplay between the historical concepts and the contemporary realities that inform the way craft is considered within architecture. I therefore found it more appropriate to use a structure of mapping the building projects, craft objects, craftspeople, and architects who came to represent instances of the successes and tensions within architectural craft. They became the basis for this book, which has extrapolated the overarching themes of material, form, scale, ornament, and identity from these specific instances. As a result, Canadian examples can speak to the global concerns of craft within architecture.

At the outset, we should note that the term "Allied Arts" has historically not been exclusively reserved for architecture and crafts. From the time of the Renaissance, when concern over manual versus intellectual skill in the arts was foregrounded, various arts were allied to raise their status; architecture, for example, was often so entangled with sculpture that artists such as Michelangelo played the roles of both architect and sculptor. Most famously, the expression *ut pictura poesis*, "as is painting so is poetry," has represented the ideal of the Allied Arts. Horace introduced this dictum, along with the idea of the "sister arts" to enhance the link between image and text.[2] The art critic and historian John Ruskin, in his 1843 book *Modern Painters*, employed Horace's principle of *ut pictura poesis* to defend the status of painting and to support his friend the painter J.M.W. Turner. To Ruskin, painting, on a par with poetry, was, as George Landow has put it, "not merely a craft or trade but a liberal art requiring mental skills capable of providing great gifts for mankind."[3] In this regard, Ruskin allied painting and poetry in opposing the prevalence of imitation that had surfaced with the Industrial Revolution, which he feared would have an impact upon the originality of artists.

In his 1797 essay "Art and Handicraft," the philosopher Johann Wolfgang von Goethe had reinforced a polarity between physical and mental labour in decrying the separation of intellectual ability from the mechanical arts (or craft and design): "Generations have succumbed to mindless imitation, false application of true experience, blind tradition, and complacent inheritance."[4] Ruskin was a significant influence in moving the discussion beyond this dualism through his efforts to raise the level of workmanship within the crafts. He, like other nineteenth-century design reformers, including A. Welby Pugin and William Morris, vehemently opposed the erosion of pride in craftsmanship that had resulted from the Industrial Revolution. Indeed, among

Ruskin's first published writings was *The Poetry of Architecture*, which appeared in *Architectural Magazine* in 1837 under the pseudonym "Kata phusin," and which addressed the growing disparity between cottage architecture and its natural surroundings.[5] To Ruskin, and later to members of the Arts and Crafts Movement, the reinstatement of good craft skills through education offered the best weapon for fighting the tyranny of poor manufacturing and design.[6]

Ruskin began lecturing on this topic in 1857 in Manchester, the seat of industry, where he presented two talks on the political economy of art titled "A Joy for Ever."[7] In these lectures he clearly allied craft with the permanence and nobility of architecture: "For there never was, nor can be, any essential beauty possessed by a work of art, which is not based on the conception of its honoured permanence, and local influence, as a part of appointed and precious furniture, either in the cathedral, the house, or the joyful thoroughfare, of nations which enter their gates with thanksgiving, and their courts with praise."[8] In March 1859, by the time Ruskin was lecturing to design students in Bradford, he had fully developed his views on the alliance between craft and architecture: "Observe, then, first – the only essential distinction between Decorative and other art is the being fitted for a fixed place; and in that place, related, either in subordination or command, to the effect of other pieces of art."[9] So intimately related were craft and architecture in Ruskin's view that he declared: "The best sculpture yet produced has been the decoration of a temple front – the best painting, the decoration of a room." Indeed, he emphasized, "There is no existing highest-order art but is decorative."[10]

William Morris, considered the father of the Arts and Crafts movement, was highly influenced by Ruskin's writings and took up his cry for unity in the arts. Harmony between architecture and all other arts became the central tenet of his design philosophy. In addition, while apprenticing at the firm of renowned Gothic Revival architect George Edmund Street in 1856, Morris was instilled with the importance of architects' understanding the potential of the full scope of materials. He learned to execute designs for a wide range of craft materials employed in Street's buildings, among which were cartoons for stained glass.[11] But after his brief architectural apprenticeship he reached the conclusion that "by no possibility could one man do [all of] it, however gifted he might be."[12] As the leading Arts and Crafts figure, he wrote extensively on his views of the relationship between architecture and craft. His address to the National Association for the Advancement of Art in 1889 encapsulates his ideals:

The very masons laying day by day their due tale of rubble and ashlar[13] may help [the architect] to fill the souls of all beholders with satisfaction, or may make his paper design a folly or a nullity. They and all the workmen engaged in the work will bring that disaster about in spite of the master's mighty genius, unless they are instinct with intelligent tradition; unless they have that tradition, whatever pretence of art there is in it will be worthless. But if they are working backed by intelligent tradition, their work is the expression of their harmonious co-operation and the pleasure which they took in it: no intelligence, even of the lowest kind, has been crushed in it, but rather subordinated and used, so that no one from the master designer downwards could say, This is my work, but every one could say truly, This is our work. Try to conceive, if you can, the mass of pleasure which the production of such a work of art would give to all concerned in making it, through years and years it may be (for such a work cannot be hurried); and when made there it is for a perennial pleasure to the citizens, to look at, to use, to care for, from day to day and year to year.[14]

The fact that the word "pleasure" occurs repeatedly throughout this text is no accident; the necessity for all levels of artistic producers to enjoy their work was embedded in one of Morris's most famous aphorisms, "Joy in Labour." In his thinking, the satisfaction of crafting an object would be visible and spiritually present in the finished work of art, from the humblest to the most grand; it would radiate out to future users, validating the care taken in the construction and handicraft. Morris was also careful to include the word "intelligent" in relation to tradition, in an effort to offset accusations such as those of Goethe that contemporary craftsmanship was simply following repetitive, blind tradition.

Ruskin and Morris's principles went on to influence generations of architects and designers, most famously Walter Gropius, director of the Bauhaus, whose impassioned plea for architects to return to the crafts was heard until the mid-1920s. In the early twentieth century, the Arts and Crafts ideals were also at play in North American architecture, particularly on the West Coast, where they inspired the "Craftsman Bungalow," a popular style of domestic architecture that offered "a sense of containment, stability and joy of place in what is often a rugged, brooding environment."[15] Architecture historian Nikolaus Pevsner traced these developments in his influential 1968 book *The Sources of Modern Architecture and Design*. Pevsner was critical, however, of Ruskin and Morris's dependence on romanticized views of the Middle Ages. Ruskin had argued that during that period art was not "divided among great men, lesser men, and little men,"[16] and while Pevsner agreed that the artistic hierarchy was unfair, he called Morris's insistence upon a joy in labour that would lead to a recognition of the importance of craft in relation to architecture and design "a strange system or theory to be guided by for a man in the mid-nineteenth century." He added that this seeming anachronism could "only be understood as a demonstration of opposition to the standard and the taste of design as it was exhibited at the Great Exhibition of London in 1851."[17] Indeed, most of the writings of Ruskin and Morris could be read as deriving from their position that industry was degrading art, craft, design, and architecture. But what cannot be underestimated is the significance of their shared view that an important way to correct the aesthetic and societal problems wrought by industry was to re-imagine the role of craft within architecture.

Architekton

There is no doubt that nineteenth-century Canadian architects and craftspeople were familiar with the philosophies of Ruskin and Morris, as their writings formed part of the curriculum at major universities and art colleges across the country, and were present in the libraries of leading Canadian architects.[18] However, despite Ruskin's strong arguments that craft and architecture be regarded as Allied Arts, the lived reality was quite different. In *From Craft to Profession: The Practice of Architecture in Nineteenth-Century America*, Mary N. Woods traces the reasons for which craft and architecture had grown apart during the period of Ruskin's writing and lecturing. The establishment of the architect as a solitary artist, as architecture became a profession in the United States between 1820 and 1860 (the antebellum period), brought increased status.[19] The new professional architect was "a designer and supervisor standing between clients who commissioned the work and artisans who constructed it."[20] The crafts became viewed as trades to support architecture, rather than part of an architect's knowledge base. Thus a different approach emerged in distinction to the long tradition stemming from Greek times when the term *architekton* meant "master carpenter."[21]

As late as the eighteenth century in the United States, Woods points out, the first architects for the earliest settlements on the East Coast had been building artisans; "gentlemen without craft training competed with these artisans only in the second half of the eighteenth century."[22] During the Gothic Revival of the nineteenth century, following the urgings of Ruskin and Pugin, future architects were encouraged to train in a complete variety of craft materials and techniques to help them better understand the close ties of their profession to craft.[23] Ruskin and Morris had turned to Medieval guild models to reinforce the idea of the architect craftsperson, an individual whose power was based upon access to materials and geographical location.[24] As the Industrial Revolution increased the international exchange of goods, however, architects were no longer restricted to using vernacular materials, and with a wider pool to draw upon, it became easier to import skilled artisans to execute their designs. In the face of expanding trade, while Ruskin and Morris's nostalgic archetype of the united architect/craftsperson sounded like a positive force to fight industrial capitalism, it remained a romanticized ideal.

Their terminology, however, persisted, appearing particularly in the annual *Guild Sourcebooks* of the late twentieth century. One of the most successful marketing enterprises for North American craftspeople, *The Guild Sourcebook of Architectural & Interior Art* was established in 1985 and is still a strong player in promoting a relationship between craft and architecture. Paraphrasing Ruskin's plea in late twentieth-century business terms, guild president and publisher Toni Fountain waxed poetic about the design revolution that she saw opening up new opportunities to "celebrate the soaring inventiveness of the human mind and the practiced skill of the human hand in creating beautiful, one-of-a-kind solutions to design problems."[25] In 1991 the guild featured an article entitled "The Personalization of Crafts" by weaver and teacher Jack Lenor Larsen, an icon of American craft. Larsen's impassioned essay encouraged architects to seek out craftspeople: "They can read plans, analyze needs and provide solutions. Models and actual-scale samples are within their grasp ... Craftsmen are, by definition, problem solvers."[26] Unfortunately, Larsen had to acknowledge that such collaborations were "still a relatively underground movement,"[27] despite the centuries-old history the term "guild" invoked.

In Canada the phrase "Allied Arts" became popular in art circles in the mid-twentieth century, particularly in the west. Alberta still maintains a number of active Allied Arts Councils, most notably the City of Calgary's Allied Arts Foundation, established in 1946 (incorporated 1954), with the mandate of protecting and growing the city's Civic Art Collection in public spaces throughout Calgary, envisioned as a "gallery without walls."[28] The most significant use of the term "Allied Arts" is found in its association with the Royal Architectural Institute of Canada from the 1950s forward.

The Allied Arts Medal

In a 1960 booklet "The Architect Looks at Public Relations," the Royal Architectural Institute of Canada stressed the need for architects to "develop a greater spirit of cooperation [and] help the press, radio and TV cover architectural activities fully and accurately." The publication noted that the granting of awards and citations "for such categories as craftsmen, draftsmen, allied professions and allied arts" would help to accomplish this task.[29] The Royal Architectural Institute had implemented a major award, the Allied Arts Medal, in 1953. In a January meeting that year, the RAIC Executive Committee moved that: "The institute recognize and honour outstanding achievement in the Arts which are allied to Architecture, such as Mural Painting, Sculpture, Decoration, Stained Glass, Industrial Design and the like, by the award of a medal to be known as the R.A.I.C. Allied Arts Medal."[30] The variety of media included for consideration was remarkably broad, and all craft materials were included. Apart from the public relations possibilities it offered, the award was intended to establish a significant high-profile relationship between artists and architects, so that "the Canadian architects in honouring their fellow artists will bring honour upon themselves."[31] To raise the prestige of the award, the Royal Architectural Institute sponsored a competition to commission a formal Allied Arts medal. Six designs were submitted through the Sculptors' Society of Canada, and the jury for the award medal consisted of five prominent members of Canada's architectural and artistic communities.[32] The winner of the commission was Montreal industrial designer and sculptor Julien Hébert, winner of the 1951 Canadian Industrial Design Competition.[33] One face of the three-inch diameter medal read "The Royal Architectural Institute of Canada – Allied Arts Medal," and the other, "Mural Painting, Sculpture, Decoration, Stained Glass, Industrial Design." Silver was chosen as the metal, "in keeping with the dignity and importance of the award."[34]

The winner of the first RAIC Allied Arts medal was Armand Filion, a respected stone sculptor from Quebec (for a full list of winners see Appendix). Considered to be a member of Quebec's religious art revival movement, Filion created stone relief sculpture in a style resembling Art Deco, and his works already graced churches, hospitals, recreation centres and other public buildings, predominantly in Montreal. In his letter of recognition to Filion on winning the first Allied Arts award, RAIC President Morris congratulated him on "the great merit of [his] work which adds embellishment to many Canadian buildings."[35] As Filion was a professor of sculpture at Montreal's École des Beaux-Arts, the Royal Architectural Institute was well aware of his influence on many emerging sculptors, and his prominence within Canada's relatively small artistic community.

The jury for the Allied Arts medal was selected from members of the RAIC Executive Committee. Each provincial architectural association was asked to submit nominations to the Executive Committee for the annual award, and various memos made clear that the selection process was to be kept "informal."[36] The Royal Architectural Institute was proud that its award was the first of its kind in North America (the American Institute of Architects introduced its fine arts medal and craftsmanship awards in June 1954),[37] and it worked hard to ensure that the Allied Arts award inspired architects and architectural associations to think in terms of the professional relationships they shared with artists. In the first few years of the award, however, the selection process caused some problems among the members of the Executive Committee. A 1954 memorandum urged the committee to place emphasis "upon some of the other allied arts" in addition to sculpture and landscape architecture, which had been awarded in the first two years. The first decade of the award demonstrates that the medal was indeed given to artists working in a wide variety of media, and the five winning sculptors even worked in diverse materials.

At a 1959 meeting of the Executive Committee another question arose: "There is an inference (however slight) that the Medal has been passed around among the various Arts, and rotated geographically, rather than strictly on a merit basis."[38] The award was granted annually at the RAIC regional meeting, which moved from region to region throughout the country. The organization was aware of the expense of flying artists to the meetings, and so they supported the idea of selecting the winning artist from the region where the yearly meeting was being planned, citing the "advantages of making awards to Artists in the area of the assembly."[39] What made the issue relatively unimportant was the fact that despite heavy promotion, not many nominations were being received for the Allied Arts medal.

During the 1950s the Executive Committee received an average of only five annual nominations to review. While this low recommendation level may have had a number of causes, correspondence from various architects and associations suggests a cynical response to the lack of artists supported through nominations. George W. Lord of the Alberta Association of Architects wrote in 1953 that he regretted being unable to suggest any nominations from his province for the Allied Arts award, for, "with the possible exception of artists who paint we have few, if any, people in this province who contribute to arts allied to architecture."[40] In 1971 Clifford Wiens, president of the Saskatchewan Association of Architects, took a pessimistic view: "Generally architects and artists do very little *together* that is outstanding. It did occur to me that 'Muzak' (canned music) has probably contributed more to the environment of contemporary architecture than any other 'art' form and I would personally make that 'tongue-in-cheek' nomination."[41]

Nominated artists were nevertheless grateful for the recognition, the publicity, and the opportunity to have their work considered in terms of its relationship to architecture. Gerald Trottier, the 1967 medal winner for his glass mosaics, and bronze and stone sculptures, wrote: "It has always been my belief that the key to the public dilemma in the face of 'Fine Art' is a greater balance between fine art and the practical arts. I consider art incorporated in our buildings not as decoration but as an integral part of the whole to be practical in nature. To be selected for the Allied Arts Medal for my work in this area gives me a great deal of pleasure and satisfaction."[42]

Business or Art? Thor Hansen and British-American Oil

Of course the lack of connection between architects and artists could be traced to the way each group was educated and their respective lack of opportunity to learn how to work collaboratively. Commercialism has also been a factor, as well as a widely felt disdain among artists for public craft commissions deemed to be at the mercy of business or industry. Nowhere was this point better illustrated than in the work of Thor Hansen, art director of the British-American Oil Company in the 1950s and 1960s. Hansen had immigrated to Canada from Denmark in 1928 and settled outside Regina, where he and his wife, Donna, had earned additional income making embroidery and needlepoint works, and hats and scarves.[43] In her 2005

Fig. 1.1
Installation of Thor Hansen's "Canadiana,"
interior design, 1954.

exhibition and catalogue *Thor Hansen: Crafting a Canadian Style*, Rachel Gotlieb recounts how this self-taught artist was forced to find clerical work at the British-American Oil Company in Regina when his craft business failed during the Great Depression. Hansen's talents were recognized, and in 1938 he was transferred to the British-American Oil Company's head office in Toronto, where he started as an artist in the Department of Advertising and Sales Promotion.[44] Passionate in his belief that craft had the power to remedy many of the world's problems, he wrote: "We could cut down the admittance to mental hospitals by 50 per cent if we could get people back to using their hands creatively as they did in former days."[45] Hansen was disgruntled by the lack of distinctly Canadian crafts: "The first fall I was here I went to Regina to find something to send home to Denmark for Christmas. I wanted to send something that would show my people at home what Canada and Canadians were like. In other words – Canadian souvenirs …

They didn't exist ... Now, I am inquisitive, so I turned everything upside-down and what did I see: 'Made in Japan,' 'Made in Germany,' 'Made in Czechoslovakia' – made everywhere else but in Canada."[46]

As an admirer of William Morris,[47] Hansen began lecturing on the importance of craft, and the idea of creating a "Canadian" craft identity, to communities across Ontario, most significantly in 1948 to the newly formed Simcoe County Artist Crafts Association. According to the Huronia Museum, after his lecture Hansen offered to create patterns for association members to produce in quilts and rugs based on the theme "Canada in Design."[48] In illustrating the story of the Huronia area (near Georgian Bay in Ontario) and its surrounding nature and wildlife, he came up with patterns for Huronia Trails, The Old Grist Mill, and very "Canadian" images such as Lumberjack, Trillium, Canada Goose, and Kitchikewana, the god of Ojibway legend who threw the 30,000 islands into Georgian Bay.[49] In 1949 British-American Oil Company vice-president, Gerald Godsoe, and his wife visited the Simcoe County Arts and Crafts Association fair. Having seen Hansen's designs, Godsoe invited the artist to create designs for the company's new headquarters being built in Toronto.[50]

Thus began Hansen's first collaboration with industry, developing what he called "the idea of decorating an industrial building with Canadian crafts."[51] British-American Oil gave Hansen free rein to combine his interests in craft, folklore, and the creation of a truly "Canadian" aesthetic with the interior designs of their buildings. Soon Hansen's designs were found in the company's buildings beyond the Toronto headquarters, and extended into fully realized interiors for the Vancouver and Montreal offices, as well as smaller decorative craft objects in their offices across the country. As Hansen recalled: "B-A has always considered its Canadian origin and heritage as an important factor in its relation with the public. When in 1949 we began to make plans for a new head office building, W.K. Whiteford wanted some visual evidence of our strong Canadian ties incorporated in the interior decoration of the building."[52] Gotlieb argues that Hansen was "in an enviable position to implement his ideas,"[53] thanks to the scale of British-American Oil's investment in a unified "Canadiana" theme throughout all its buildings. She notes how Hansen's craft aesthetic at first seemed at odds with the "gleaming glass and concrete" eight-storey modernist building on the corner of College and Bay by the architectural firm Page and Steel.[54] However, the impact of Hansen's "Canadiana" craft theme throughout the building was immediately popular with the public and the press (fig. 1.1). As Gotlieb recounts:

Hansen selected a colour scheme of "cherry, terra cotta, olive-beige and purplish Chocolate" to capture "the essence of Canada in the autumn." Canadian artisans adapted his designs to everything from woodcarvings to wall murals, and even drapery. Leading metalsmiths Nancy Meek Pocock and her husband John Pocock hand-pierced floral patterns of Indian pipe and skunk cabbage in 24 copper radiator grills for the president's office. Archibald Chisholm, of the T. Eaton Company, built the boardroom table, reception furniture and president's desk … The hooked rug *Geese in Flight*, also known as *Sunridge*, hung in the reception area and it would become Hansen's signature design. Inspired by the Georgian Bay region, Hansen created a dynamic composition depicting flying geese in a curvilinear landscape of trees, horizon and clouds. Cheticamp Island [sic] craftspeople in Nova Scotia hooked *Sunridge* for both Toronto and Ottawa offices, and A.B. Caya of Kitchener issued the design as a printed fabric for the residential market.[55]

Thousands of Canadians came to visit the British-American Oil Company's head office in Toronto to take a look at Hansen's heavily promoted vision of "Canadiana." As Hansen proudly wrote in 1958: "The idea caught on in the imagination of the public … I doubt that any other building in Canada has ever received as much publicity. Scores of people asked permission to come and see the décor of the building."[56] Soon he was travelling the country to endorse his unifying vision for Canadian interior design. When the Vancouver office opened in 1954 he followed up its success by delivering lectures to sixty-one groups and societies in British Columbia,[57] moving on to lecture throughout Quebec when the Montreal building opened. Hansen and his corporate sponsor were recognized for their vision of the Allied Arts in 1954 at the annual conference of the American Public Relations Association by their award for corporate relations, the first time that award had been given to a Canadian firm.[58] To Hansen, this acknowledgment proved he had succeeded in uniting architecture and craft, with the result that "our Canadiana program has been accepted and recommended by people everywhere."[59] After speaking to over 45,000 Canadians between 1948 and 1954[60] (Gotlieb's research indicates that Hansen gave more than a thousand lectures), Hansen was invited to lecture at Harvard University's Graduate School of Business Administration, a highlight in his career as a public lecturer.

But accolades were not unanimous. Perhaps it was because of the overt commercial support for his designs, their tremendous popularity, or their obvious links to the decorative impulses of the Arts and Crafts Movement, but the Canadian art scene was not supportive of Thor Hansen. His work ran contrary to the trend toward modern building designs of the International Style, which, although slow in taking hold in Canada, was by then being used in most large architecture projects. As architectural historian Harold Kalman observed: "In Canada the International Style did not reach its full flowering until the 1950s and 1960s."[61] Hansen's ornamental interiors must have appeared retrograde to architects and artists fully committed to a simplified aesthetic. Although the esteemed Canadian artist Lawren Harris personally wrote to Hansen about the Vancouver office, stating "the whole scheme looks good to me and I congratulate you on the result,"[62] Hansen's work received little or no coverage in Canada's leading art magazines. An image of the mural in the foyer of the British-American Oil office in Toronto "executed" by Art Thorne, but obviously designed by Thor Hansen, was reproduced in *Canadian Art* magazine in 1961, without any mention of Hansen.[63] No articles on his interiors were published in the *Journal* of the Royal Architectural Institute of Canada, and most significantly, Hansen's work was not collected by any major art galleries or museums.

Even Lawren Harris's praise needs to be qualified. In 1954, the same year Hansen's designs were unveiled in the Vancouver office, Harris wrote an article in *Canadian Art* called "What the Public Wants." He separated art into four styles: commercial, academic, derivative, and creative. "The function of commercial art," wrote Harris, "is a different one from that of the other three kinds of art. Its purpose is to achieve a direct, instantaneous appeal to the widest possible public."[64] The creative artist, Harris argued, does not think in terms of the public, and furthermore, "there is not just one undifferentiated public."[65] Most damaging in terms of his praise of Hansen's popular designs was Harris's assertion that "the best in art in any country never originates in terms of 'what the public wants.' No creative artist paints to please the public although he may be very gratified when his work finds favour with some part of the public."[66] Obviously, to Harris, Hansen was not a creative artist but a commercial one, and occupied a very different role as a result. Sadly, few of his designs for British-American Oil Company's offices are still in existence,[67] and Hansen had to bear witness to the declining popularity of his aesthetic when the company's successor, Gulf Canada, dispersed its collection in the mid-1970s.

Interior Design

We could conjecture that the artistic community read Hansen's work as overly romanticizing "Canadiana" through clichéd images and motifs, but another problem was the blurring of boundaries between Hansen, artist and designer, and Hansen as interior designer for a major corporation. Interior design was a relatively new professional field in Canada and received absolutely no coverage in the country's art publications. Unlike architecture, which was comfortably professional and masculine, the field of interior design was fraught with the baggage of gender and materials. As the design historian Penny Sparke comments, the bias against interior design was predicated upon "the problematical nineteenth-century notion of the 'separate spheres,' the idea, that is, that with the advent of industrialisation middle-class men and women came to inhabit distinct environments – the public sphere of work and the private sphere of home."[68] How, therefore, to classify the work of Hansen, which blurred the boundaries between "cozy" domestic materials and practices and the modern glass and steel business environment?

This book is not about interior design, and intentionally states its area of investigation as the relationship between craft and architecture, but it is impossible to neatly separate these fields. Not only were interior and commercial designers like Hansen among the chief promoters of the crafts within architecture but they played a sometimes invisible role mediating craft in built spaces. Once a craftsperson has completed a public commission, it can be hung according to the directions of an interior designer rather than according to the preferences of the artist or the architect. A more noticeable finding in my research for this book were the frequent instances when an often anonymous interior designer was responsible for the removal of public artworks when they did not fit with the updated colour and furnishing schemes that corporations and businesses regularly undertake. Sparke argues that the subject of interior design is a difficult one to research because "unlike histories of product, graphic or fashion design, the object of these studies is constantly in flux … the multiplicity and variability of the interior renders it a difficult object for analysis."[69] Adding to the problems of constant stylistic updating and change within interiors is the issue of anonymity. Interior design firms are often noted in archival records, but rarely is an individual designer named. Why is this an issue? Because there have been many instances of the removal and destruction of craft objects from public buildings, and it is impossible for either the artist or the researcher to trace responsibility back to an individual interior designer. Furthermore, since the field of interior design itself is frequently left out of architectural histories, it becomes difficult to discuss the vision of the interior designer whose work may have transformed a public area into an idealized stylistic representation.

The historical anonymity and vulnerability of the interior designer is being superseded by the sort of superstardom offered by shows on Home and Garden Television, but in Canada it is still a challenge to figure out the role of the interior designer in the commissioning and decorating processes that serve as the intermediaries between architects and artists. As demonstrated by the loss of much of Hansen's body of work for the British-American Oil Company, interior design is still at risk through its association with commercial and business enterprises.

Although much has changed, the story of interior design education in Canada reveals that gender has played a major role in the frequent anonymity of the interior designer. The first university to provide an undergraduate education in interior design was the University of Manitoba, which initiated a Department of Interior Decoration in 1938.[70] The term "decoration" is significant because the students in the program were all women, and definite gender stereotypes regarding suitable course materials were in place, with many classes using Home Economics as their model. The terminology was designed to be non-threatening to the engineers and architects, who were expected to share academic quarters with these new female students. As Joan Harland, professor emeritus in the University of Manitoba's Department of Interior Design, reminds us: "Women's place in the profession … was precarious. In the early 1930s, the calendar of a leading eastern university stated: Architecture (no women), and as late as 1938 a woman graduate in Architecture (with a Gold Medal) was advised by the head of an architectural firm to take a stenographic course so she could become a valuable secretary in an architectural firm."[71] So while interior decoration was a more acceptable field of enterprise for female students, it did not take long for the first university program in Canada to realize the significance of replacing the term "decoration" with "design," and by 1945 the University of Manitoba's Department of Architecture and the Department of Interior Decoration were united to form the School of Architecture and Fine Arts, which was still housed within the Faculty of Architecture and Engineering.[72]

It is important to note that in 1959 Interior Decoration was "modernized" at the University of Manitoba when it was included in the new J.A. Russell building, which housed the School of Architecture and Fine Arts.

The Russell building, by architectural firm Smith, Carter, Parkin, was considered to be one of the earliest and most significant International Style buildings in the Prairies. The advanced architecture was interpreted as reflecting the "progressive principles" of the school.[73] These academic shifts were important in terms of professionalizing women's work, as the move to bring interior decoration together with architecture led to the 1948 renaming of the program to Department of Interior Design, and the granting of a degree of Bachelor of Interior Design, rather than a diploma of interior decoration.[74] While significant for the women who were now receiving formal degrees in the field, the change was a direct result of the entrance of male students into interior design programs following the return of veterans from the Second World War. At the University of Manitoba, enrolment in the program doubled between 1943/44 and 1945/46.[75] The Carnegie Corporation recognized the program for its contributions to Canadian design and presented the department with a set of large photographs of important European and American buildings and interiors to be used in the teaching of their decorative art courses.[76] Craft played a significant role in the requisite courses, with the result that when the graduates moved into professional careers as decorating consultants, department store designers, draftsmen in architectural or engineering firms or planning research firms, or as independent interior designers, they arrived with a knowledge of the history, materials, and processes of craft.

Craft Education

In 1945 Canadian universities offered few opportunities for students to graduate with degrees in craft. When the University of Manitoba's Fine Arts degrees were first granted in 1950 ceramics were included, but many Canadian craftspeople still felt the need to leave the country to receive formal training. The opportunity for craftspeople to learn to work with architects in an academic environment was limited; however, there were some programs, most notably at Montreal's École des Beaux-Arts and École du Meuble, where sculptors and designers were introduced to architectural concerns. The École des Beaux-Arts, established in 1922, was already a leading art institution promoting a distinctly francophone cultural profile when craft pioneer Jean-Marie Gauvreau founded the École du Meuble in 1935.

Ray Ellenwood describes the tension between these art institutions in his history of the Montreal Automatist Movement, arguing that the École des Beaux-Arts had intentionally moved away from the applied arts toward more traditional training in art history, painting, and sculpture. The École du Meuble, on the other hand, had the "goal to find a mid-road between high art and technical skill."[77] Ellenwood argues that Gauvreau's background as a cabinetmaker enabled him to hire more challenging artists like Paul-Émile Borduas and Maurice Gagnon, whose presence led to "a particularly stimulating atmosphere."[78] Under Gauvreau's leadership, the crafts played a central role in emerging debates around material, form, and abstraction. His 1929 book *Nos intérieurs de demain* (which won Quebec's *Action intellectuelle* award) stressed the need for contemporary designs to use all forms of craft materials that would project current ideals in Canadian design suitable for modern interiors.[79] As a cabinetmaker, Gauvreau was familiar with the need to understand architectural and interior spaces, and he emphasized this approach in his work as director of the École du Meuble as well as in his role as president of the Salon d'artisanat du Québec, Canada's first (1955) and leading exhibition of craft and design.

While the École du Meuble was creating intense debate around materials and space, the École des Beaux-Arts was producing some of Canada's leading sculptors such as Sylvia Daoust and Eleanor Milne, who won many competitions for public commissions. Milne broke an important gender barrier when she was hired as Canada's Dominion Sculptor in 1961, with the responsibility for the design of wood and stone carving, stone reliefs, stained glass, bronzes, and furniture for the Parliament Buildings.[80] The position of Dominion Carver had been established in 1916 following the fire that destroyed much of the Parliament Buildings, and the artist who held this position was expected to produce Gothic Revival style work that reflected national flora, fauna, and narratives.[81] Milne's formal training, completed at Montreal's École des Beaux-Arts, allowed her to compete and win the position as Canada's national sculptor, but she insisted that the formal title be changed from "Dominion Carver" to "Dominion Sculptor": "The new title reflected the belief that Milne's skills were beyond/above those of the physical labour involved in the craft of carving and stained glass cutting. The conceptual design stage, which was the area of production done exclusively by Milne, required talents specific to drawing and design. Here the separation goes beyond the art versus craft debate, and into perceptions of cultural

Fig. 1.2
Frederick J. Way, "She Carves Our History."

capital. Milne believes that the differentiation in title is important, as it reflects training and skills."[82] And so, despite the fact that Milne was trained in a range of craft materials and techniques and enjoyed the physical work, she alligned herself with the artist in architecture rather than the artisan (fig. 1.2). Given that she was hired in 1961, it is no surprise that Milne wanted to avoid the word "artisan." This was the beginning of intense debate within the craft world over outdated terms such as "handicraft" and "artisan," and Canada was no exception.

Anita Aarons

In 1965 a new voice arrived forcefully on the Canadian craft and architecture scene – Anita Aarons. Brutally honest, strong-willed, and determined to unite craft and architecture as the Allied Arts, Aarons took all previous deliberations over the role of craft in architecture and cast them aside to promote her contemporary view. Aarons came to Canada in 1964 from Australia, and immediately took a leadership role for architectural crafts. As the Australian delegate to the June 1964 First World Congress of Craftsmen in New York City (the conference that led to the formation of the World Crafts Council), Aarons met ceramist Merton Chambers, one of thirty Canadian delegates. Aarons and Chambers became life partners, "leading to her launch on unsuspecting Toronto [where] during the ensuing 21 years she promoted liaisons between art and architecture."[83] Aarons was quickly able to become a leading member of Canada's artistic community thanks to her impressive list of international credentials, not to mention her forthright assuredness. "Before moving to Canada, Aarons was the head lecturer in charge of sculpture at Caulfield College in Melbourne, Australia, and a founding member and executive secretary of the Society of Sculptors and Associates, which promoted liaison work between Australian sculptors, designers and architects. This led to her 1962 commission from the Sydney Municipal Council to execute the first playground sculpture in Australia."[84] In 1965 the Royal Architectural Institute of Canada's *Journal RAIC* hired her to write a monthly "Allied Arts" column, giving her a prominent platform for promoting craft as integral to architecture.

For the purposes of this book the importance of Aarons's voice cannot be underestimated. She occupied the public role of architectural craft advocate and she lobbied tirelessly for a critical examination of the complex relationship between art and architecture. To Aarons, the Canadian public architecture that she discovered upon her arrival in the mid-1960s was "functional, inorganic, antiseptic and colorless," and dependent upon art for signs of humanity.[85] Aarons's first "Allied Arts" column in February 1965 was an audacious critique of the esteemed Canadian artist Harold Town's painted and metal murals for the upper restaurant of the new Toronto International Airport. A large sculpted brass screen by Town was placed at a right angle to one of his painted murals, a pairing of designs and materials that Aarons called an unharmonious juxtaposition.[86] While Aarons felt that Town's large brass mural (2.4 × 3 m) made of sixty prefabricated solid brass panels, was "a successful wedding of Town's talent and commercial technique process," she levied her strongest criticism at the architects of the space for positioning the brass screen beside the painted mural. For Aarons what made the situation even worse were the "many hazards – ropes, chairs, tables, impedimenta and general clatter [that made] contemplative viewing of the painted mural impossible."[87]

And so Aarons launched herself as a critic of artists, architects, and interior designers, a position she occupied more fully as she convinced the Royal Architectural Institute to publish two volumes of her *Allied Arts Catalogues* in 1966 and 1968, to showcase artists and craftspeople who could work with architects. The introduction to Volume 1, written by "W.B.B.," praised Aarons for her "infectious enthusiasm for her work and force and candor in expressing it."[88] The catalogues were a first in Canada – carefully documented and illustrated listings of artists in all media whom Anita Aarons deemed professional enough to work with architects. The first volume included luminaries such as Louis Archambault, Ted Bieler, and Alfred Pellan, but leaned heavily toward craftspeople. W.B.B. noted in the introduction: "In Miss Aarons' philosophy the general requirement of creative imagery makes all aspects of art acceptable … Fine craft work or decorative embellishment, if original, is also eligible for publication."[89] Volume 2 (1968) was divided into six sections, and Aarons's support for the crafts is evidenced by the inclusion of Stained Glass and Architectural Craft as two of the categories (figs. 1.3 a and b).

Aarons's first column also revealed her broader philosophical mandate for the Allied Arts – for architects, interior designers, engineers, and the public to provide respectful spaces and to take the time to consider the artworks on display. No more overcrowding. No more last-minute commissions. No more lack of space for artwork. It was an ambitious goal, given that in 1965 it was still a struggle to convince architects, and particularly their clients, to become involved in commissioning artworks. Aarons recognized this and put the responsibility squarely on the artists, writing in her July 1965 column that artists had to first "produce significant forms of worthy scale to excite and make the architect forget his budget and functional inhibitions and move to greater realizations."[90] She took it upon herself to seek out and identify capable artists, and her columns introduced a wide selection of craftspeople to architects and other readers of the *Journal*.

Aarons also curated several exhibitions designed to bring artists and architects together. Her March 1967 exhibition *Crafts for Architecture*, held at the University of Toronto School of Architecture, was an outstanding success. It attracted over four hundred visitors a day and pushed the idea of architectural craft in new directions, stressing the idea of "architectural clothing" that would fuse materials and stimulate new responses in the viewing public.[91] In her exhibition Aarons showcased thirty-eight pieces representing her choice of "the best" craftspeople. She worked closely with Donald Macduff

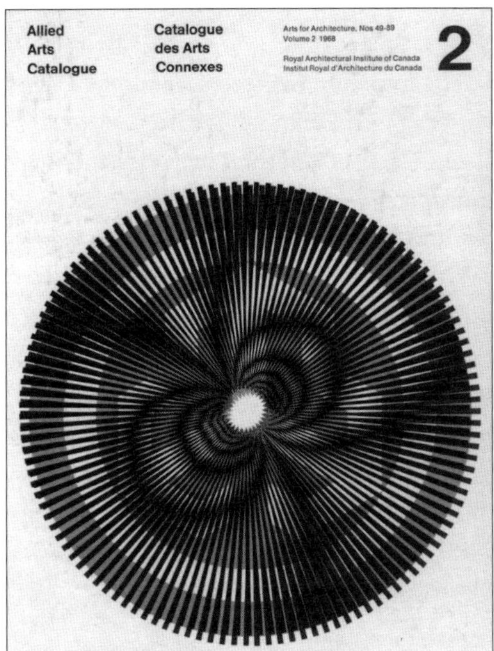

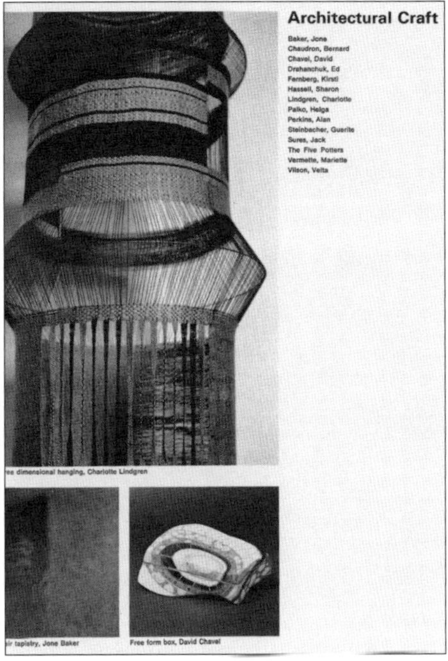

Fig. 1.3 a and b
a) Cover of Anita Aarons's *Allied Arts Catalogue*, 1968, and b) "Architectural Craft," title page.

of the Toronto design firm J & J Brook Designs, and together they created a series of mood-evoking spaces employing colour transparencies to highlight the relationship between light and object.[92] The highlight of the exhibition was 15 March, "Architects Night," when over two hundred and fifty architects and craftspeople gathered together "to celebrate past successes and future collaborations."[93] *Crafts for Architecture* was timed to initiate this discussion just before Expo '67 opened in Montreal. Considered to be Canada's introduction on the world stage, the pavilions of Expo '67 featured many integrated craft and architecture projects. Aarons used the momentum from Expo '67 to suggest that Canadian craft was coming of age, "shaking off sentimental ties of 'lost traditions' and [becoming] a true innovator of contemporary imagery with new materials as well as old," thus demonstrating the power of craft to affect public spaces.[94]

It was no accident that the Royal Architectural Institute of Canada initiated an "Allied Arts" column in the year 1965, for it coincided with the federal government's announcement of a one-percent art program for all new federal buildings in Canada. The impetus was to create modern symbols of government in time for Expo '67, and these buildings needed to contain artworks that were representative of Canada's cultural maturity and innovation. Aarons was quick to point out that it would not be an easy task to suddenly find a wealth of craftspeople and artists who were ready to work within architecture. "Please," she wrote upon the announcement of the federal program, "let us not have a rash of commissions, purchasing and ordering of this and that to decorate and embellish architecture – more jewellery for an architectural 'Mrs. Richquick' [than art]."[95] Aarons stressed the need to advance the Allied Arts at a reasonable pace – a pace based on education and the exchange of materials and ideas. With the sudden availability of spending on public buildings this was not always the case, although as subsequent chapters show, many of the craft commissions for federal buildings, and for later provincial art programs, were successful, and stand today as icons of public craft.

Modernity, Architecture, and Craft

The 1960s in Canada were a significant time for the Allied Arts – not only thanks to the institutionalization of the term through print media and exhibitions but because Canada was part of the enormous changes that were happening in the art world. As art critic Clement Greenberg (who always enjoyed provoking the craft community) pointed out during a 1979 keynote speech at "The Ceramics Symposium" in Syracuse, New York: "What happened towards the end of the 1960s ... medium scrambling and medium mixing" resulted in the "sanctity of the boundaries between the different mediums" losing its hold.[96]

Although many craft writers of the 1980s and 1990s pushed for a separation of artistic modernity from craft – most notably the jeweller and writer Bruce Metcalf, who wrote: "Status-hungry producers who manipulate craft in order to fit it into the modernist vision of 'high' art should be wary as such machinations deplete craft of its intrinsic social and material values"[97] – craft always played a role in the spaces of modernity. Just as Ruskin and Morris had advocated for the harmonious fusion of craft, architecture, and design, evidence is emerging that a wide range of modernist architects and designers shared this sentiment. "While Le Corbusier may have argued that 'the more cultivated a people become the more decoration disappears,' he never abandoned craft or interior design. Le Corbusier's desire for standardization and a typology of human needs necessarily included craft and design objects that would meet these basic human needs."[98] What appears to have taken place is a conflation of ornament and design and a misreading of a modernist dislike of decoration as an aversion to craft. The interface between craft and architecture has always contained elements of interdisciplinarity. It is often difficult to single out certain materials as being specifically craft rather than a part of the organic whole. And craft has always been regarded as the perfect vehicle for introducing "humanity," as Aarons called it, into any style of building.

Jack Lenor Larsen reinforced the views of Ruskin and Morris when he attributed to craft the power to personalize any architectural space, private or public, large or small, ornate or minimalist, thus redeeming it from the impersonal coldness of industrialization: "It is the furnishings within [spaces] that provide a sense of place, of materials and warmth, and of identity. But of all furnishings, craft particular to site and client best provides the quintessential antidote to mass production."[99] As Kalman contended, Canadian architecture was unique in one important respect: "Late Modernism did not flourish in Canada as it did in Europe and the United States. Canadian architects were never completely sold on the International Style, they showed less respect for it and its variants than their counterparts in other countries. Instead, many chose to deviate from international modernism in order to express a regional character and a personal vision, while also employing a wholly modern vocabulary and technology."[100]

This tendency to resist the International Style in favour of a more personal approach to architecture ensured that Canadian craftspeople were provided opportunities for the integration of craft materials and sensibilities into a wide range of new buildings. As the following chapter, "Material," will argue, the Allied Arts found a united voice through their dedication to exploring a complete range of materials.

2 MATERIAL

We may safely assume that in general the more advanced architects tend to prefer handicraft ... Only unreasonable dilettantism and blatant idealism would attempt to deny that each authentic and, in the broadest sense, artistic activity requires a precise understanding of the materials and techniques at the artist's disposal, and to be sure, at the most advanced level.
Theodor W. Adorno[1]

The crafts have always been based in materials. Until relatively recently this grounding in material was perceived as a limitation, a reflection of a lack of conceptual ability. While this essentialized vision of the crafts persists, it is slowly eroding as craft materials become increasingly co-opted by artists of all backgrounds.[2] Critical thinkers have argued that the material basis of craft is its strength, and that this basis is closely shared with architecture. The craft community has only recently rediscovered some of the literature expressing this view. The writings of the nineteenth-century German architect and critic Gottfried Semper were particularly influential in bringing a focus to the properties of craft that relate it to architecture.

Two central problems had prevented the material link between craft and architecture from being recognized: the conflation of craft and ornament, and the assumption that high Modernism negated craft. A line of German philosophers, starting with Semper and later Martin Heidegger, the latter's pupil Hans-Georg Gadamer, and the Frankfurt School's Theodor Adorno, connected craft with architecture, privileging its materials and skills as fundamental to the development of building. How ironic, then, that it has taken well over a century for the privileged position of craft within architecture to be understood. Why is it that the shared material concerns of craft and architecture have been overlooked? As I shall outline in this chapter, Semper's argument that craft lays the foundation for architecture may have waxed and waned in popularity, but it proves enduring, particularly in relation to the strong metaphysical link between the creation of spaces of contemplation by architects, and the reflective objects employed in these spaces as conceptualized by craftspeople. Through an examination of specific shared materials such as concrete, and a study of Heidegger's emphasis upon *techne*, I will propose that matter, material, and the immaterial are inseparable within the Allied Arts. An opening will appear for an argument that the ideal types underlying materials and their subsequent use, institutionalization, and reception are at fault for the isolation of craft from architecture.

Gottfried Semper

In addition to being a talented architect and critic, Gottfried Semper was experienced in a variety of craft materials. He designed porcelain for the Meissen factory in Dresden, and after moving to London, England, he taught metalwork and furniture design.[3] Semper's involvement in the 1851 Great Exhibition and in the subsequent founding of the South Kensington Museum (today the Victoria and Albert Museum) established him as a leading supporter of the crafts. In his influential two-volume publication, *Style in the Technical and Tectonic Arts*, completed between 1860 and 1863, he made a major assertion: "Without an appreciation of this early influence of the technical arts on the genesis of traditional forms and types in architecture, no proper understanding of architecture is possible."[4] Semper argued that the crafts form the basis for architecture, and he provided four categories for the foundational raw materials of building: first, Textile Art, specifically weaving and the patterns derived from weaving; second, Ceramic Art, which he related to molding; third, Tectonics, or carpentry and framed structure; and fourth, Stereotomy, or masonry, specifically stone.[5] Although he did not classify metal as one of the four categories, Semper assigned it a universal role: "Of all the materials that are used to serve human ends, it is metal that unites all the properties listed above. It can be made plastic and then hardened; it is flexible and tough, with a high tensile strength ... As a result of this versatility, metalwork combines all four technical classes within itself."[6] Furthermore, he posited that woven textiles gave rise to archetypal patterns of wallcoverings that evolved well before timber frames and masonry, and were examples of universally shared materials.[7] According to Semper's thinking, the crafts were not simply addenda to built space; they informed the development of architecture itself.

Semper's interest in patterns and wallcoverings reflected their close relationship to ornament, and it could be argued that the conflation between the materials of craft and ornament in the twentieth century stems back to his early writings. This linkage was detrimental to the project of studio craft, for it gave rise to the erroneous impression that craft products were synonymous with ornamentation. In Adolf Loos's 1908 essay "Ornament and Crime," his sweeping condemnation of ornament, although craft is not overtly referenced, material objects that suggest craft are blamed for "the enormous damage and devastation caused in aesthetic development by the revival of ornament."[8] It was not until Adorno's 1965 lecture "Functionalism Today" that Loos's argument was reassessed in relation to craft and architecture. In the interim, a conceptual cleavage between craft and architecture was supposed; however, as their shared materials and philosophical foundations will demonstrate, this was a false suggestion.

Metaphysics

What was not false was the reality that architects had moved away from their historical role as builders. While William Morris spent 1856–57 apprenticing in the Gothic Revival architectural firm of George Edmund Street and learning firsthand how each of the materials used in a Street building were manipulated, over a century later when Adorno wrote "Functionalism Today" it was recognized that the architect could operate as a hands-off designer. "The syllable 'hand,'" he wrote, "exposes a past means of production; it recalls a simple economy of wares. These means of production have since disappeared."[9] Although this was the lived experience of architects, Adorno nevertheless believed that engagement with craft and a respect for materials were essential to avoid commodification and pandering to the dominant stylistic orders within architectures, which were simply reflections of the capitalist hierarchy. Adorno avoided John Ruskin and William Morris's romanticized and over-simplified edict that the world must return to pre-industrial crafts to correct the mistakes of capitalist industrialism, acknowledging that it was "impossible in this age of commercial means of production to recreate that state before the division of labour which society has irretrievably obliterated." However, making the architect into an unquestioned expert was equally problematic, for the architect's "disillusioned modernity, which claims to have shed all ideologies, is easily appropriated into the mask of the petty bourgeois routine."[10] What Adorno suggested should replace these polarized positions for craft and architecture was a healthy respect for shared materials which embodied the imaginations of all artists. To this end "Functionalism Today" employs an almost metaphysical tone in evoking the power of the imagination to manipulate materials into powerful socio-political symbols: "Clearly there exists, perhaps imperceptible in the materials and forms which the artist acquires and develops something more than material ... Imagination means to innervate this something. This is not as absurd a notion as it may sound. For the forms, even the materials, are by no means merely given by nature, as an unreflective artist might easily presume. History has accumulated in them, and spirit permeates them ... Artistic imagination awakens these accumulated elements by becoming aware of the innate problematic of the material."[11]

Interestingly, the year Adorno delivered this lecture was the same year that Aarons began urging Canadian artists and architects to explore their shared materials through a metaphysical lens. For her, public art commissions were not simply decorative art objects designed to break up space; she felt that large-scale artworks had an obligation to provide the public with reflective moments in their everyday lives. More specifically, it was the responsibility of the artist to produce "conceptual images and symbols of our time" that would inspire introspection, and it was incumbent upon the architect to provide "functionless, purposeless areas; courtyards, corridors, even empty rooms – non-competitive and anonymous – housing one significant form for contemplation."[12]

Adorno and Aarons shared the view that architectural spaces and the art objects they contained had the potential to provide conceptual inspiration for the occupants of those spaces. Adorno, for his part, compared the concept of space to musicality: "Musicality cannot be reduced to an abstract conception of time – for example, the ability, however beneficial, to conceive of the time units of a metronome without having to listen to one. Similarly, the sense of space is not limited to spatial images, even though these are probably a prerequisite for every architect if he is to read his outlines and blueprints the way a musician reads his score. A sense of space seems to demand more, namely that something can occur to the artist out of space itself; this cannot be something arbitrary in space and indifferent toward space."[13] Aarons expressed the same idea in her monthly "Allied Arts" columns, which again and again reminded artists and architects that the integrated materials of art and architecture could provide viewers with moments of metaphysical reflection. For

Aarons, successful manipulation of materials into metaphysical artworks not only elicited spontaneous moments of contemplation but engendered community. Public craft could "combine to the pleasure of mankind" through "delightful and happy coincidence" as a result of unplanned but responsive action. "Sensitivity responds to sensitivity and faith and confidence breed positive contribution in a community."[14] The architect and artist possessed the power to introduce vast audiences to conceptual images and symbols that were vital signs of contemporary society.

The artist whom Aarons most admired for his metaphysical abilities was Jordi Bonet. Born in Barcelona in 1932, Bonet immigrated to Canada in 1954 and settled in Quebec. Bonet was an exotic figure on the Canadian art scene, an artist with only one arm, dramatic Spanish flair, and tremendous skill in a range of materials, from drawing to ceramics and concrete to aluminium.[15] Art critic Guy Robert's 1975 monograph on Bonet is eloquent about the artist's ability to convey deep meaning in all his artworks: "The work germinates and rises, sputters and explodes, frets and rejoices, strained to the breaking point between these two extremes – Life and Death."[16] Bonet undertook his first large public mural commissions in the mid-1960s. The renowned Quebec sculptor Julien Hébert helped him establish his workshop, which at times employed a dozen assistants.[17] His first large commission, the 1963 ceramic mural "Hommage à Gaudi (Three tympana)" in the Place des Arts in Montreal was followed by ceramic works, including one for the Sierra Leone pavilion at the 1964 New York World's Fair.[18]

Bonet's work received much critical attention, and he was hired to teach art at the University of Montreal's School of Architecture between 1966 and 1968.[19] In 1965 Bonet was awarded the Royal Architectural Institute of Canada's Allied Arts medal, and Aarons singled him out for praise in her column. She noted that his mural commissions were international in scope and growing in number, and credited his virtuosity with materials that created full sensory experiences for viewers. "Full and complete rapport with his material [ceramics and concrete], plus a burning passion and expressionism have given him supremacy as a decorator." According to Aarons, the results were "evocative caballistic cryptograms declaring walls as sacred sepulchres for bodies and gods yet uninterred. His Spanish 'love of death' is manifest."[20] Aarons had finally found an artist whose passion for materials and understanding of architecture encapsulated the goal of the Allied Arts: "Above all, by collaboration with architects he excites the designers and elevates the building beyond function to true architecture. The most important factor is that architects have recognized the worth of this passionate artist to excite them and by material recognition, say so. True collaboration is more dependent on spirit than techniques and ways and means. Bonet, truly professional, rises above competence and by inspiration can give heart to other metaphysical designers, for such approval lends new heart."[21]

Aarons also noted that Montreal was establishing itself as a leading city in terms of public art. But Toronto was, as always, competing with Montreal for this title, and in 1968 it unveiled one of Canada's most ambitious Allied Arts projects, the MacDonald Block. This complex, located at the corner of Bay Street and Wellesley streets, was a new Ontario Government building filled with sculptures, paintings, ceramic murals, and tapestries. The *Toronto Star* commented: "Like a modern-day Medici, Premier John Robarts is building a $55 million, marble-lined office complex and filling it with $330,000 in art, more art than the Art Gallery of Ontario has bought in the last 15 years."[22] The MacDonald Block was representative of the watered-down version of International Style architecture favoured by provincial and federal departments of Public Works. As architectural historian Janet Wright comments, buildings like this "were built to project a suitably dignified architectural image that would reflect creditably on the state,"[23] and this structure employed high-end materials such as marble to ensure a majestic set of buildings.

Designed by Shore, Tilbe, Henschel and Irwin Architects and Engineers, the MacDonald Block was one of four connected buildings that together created the largest single office building space in Toronto when it was opened.[24] It was fundamental to the stateliness of the architecture to ensure that high-quality artworks were commissioned. In 1965 an art consultant committee was formed, consisting of Cleeve Horne, chairman of the Royal Canadian Academy of artists, and fellow Academy members Peter Haworth and Clare Bice.[25] This committee worked for a year inviting artists to submit maquettes, and selecting final artworks. Featured in the main Wellesley Street entrance to the MacDonald Block was Bonet's huge ceramic wall mural (fig. 2.1), which today still captures attention as one enters the building. The mural features a complex patterned surface covered in protrusions of various sizes, and glazed in a range of browns and bronzes. The mural can be viewed from the ground floor or the mezzanine, and consists of a variety of imprinted patterns that suggest leaves, fossils, and other natural references. Arnold Edinborough, the art critic for the *Financial Post*, described Bonet's piece in a 1971 article: it looked "like a picture of the moon's surface taken from

Apollo XIV; on other days, one might think of it as part of the bed of an ancient lake with encrusted fossils. To some, it might seem a recreation of some archaeological dig in Egypt; to others, it might appear as a geological specimen case."[26] This work continues to have a striking impact. People take the time to stop and surreptitiously caress the intriguing surfaces, and the workers who interact with the mural daily, from the security guards to the government employees, keep a watchful eye on people touching or photographing the piece. In such a busy lobby one might question whether the "Life and Death" impulses in Bonet's work still resonate, but given the continuing ability of this mural to stop people in their tracks, the metaphysical potential appears to remain strong.[27]

Concrete

Bonet was always experimenting with new materials, and he combined ceramics and concrete in his mural work before abandoning them for aluminium in the 1970s. Ceramics and concrete are both malleable materials with great expressive potential. Bonet's murals depended on extruded forms, both small and large, and sgraffito markings that alternated between deep active lines and careful, delicate impressions. It was significant that one of Canada's most celebrated muralists was drawn to concrete, for this was the symbolic material of modern architecture. In his book *Concrete: The Vision of a New Architecture*, Peter Collins traces the long history of concrete back to Roman times, but emphasizes the symbolic newness of concrete since 1914 and the rush to develop new materials for the war effort. Concrete allowed for molded buildings and, while the material itself was not new, the techniques being developed were innovative.[28] One of the earliest proponents of concrete, Jean-Auguste Lebrun, described in 1836 the decorative, or craft, potentials of this material: "Concrete will lend itself easily to every kind of decorative design; it will suffice to model the centring with the compartments or coffers required, for these to be faithfully reproduced after the centring's removal. This type of masonry, covered with a coat of plaster, retains perfectly every kind of painting with which one could wish to decorate it."[29]

Collins describes how Ruskin, rather ironically given his edict of "truth to materials," actually provided an opening for architects and builders to begin decorating with concrete, through his chapter on "Surface Deceits" in *The Seven Lamps of Architecture*. Ruskin was opposed to deception; however,

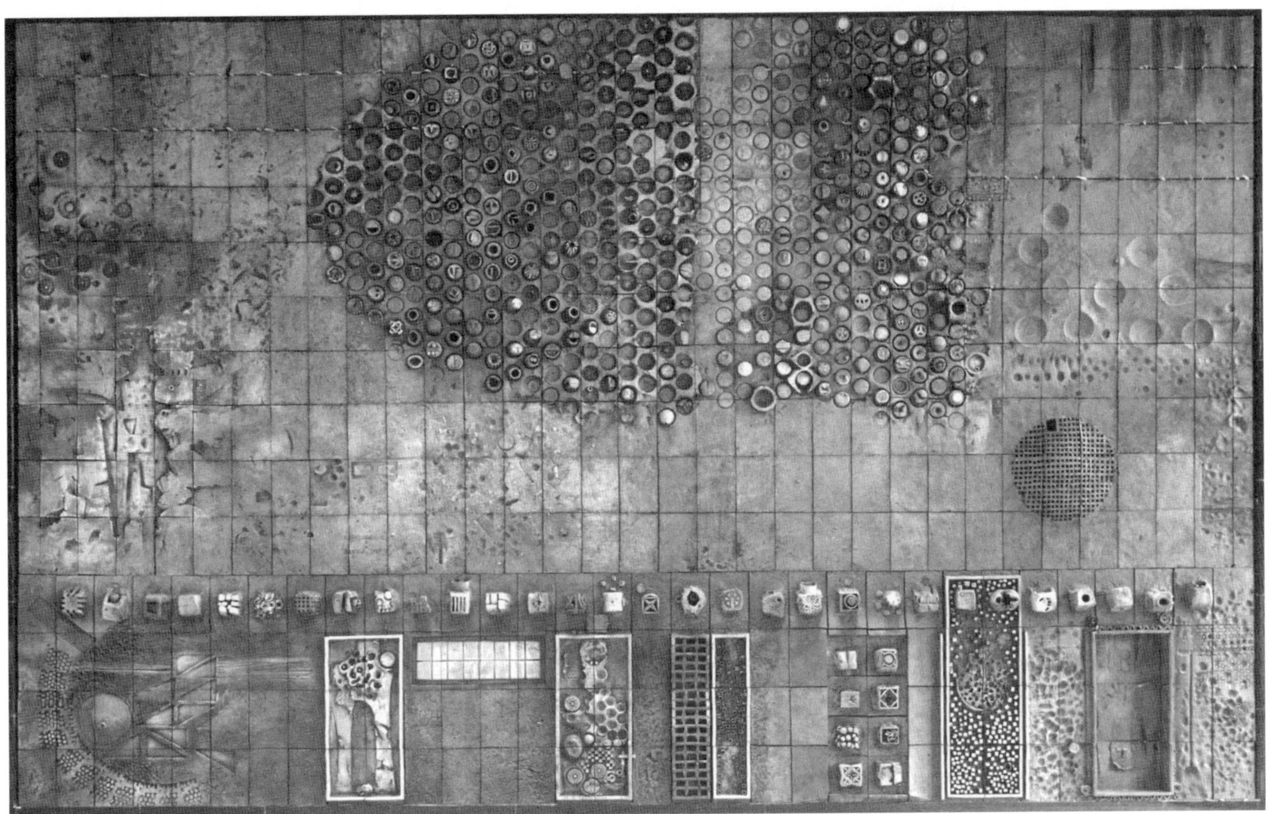

Fig. 2.1
Jordi Bonet, "The End of Time" (6.6 x 9.4 m), ceramic mural, 1968. MacDonald Block, Toronto.

"provided one did not cover the wall with a material which looked like some other material, then virtue was saved."[30] So if concrete was devoid of its structural characteristics it provided an ideal surface for decoration. Throughout the nineteenth century, debate raged over the use of concrete and its attendant decoration. It was in Madrid, Spain, at the sixth International Congress of Architects in 1904 that Maurice Jalvo, one of the Spanish delegates, argued that the material properties of concrete made it the same as any other art material.[31] And so it was the interconnected architecture and craft works of Barcelona School artists like Antonio Gaudi that prompted the Congress to pass the resolution: "That decorative forms must bring out both the material employed and the structure; that to be beautiful, these forms must be in harmony with the quality of the material; and that of all modern processes, reinforced concrete was one of those which united the most conditions adaptable to numerous applications."[32]

It was quite fitting, then, that Bonet's first large-scale ceramic and concrete mural in Canada at the Place des Arts in Montreal was titled "Hommage à Gaudi (Three tympana)." While other Canadian artists executed works in concrete, such as the planter experiments by Merton Chambers and Luke Lindoe's native petroglyph designs etched into the concrete exterior of the Royal Alberta Museum and Archives building (fig. 2.2), it was Bonet who was credited with reconnecting architects with the spiritual potential of concrete and ceramics. These artworks in concrete are united through the standardized modern interiors and exteriors that promoted this material.

Lindoe's petroglyph designs rest easily on Australian architect Raymond O. Harrison's low flat-fronted Royal Alberta Museum and Archives building (1964–67). Built of light beige concrete, the façade featuring Lindoe's "Petroglyph Mural" extends east of the main entrance along five huge grids. The material of the building's surface is perfect for petroglyphs as it reflects a stone-like quality. Lindoe was the ideal craftsperson to undertake this commission. Although he was not an Aboriginal artist, a fact that was not of concern to anyone involved in the building project, he was known for his sparse, modern ceramic style, which fit with Harrison's minimalist architecture. Lindoe did extensive research on the Writing-on-Stone petroglyphs in Southern Alberta and brought replicas into his mural: "Each figure is accurate in its details, although enlarged (in some instances by a factor of ten) from the original."[33] Despite Lindoe's enlargement of the petroglyph figures, the materials and modern minimalism of the Royal Alberta Museum and Archives building provide the perfect setting to highlight the spiritual nature of these images. Sunlight catches them, shadows deepen them, and rain acts like wash of paint, making them pop out from the side of the building.

Techne

As mentioned earlier, Adorno and Aarons were certainly not alone in espousing the poetic power of materials. Other German philosophers such as Heidegger and his pupil Gadamer were also using craft references to discuss the spiritual potential of architecture. Heidegger held a deep concern for the power of architecture to situate people in their specific contexts, writing about the connection between "Space" and "Being." He used the Greek term *techne* to describe the process that transforms materials into visible, inhabitable reminders of the world. In his discussion of *techne* in 1951, Heidegger referred to the virtues of handicraft: "The creation of a work requires craftsmanship. Great artists prize craftsmanship most highly … It has often enough been pointed out that the Greeks, who knew quite a bit about works of art, use the same word *techne* for craft and art and call the craftsman and the artist by the same name: technites."[34] Heidegger suggested that it was advisable to "define the nature of creative work in terms of its craft aspect" but reminded readers that *techne* was really about a mode of knowing, of revealing being, not simply the act of making.[35] It follows that craft is intrinsic to architecture as a necessary part of the revealing process, and that they naturally share materials and visual concerns.

Gadamer expanded upon this thesis, arguing that the Allied Arts could create spaces of being and identity, and that ornament was crucial to the task: "Hence the comprehensive situation of architecture in relation to all the arts involves a twofold mediation. As the art which creates space it both shapes it and leaves it free. It not only embraces all the decorative aspects of the shaping of space, including ornament, but is itself decorative in nature. The nature of decoration consists in performing that two-sided mediation; namely to draw the attention of the viewer itself, to satisfy his taste, and then to redirect it away from itself to the greater whole of the context of life which it accompanies ... One also sees that the usual distinction between a proper work of art and mere decoration demands revision."[36] These are strong words, and it is surprising that the craft community has overlooked them for five decades (Gadamer wrote this essay in 1960). Perhaps not that surprising, however, given the emphasis that the crafts have placed on seeking parity with the fine arts worlds of painting and sculpture in the time since then. What does an exploration of public craft commissions in architecture and the philosophical writings related to the role of art within architecture reveal? That the materiality of craft, rather than being a liability, is central to the architectural process. Furthermore, delineating craft materials into mutually exclusive categories becomes an impossible task when discussing the Allied Arts. How, then, can concrete be understood ... or aluminum?

While the craft world, with the exception of Glenn Adamson in his 2007 book *Thinking through Craft*, has largely neglected the relationship between craft and architecture, several architects and architectural historians have been giving it attention. Adamson's chapter "Material" offers a sustained discussion of the interplay between craft and sculpture, setting up a tension between the material specificity of craft and the opticality of modern painting and sculpture, and he places his exploration of architecture under the chapter on "Skill," referring to Heidegger's arguments about *techne*. According to Adamson, Heidegger presumed that building was a form of craft activity: "Just as the creation of a structure results in a dwelling that reveals both the character of the place and that of the people who inhabit it, in craft, the making of a thing 'reveals' both the material and the maker simultaneously."[37] Adamson also refers to Semper's discussion of process and materials and his argument that textiles formed the basis for architecture. Semper, it appears, has the potential to be the philosophical unifier between craft and architectural historians.

Matter, Material, and the Immaterial

The Institute for Contemporary Canadian Craft in 1997 held a symposium entitled "Common Ground: Contemporary Craft, Architecture and the Decorative Arts" at the Musée des Beaux-Arts and the Canadian Centre for

Architecture in Montreal. The accompanying book of the same name, published in 1999, contains an introduction by editor Gloria Hickey that gives an excellent survey of the views shared by craft and architecture at that particular moment. Hickey outlines the perspectives of craft and architecture: "Craftspeople saw architecture in terms of lost opportunities ... Architects, on the other hand, were concerned about the loss of the craft of building – architecture was no longer an integrated act of designing and making a building."[38] The infusion of government money into public craft in the 1960s was perceived to have been lost by 1999: "Current academic writing substantiates this lack of public appreciation for the skills of craftspeople and architects, citing the classification of craft and architecture as luxuries and the shrinking support at the government level – in terms of education, taxes or legislation. It seems that craft and architecture had assumed a culture space where 'real people visit in their spare, fringe time but that only fringe, spare people inhabit in their real time.'"[39] Despite this negative assessment, *Common Ground* contains a wide range of essays from architects, craftspeople, and curators, and the individual chapters offer some optimism regarding the Allied Arts (a term that was not used in the publication, a sign of its waning popularity).

Myriam Blais, a professor of architecture at Laval University, outlined the historical links between craft and architecture in her essay "The Meaning of Techniques and Materials." While references to historical models or thinkers were absent from many of the essays by craftspeople, Blais suggests that "recovering architecture's meaning may depend ... on a reconsideration and reinterpretation of the history and tradition of ... crafts."[40] Blais makes the important point that architects do not write the history of architecture, and thus are not directly responsible for its rupture with materials and craft. Indeed, it was the emphasis on style in architecture, rather than materials and techniques, that led to the marginalization of this discussion within art and architectural history. Blais emphasizes that the large number of new construction materials developed during the twentieth century transformed ways of building and further separated traditional craft materials from the gaze of architects. Finally, Blais reminds craftspeople that architects are no longer trained as artisans, and that the loss of hands-on training has resulted in a neutral attitude toward materials. She relies on Semper to answer her question: "Is it possible to give meaning back to the way materials and techniques of construction are to be thought of and used?" It appears that the answer is yes. Semper's notion of "truth of construction" redirects attention to the "logic that goes directly from means to buildings."[41] In order to achieve "truth of construction," Blais explains, one must differentiate between matter and material and the ways that artists and architects approach this difference:

> Matter is a mere substance, whereas the term material represents the aptitude that the artist recognizes in matter to be assembled in construction. A material is always thought of in terms of construction, and the artist invents materials, as a synthesis between the matter of which it is constituted and the specific culture that gives it meaning in construction. Turning matter into materials constitutes the very first artistic and creative gesture: it is the origin of construction and, consequently, of architecture. Architects bear very little if any such responsibility anymore, new materials are provided beforehand, according to the rules of the market. This represents an important and damaging loss for the architect, and for architecture as well, because the cultural prefiguration of construction that was traditionally implicit in the making of materials does not seem relevant for today's architectural work.[42]

This is a tremendously important observation. So often the architect receives the blame for the lack of craft commissions within public spaces; however, given the constraints provided by clients' budgets, a general lack of material knowledge provided through architectural education, and the expedience and availability of ready-made construction materials, it is no wonder this gap exists.

The only essay in *Common Ground* by a craftsperson which contains a sustained exploration of materials is by Lutz Haufschild, a glass artist from Vancouver who has executed over two hundred large-scale glass commissions. Haufschild is lyrical about the complex relationship between the materiality of glass and the immaterial effects created by this light-giving substance: "In all art forms light is the essential element but in architecture light seen through art glass windows suggests a dialogue between the material and the ephemeral, the physical and the metaphysical, the profane and the sacred."[43] Haufschild's work is dramatic but obtains this effect through the cleanness of its elements. His essay "Inspired Light, Space Inspired Thoughts About Light in Architecture" focuses on his vast art glass window (13.7×10.7 m) for Toronto's Bata Shoe Museum, which architect Raymond Moriyama described as the "eyelids" of the building.[44] Haufschild is careful to separate himself from traditional stained glass artists, stressing the importance of

Fig. 2.3
Lutz Haufschild, "The Great Wave Wall" (10.7 x 41.2 m), glass, 1996. Vancouver International Airport.

simplicity in his designs. This simplicity, he argues, is what allows his pieces "to empower the ultimate creative source, namely light, to transform the material, to de-materialize glass into spectral colours as elusive as those of the rainbow. The result is not an opaque window, nor is it a transparent wall, but rather a magically suspended veil of light."[45] Because the artist is so capable of placing his work in relation to an architect's vision of a space, his pieces work well in a wide variety of contexts.

One of Haufschild's most prominent works is "The Great Wave Wall" at the Vancouver International Airport (fig. 2.3). Composed of thousands of pieces of rough-edged glass, this massive window (10.7×41.2 m) features a simple colour palette of whites and blues in a dramatic wave pattern that evokes the ocean. Haufschild based his composition on the Hokusai print "The Great Wave of Kanagawa," and the work links not only to Vancouver's strong maritime connection but also to the importance of the ocean within West Coast First Nations' cultures. This is made clear by the placement of "The Great Wave Wall" behind Bill Reid's celebrated bronze statue "The Spirit of Haida Gwaii, the Jade Canoe." The Vancouver Airport Authority has allocated spaces for public art, and part of their mandate is to create "places of repose for travelers while providing public art without the elitism."[46] In this space "The Spirit of Haida Gwaii: The Jade Canoe" sits in an amphitheatre-like setting on a mezzanine overlooking the busy international departures area. Above it is Haufschild's wave window, which bathes Reid's sculpture in an ever-changing range of light and shadow. Together these pieces evoke a strong atmosphere that is appreciated by the thousands of travellers who pass by every day, some of whom sit for minutes, others for hours, simply enjoying the effect. Observing this placid interaction between viewer and object in the midst of the pandemonium of an international airport, one is struck by Haufschild's assertion that "it is possible, perhaps even unavoidable, that the ambience created by light filtering through artistically treated glass, contributes something very significant to architecture. Truly illuminating light not only enhances and completes space within a built environment but also embraces the viewer. It elevates the accident of light to higher meaning."[47]

The impact of Haufschild's "The Great Wave Wall" reinforces Heidegger's concept that architecture contributes to the situatedness of people in the world. While Heidegger's writing focused on dwellings, the idea that certain truths about the world can be revealed through architecture is valid for public spaces like the Vancouver International Airport. There, a space has been created to encourage harried travellers to take a moment to situate themselves in the specific context of the west coast of Canada, in Vancouver, British Columbia. This regional approach contrasts strongly with early postwar efforts to build Canadian airports that were progressive through their standardized International Style aesthetic.

In 1958 the federal government of Canada built the first major air terminal of its new national program in Gander, Newfoundland; it was followed by airports in Halifax, Montreal, and Ottawa in 1961, Toronto, Winnipeg, and Edmonton in 1964, and Vancouver in 1964.[48] As architectural historian Bernard Flaman relates, each of these "new terminals shared a common design theme that employed the latest Canadian and international furniture and lighting within a backdrop of modernist architecture in the international style."[49] Flaman compares these terminals to art gallery spaces, in that they are both neutral environments in which to showcase modern art and design. The crafts did not fit easily into these spaces, with their modernist aesthetic that encouraged abstract art and industrial design. As Flaman argues, "public art at this time was understood as mural painting and architectural sculpture," and while the Canadian landscape still provided inspiration, it was "brilliantly reinterpreted in the modernist idiom."[50] Ironically, most of these terminals and their art commissions have been destroyed, despite the important role they played in projecting Canada onto the world stage.

Today, the Vancouver International Airport is much more literal in terms of regionalism: materials, sounds, smells, and sights are all specific to the "safe" vision of West Coast flora, fauna, and First Nations – a vision that is produced through craft materials, techniques, and forms. Perhaps the emphasis on regional identity can be read as symbolic of Canada's achieving its place on the world stage. This regionalism is made even more comforting when it is packaged and resold to tourists in the form of souvenir reproductions of the art objects on display in the airport. Despite the commercialization of the airport's strong regional identity, its artworks and Haufschild's use of glass to produce the immaterial magic of light have the potential to encourage sensitive observers to contemplate their own being – or, as Heidegger would argue, their own temporary space in the world. Heidegger's emphasis on dwellings, however, introduced a key problematic relating to the discussion of craft materials in public spaces – domesticity.

Textiles

While Haufschild's use of large-scale glass installations has a long history of precedents within architecture, some craft materials, like textiles, suffer from domestic stereotypes despite a long history of use within a variety of building genres. Semper's insistence that textiles formed the basis of early architecture has been long neglected, and in many instances textiles are seen as too fragile, ephemeral, and feminine to work effectively in public spaces. The use of utilitarian fabrics such as window coverings, upholstery, and carpets is widely accepted in buildings, but the idea of a large-scale textile piece being installed as an art object can still meet with resistance. Textiles are often perceived, for example, as being too difficult to clean – Halifax fibre artist Charlotte Lindgren had to remind many of her clients and the building managers responsible for her pieces that "all it takes is a beating with a broom and it's clean. That's it."[51] The real problem with textiles appears to be the ease with which they are destroyed, removed, or lost. Mariette Rousseau-Vermette, one of Canada's leading architectural textile artists, worked closely with a number of architects during her career, yet was a sad and often powerless witness to the removal of some of her major commissions, including notably her acoustic textile panels for Roy Thomson Hall (completed with Arthur Erickson) in Toronto (fig. 2.4). Although Rousseau-Vermette demonstrated professionalism at every stage of her architectural work, from maquettes through to the finished piece (fig. 2.5), she was not always able to work with the architect from the concept stage. "The architect should be your friend,"

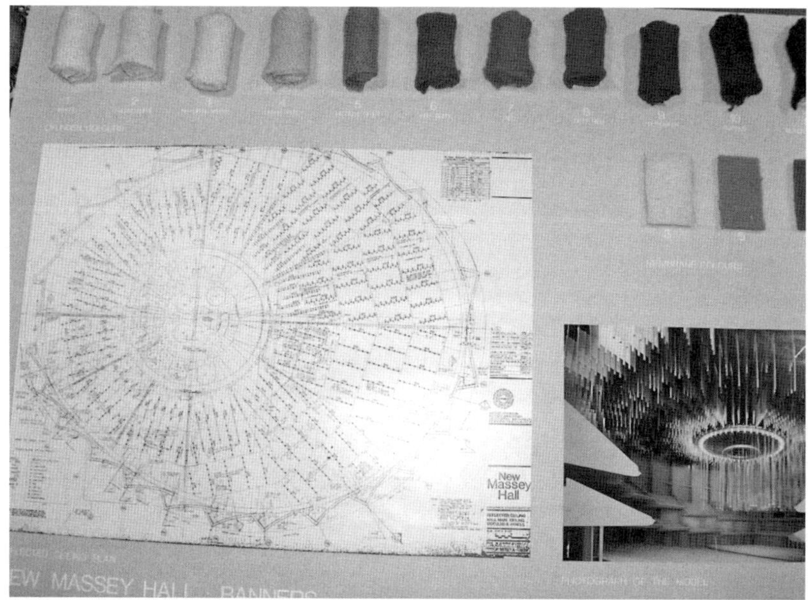

Fig. 2.4
Mariette Rousseau-Vermette,
maquette for her acoustic
textiles for Roy Thomson
Hall, 1980–82.

Right Fig. 2.5
Mariette Rousseau-Vermette
in her studio, Ste-Adèle,
Quebec, 2006.

she argued. "If you come in after the building is completed and they simply want your piece for the wall then the artist is only a jewel in the hand."[52] Despite her close working relationship with a number of architects, including Erickson, Rousseau-Vermette was dismayed by the power of the interior designers over the vision of the artist, especially given the whims of changing interior design styles: "That hurts – they come into the building and want to change things, they don't understand that art is art."[53] In the course of her fifty-two-year career, she witnessed a wide range of reactions to her work, from the response of secretaries in a bank in Quebec City during an installation ("What are you putting up? We wanted a bathroom!") to the celebration and preservation of her monumental curtain in the Eisenhower Theater at the Kennedy Center in Washington, the official gift from Canada to the United States.[54]

Early on, Rousseau-Vermette realized that pursuing a professional career as a textile artist would require leaving Canada for her training. She was attending art school in Quebec City in 1944 when her father brought home a copy of *Life Magazine* and she saw an article on the American textile artist Dorothy Liebes, which inspired her not only to paste it on her bedroom walls, but to leave and study in San Francisco. Liebes ran a textile studio that specialized in collaborations with architects and interior designers, and during Rousseau-Vermette's time with the artist (1948–49) she learned how to market textiles to this audience, and how important professionalism was in securing commissions.[55]

Throughout her career Rousseau-Vermette was a leader in the Canadian craft scene, and she used her architectural knowledge to create works that integrated new materials and worked with contemporary architectural spaces. In 2002 she completed a large-scale commission for the Imperial Tobacco building in Montreal, using rolls of silk and wool on aluminium to support fibre optics (fig. 2.6). This was one of Canada's first successful fibre optic textile pieces, completed in delicate shades of white, silver, and grey with cascading fibre optics underneath and over the top. Placed in the main lobby of a standard high-rise building, this work dominates the space and provides the only visual stimulation in an otherwise austere entrance; at night it dances and plays with light (fig. 2.7). American fibre artist Jack Lenor Larsen introduced Rousseau-Vermette to fibre optics, and a friend in New York (an architect whose husband was a distributor of electrical threads) commissioned her to complete two early pieces. "I was brought to a warehouse that was like a candy shop full of colours and I said to myself 'I want to work with this.' That was about ten years ago and at first I used wires, weaving the tapestry on top then installing wires in a big circle. Then I was sent a box full of fibre optic threads which I could weave into pieces and easily manipulate."[56]

Rousseau-Vermette's interest in new materials contributed to the digital direction of Canadian textiles, leading to projects like Ingrid Bachmann's early 1995 contribution, "Fault Lines: A Montreal and Los Angeles Link,"

at Galerie La Centrale in Montreal, for which computerized looms connected Montreal and Los Angeles by weaving seismic activity charts. Another example is Robin Muller and Sarah Bonnemaison's "Centre for Cultural Technology and Innovation" at NSCAD University, in which the architectural application of electronic textiles is the focus, and researchers and artists are working on developing "Smart Textiles" responsive to sound and movement through lights and sensors, which are interwoven into curtains, freestanding walls, and hung ceilings (fig. 2.8). Muller describes the pressure that came from European textile artists to employ new technologies like rapid prototyping: "I wanted to learn more and after bringing in visitors like the textile

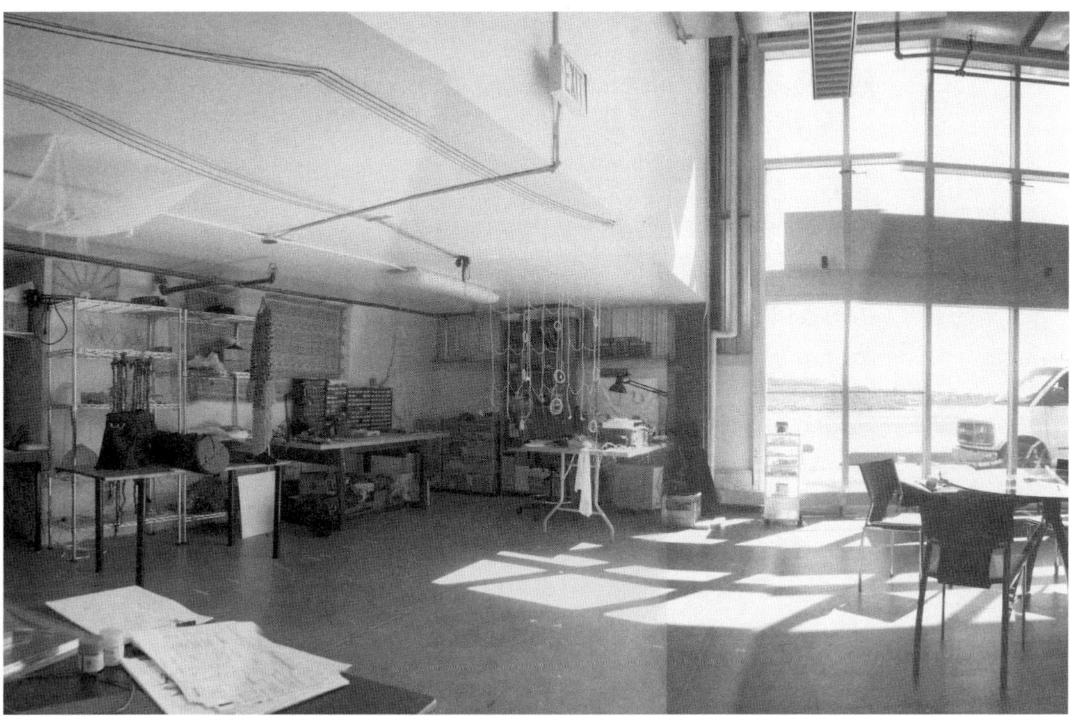

Fig. 2.8
Centre for Cultural Technology and Innovation,
NSCAD University, Halifax, 2009.

engineer and chemist Joy Boutrop from Denmark we realized it was time to pursue architectural investigations."[57]

In collaboration with Sarah Bonnemaison and Christine Macy of Dalhousie University's School of Architecture, NSCAD University established Architextile and began working on smart textile prototypes. They have developed close relationships with engineers, who unite the artistic and architectural through objects, including Mondrian shades that light up with electro luminescent wire, and body sensor sets and costume designs (fig. 2.9). The Flamenco dancer Maria Osende helped Architextile prototype a portable set with ribs, which collapses down into a simple base. Triggered by body movements and constantly changing colours, Osende's costume and set use sophisticated fibre technologies to create scenes reminiscent of dancing around a campfire. There is a certain irony in the cutting-edge position that architectural textiles now occupy, given the gendered and stereotyped history relating to textile production.

One of the most influential books published in the field of craft history is Rozsika Parker's 1984 *The Subversive Stitch: Embroidery and the Making of the Feminine*. Parker traces how embroidery was enforced as a "proper" activity for women, but argued that for centuries women had been manipulating needlework and inverting it into a subversive form of personal and political expression. Her thesis draws a parallel with the feminist art movements that had co-opted embroidery and textiles to reclaim agency for women artists, and sets up an interesting comparison between the "background" architectural textiles of artists like Rousseau-Vermette and the overtly feminist textile art objects by artists such as New York's Elaine Reichek, and most famously Judy Chicago, whose 1979 "Dinner Party" featured embroidered and appliquéd runners underneath each of the ceramic dinner settings.

Fig. 2.9
Architextile Lab, interactive collapsible set and costume for Flamenco dancer Maria Osende, 2009.

Fig. 2.10
Joyce Wieland, "Barren Ground Caribou" (2.4 x 9.1 m), quilt, 1978.
Spadina Subway Station, Toronto.

Canada has a long history of women producing monumental and striking textile pieces for architectural spaces, and while these works create important and strong statements about women manipulating traditional textile materials into architectural art, rarely do they contain overtly political or feminist statements. However, the works themselves can be read as feminist, or as the ceramic artist and craft historian Susan Surette notes: "As a woman maker, I really believe that just making these works and having them in such architectural spaces is a strong feminist statement, especially during this time period in Toronto."[58] These are often abstracted, colourful works that suggest a more metaphysical than political interaction with the viewer.

Possibly the most overtly political textile statement made by a Canadian female artist during the late twentieth century was Joyce Wieland's "O Canada," a series of lip imprints mouthing the national anthem that were embroidered into a cloth wall hanging. Scholars agree that Wieland's intention was to juxtapose the competing ideologies of nationalism and feminism,[59] and so one might assume that her massive quilted commission (2.4 × 9.1 m) for the Toronto Transit Commission's Spadina subway station, titled "Barren Ground Caribou," contains an equally political statement (fig. 2.10). If so, the subtlety of this statement would possibly be lost on the legions of commuters who pass by this work, as it features majestic caribou grazing on a colourful tundra background. Today Wieland's piece is carefully protected behind glass, but unsubstantiated rumour has it that when it was originally unveiled the Toronto Transit Authority was concerned about the potential impact of thousands of hands touching the exposed cloth and the piece was removed from view for a period of time. Whether Wieland intended it or not, the juxtaposition between the materiality of quilting, the wild majesty of the imagery, and the contained, hurried urban atmosphere of the subway tunnel is startling. "Barren Ground Caribou" forces the viewer into considering how far removed commuters are from the domestic comforts of home and the natural settings of the North by revealing the sterility of the ceramic tiled and fluorescent lit tunnels we occupy throughout the day. One can only imagine how immediate this sensation would be if the glass barrier separating the piece from viewers was removed. In some respects encasing it in glass protects commuters from having to read the work as a critique of their urban surroundings.

Joyce Wieland was considered first and foremost an artist, and was not classified as a craftsperson (she hired her sister to quilt "Barren Ground Caribou"). She used textiles to convey her political concepts, thereby positioning her ideas and her work in the history of a continued debate. How does the idea of materiality function within the context of craft? How do biases and assumptions affect the integration of craft within architecture and the ideal of the Allied Arts? All crafts are fundamentally sensual pursuits, and meaning is embedded in their materiality, but their omission from the art historical cannon has meant that this relationship has traditionally been overlooked. Craft ideals and materials are being introduced into art history at an unprecedented rate; nevertheless, there are many pitfalls in the discussion of craft and materiality as part of the post-modern or post-conceptual reassessment of art. These only become more complicated when we consider craft in relation to the field of architecture.

Not all art historians and curators privilege theory and concept over objects and materiality; even so, there is a lingering suspicion that craft is anti-intellectual because it is materially rooted. When craft is juxtaposed with architecture, dogmatic distinctions between materiality and concept dissolve – a benefit of interdisciplinarity. Indeed, interdisciplinarity is the strength of craft. Some may call it chaotic, but it can be viewed as an exciting lens through which to consider materiality and meaning through a multiplicity of methods.

As historical examples like those of Semper and Ruskin demonstrate, granting intellectual validity to craft materials is not a new idea or approach; however, for too long craft has been the preserve of the apologetic – a strange situation, given that the field of craft has long provided alternatives to moribund ideas related to art and architecture. A four-part framework is useful for considering how craft successfully roots itself in material identity: materials themselves; the way the craftsperson employs these materials; the institutionalization of materials; and the reception of materials.

Material Identity

As mentioned earlier in this chapter, boundaries are frequently placed around materials, whether they are based on social, economic, or gendered hierarchies. During the postwar period, Canadian art history and criticism prescribed its own set of material boundaries for public art, described by art historian Annie Gérin as "sculpture, painting or mosaic – in abstraction from the temporality and environment in which they evolve."[60] It wasn't until 1966, when Aarons published the first *Allied Arts Catalogue* for the Royal Architectural Institute of Canada, that craft materials were included in any official list of materials acceptable for architectural commissions beyond the traditional ideas related to architectural craft like stonemasonry and stained glass. Even then it was not a straightforward matter of opening up restrictions on materials. While craft materials provide layers of meaning and specific cultural references, every craft material has its own language. This specificity can be a problem. The discourse around craft materials needs to be better analysed in order to equip the crafts with the tools for understanding the diminishment of craft that has caused such apprehension among craftspeople.[61]

Why is the use of craft materials within contemporary art problematic, while the use of the same materials within architecture is celebrated as Allied Arts? The answer has to do with empowerment – craft is emboldened by its alliance with architecture when a craftsperson receives a commission, whereas the craftsperson loses prestige when his or her materials are co-opted for use without skill or expertise. I should note that this discussion of the artistic hierarchy is based entirely in the Eurocentric craft traditions employed in North America, the United Kingdom, Australia, and Europe. This is a very limited approach when contrasted with the exciting craft developments in countries like South Korea, host to the world's largest craft biennale; however, the Eurocentric traditions are those most commonly used in the training of Western craft, art, and architectural historians, and so they provide the basis for this discussion of materiality.

The dominant imperative for the crafts in Western culture is "truth to materials." Although Denis Diderot and Jean d'Alembert wrote extensively on the differences between the mechanical arts (craft included) and the liberal arts in their 1751 *Encyclopédie*, dividing the two along material lines, it was Ruskin's assertion of truth to materials (following designer A. Welby Pugin's lead) that established the basic tenet of the Arts and Crafts Movement. Truth to materials is based on the following "truths":[62] first, all forms must be faithful to nature and the materials of their construction; second, a morality in design is necessary (it must be reflective of society, thus, no art for art's sake); third, goodness and truth are expressed in form and material. According to Pugin and Ruskin, the craft ideal hearkens back to the Middle Ages, when the manner of execution of objects was "admirably suited to the material."[63]

Morris picked up on this theme of truth to materials. He followed Ruskin's admonishment that: "No person is able to give useful and definite help towards such special applications of art, unless he is entirely familiar with the conditions of labour and nature of materials involved in the work."[64] Morris was equally passionate about architecture, specifically the preservation of historic buildings, and he soon associated craft materials and the restoration of historic properties with larger social goals, associating truth to materials with the anti-industry sentiment of design reform and the Arts and Crafts Movement; however, Morris also emphasized the link between craft and socialism. He took it upon himself to educate his audiences on the importance of architecture and ethical craft materials as well as production practices in relation to the socialist reconsideration of industry. In fact his first major project, architect Philip Webb's 1859 Red House constructed for Morris and his bride, Jane Burden, was an attempt to fully harmonize architecture and craft.

Tom Crook, in his article "Craft and the Dialogics of Modernity: The Arts and Crafts Movement in Late-Victorian and Edwardian England," does an excellent job of arguing that it is too simplistic to merely set up a binary opposition between craft and modernity. Instead, Crook traces how the movement provided an alternative form of modernity, one based on a multiplicity of dialogues, which has led to historiographical confusion: "On the one hand, craft is conceived of as 'antimodern,' as opposed to, and critical of, industrial modernity. In this way, it is also seen as backward-looking, nostalgic and anachronistic. On the other hand, its very critical posture towards industrial modernity is taken as evidence of its modernity, of a forward-looking, transformative ethos which seeks to foster change, innovation and reform."[65]

This tension between nostalgia and progress can be seen in the debates over West Coast architecture with its tributes to the Arts and Crafts movement, specifically the Craftsman Bungalow. Is the Vancouver International Airport retrograde for its use of natural woods, warm interiors, and inviting lighting? Or is it simply adapting vernacular materials on a grand scale? Crook gives an apt description of the tension between modernity and the Arts and Crafts Movement; it is a tension that continues to haunt craft materials within architecture, where textiles, for example, are perceived as both outdated feminine nuisances that are hard to maintain and as cutting-edge technological tools capable of transforming spaces into sensory experiments.

It is no accident that textiles were Semper's choice in the formulation of his architectural hut theories; nor was it mere coincidence that Morris's socialist mentor, Karl Marx, used weaving as a favourite metaphor. Weaving remains an ideal ethical material. Plato is famous for using the analogy of weaving in his "Dialogues" and the *Phaedo*; Homer employed it in *The Odyssey*.[66] Of course Plato and Homer used an entirely gendered approach to weaving but, as Lisa Pace Vetter argues in her book *Women's Work as Political Art*, "the gendered aspects of Plato's dialectical weavings also reveal unexpected alliance[s]."[67] Therefore, the materiality of weaving – the warp and weft, the feel of the shuttle, the repetitive motion – becomes a democratic symbol of inclusiveness, and provides the link between the traditionally masculine preserve of architecture and the feminine spaces of textile art. It also became a particularly silly analogy in the writings of Sigmund Freud, who conjectured:

It seems that women have made few contributions to the discoveries and inventions in the history of civilization; there is, however, one technique which they may have invented – that of plaiting and weaving. If that is so, we should be tempted to guess the unconscious motive for the achievement. Nature herself would seem to have given the model which this achievement imitates by causing the growth at maturity of the pubic hair that conceals the genitals. The step that remained to be taken lay in making the threads adhere to one another, while on the body they stick into the skin and are only matted together. If you reject this idea as fantastic and regard my belief in the influence of the lack of a penis on the configuration of femininity as an idée fixe, I am of course defenseless.[68]

Inclusiveness was not the dominant imperative for Ruskin, Morris, or especially Marx. For these nineteenth-century writers, the materials of craft were universalizing in their truths; but they only applied when considered in terms of the dominant group of white, male Europeans who were leading the fight against the tyranny of industry. One can only speculate that this bias may have been tied in to the significant loss of jobs and skill sets that the industrial revolution brought traditional male weavers, but what is certain is that any craft materials that are not traditional, that are not employed by the expected group of artisans, and which deviate from ethical utility could not – and still cannot – be accommodated under the universalizing idea of truth to material.

Employing Materials

The craft ideals of industrialized nations have been heavily influenced by the philosophies of the Arts and Crafts Movement and the moral underpinnings of the concept of truth to materials. How does this legacy contribute to the contemporary classification of materials traditionally associated with the crafts, and how does it relate to architecture? Are contemporary classifications entirely based on imperatives stemming from the European enlightenment, or are they more related to Le Corbusier's exhortation that modern designers need to: "open our eyes and rid ourselves of all the romantic and Ruskinian baggage that formed our education … freed from all reminiscence and traditional preconception" by applying "a rational and reassuring rigour [to our designs]"?[69]

While Ruskin had called for a clear, crisp typology of materials, Le Corbusier took this approach a step further, becoming an advocate of standardization. Whereas Ruskin created entire texts based on his opposition to materials that blurred the boundaries between traditional craftsmanship and industrial production (famously Ruskin disliked any ornamented craftsmanship to do with trains or train stations, writing, "Another of the strange and evil tendencies of the present day is to the decoration of the railroad station"[70]), Le Corbusier was equally dogmatic about unnecessary decoration. By the early twentieth century Ruskin's aesthetic had become Le Corbusier's baggage. However, both men purposefully limited the materials they considered acceptable to their social and aesthetic agendas. Many of today's architects, unlike the examples of Ruskin and Le Corbusier, draw upon diverse approaches.

Fig. 2.11
Suzanne Swannie in her studio, 2004.

The sleek modernist aesthetic of Nova Scotia's Brian MacKay-Lyons, for instance, is interspersed with material references to the Atlantic land- and seascapes that surround him. For MacKay-Lyons, differentiating between architecture and craft is less important than finding the connections between them and he finds such links through guild traditions, from which both fields have too greatly diverged: "In North America the term designer-craftsman is an oxymoron, they are rarely both, whereas in European apprenticeships you learn both." His views on architecture as a profession "grew out of guild traditions, a long and distinguished tradition in architecture but these days … not seen as such."[71] MacKay-Lyons has established the Ghost internship on a farm in Lunenburg County as an "international laboratory based on the apprenticeship model." The Ghost project requires interns to design and build structures based on four-hundred-year-old ruins, and on the middle Saturday night of July they host a community concert that reinterprets in musical form the material culture history they have explored.[72] MacKay-Lyons believes it is important to "take architectural education out of the ivory tower and back to the guild tradition"; as part of that mandate he has worked collaboratively with craftspeople he believes understand these guild ideals.[73] He has undertaken collaborations with the weaver and designer Suzanne Swannie, with whom he shares not only an understanding of guild history but also an interest in the landscape as a source of inspiration (fig. 2.11).

Swannie's wall hangings and carpets are aesthetically similar to MacKay-Lyons's built structures in their elegant simplicity and bold modular designs, and her six thousand hours of training in the Danish weaving workshop of John Becker from 1960–63 certainly qualified her as the type of traditionally educated craftsperson that MacKay-Lyons has a desire to work with.[74] Swannie's "Brud II" (fig. 2.12) employs dramatic vertical lines to break up horizontal bands of richly hued greens. Bold blacks and whites demonstrate the mathematical intricacy of weaving. While this object is not permanently installed in a building (it resides in the collection of the Art Gallery of Nova Scotia) it has been displayed both on the wall and on the floor, and shows a remarkable ability to engage architecturally on both surfaces. While MacKay-Lyons stresses that the Ghost workshops utilize the materials of architecture, he is open to the use of textiles. Nevertheless, he reminds us realistically that "the parallels between architecture and craft could be there if people shared values but they are not there – the apprenticeship system is needed to achieve this."[75]

Just as Le Corbusier's typology of materials led to a divide between craft and architecture, MacKay-Lyons's opinion of the contemporary university education of craftspeople and architects reinforces this distinction. Ironically, his view of the need to return to the guild model is a direct echo of Ruskin and Morris's nineteenth-century urgings. It must be admitted that this romanticizing continues to be a problem within the history of art, craft, design, and architecture, despite supposed interdisciplinary advances. Even more frustrating for the crafts is the fact that, despite decades of scholarship on the shifting range of materials and practices, other disciplines continue to minimize and essentialize craft. For example, the prominent sociologist Richard Sennett, in his book *The Craftsman*, begins with the statement, "The Craftsman summons an immediate image,"[76] and then proceeds to reinforce every stereotype of handcraftsmanship and materials put forth by Ruskin and his peers over a century ago. Despite this theoretical setback for the crafts by such a prominent sociologist, the field of sociology is helpful in the larger project of discussing materiality and meaning in the crafts.

Art historians often employ theories by sociologists who use heuristic devices to set up categories of meaning. A popular example is the work of French sociologist Pierre Bourdieu, who identified three categories of capital that people can possess: cultural, economic, and symbolic. Bourdieu describes the men and women who occupy privileged positions in the arts as "the most favourable agents in cultural production … sufficiently secure to be able … to take on the risks of an occupation which is not a job."[77] Although it is not common to discuss heuristic devices within art historical

Fig. 2.12
Suzanne Swannie, "Brud II (green)" (1.8 x 1.2 m), hand-dyed Spelzau wool on linen warp, 2004.

methodology, the Renaissance development of art academies and the publication of Giorgio Vasari's *Lives of Artists* in 1550 created a typology of art that can be read as marginalizing craft. Vasari's classification of particular artists and materials could be considered a heuristic device, one that still haunts craftspeople.[78] Despite protestations against Vasari's typologies of art, craft historians and craftspeople are busily applying a similar attitude to craft materials today, often in a protectionist stance.

Working with architects or receiving commissions to fit a particular predetermined aesthetic space can be seen as problematic by practitioners who perceive themselves as independent artists. There is much debate at international craft conferences about the relationship between rapid prototyping and handcraftsmanship: Do new technologies strip away the materiality of craft while stealing craft processes?[79] Another heated source of debate is fine art's "poaching" of craft. Can Kiki Smith be considered a textile artist when she openly confesses "I'm not particularly adept at making things?"[80] What level of resentment do craftspeople hold toward artists who are not formally trained in craft but borrow certain techniques and materials, which are in turn embraced by curators and high-end art galleries that otherwise would exclude makers labelled "craftspeople"? How do these prejudices play out in the selection committees for architectural commissions, where the art-historical education of jurors may have unwittingly reinforced these age-old biases?

If heuristic devices can be considered research tools to be used by both researchers and makers, they allow for the deconstruction of meta-narratives of materials taken for granted in the crafts. They permit the recognition that the idea of truth to materials can be read as a moralistic ideal rooted in nineteenth-century Anglocentric fears for craftsmanship in the age of industry. They can help explain the continued irony of projecting craft materials as a metaphysical cure for the busy nature of twenty-first-century life, in ways such as placing a majestic Haida carved totem pole in the middle of a busy modernist glass and steel Toronto shopping mall. Heuristic devices allow for the re-examination of the assumption that craft materials are more moral, or closer to nature, than art and architectural materials. This re-examination can challenge the presumptions surrounding craft materials that are deeply embedded in philosophy. Take, for example, Heidegger's statement in his essay "The Thing" that "the potter makes the earthen jug out of earth that he has specially chosen and prepared for it. The jug consists of earth."[81] Following Heidegger's thinking, the materiality of the jug is about the earth – the clay – and not about form, surface, utility, or concept; there is little room in this formulation for the ceramist who deviates from clay. Nor does it open up a discussion of how architectural materials are also related to natural sources from the earth. Heidegger provides one possible typology for the jug, but more important, his essay operates as a useful framework for researching the ideal types that have developed in the crafts.

German political economist and sociologist Max Weber developed the notion of the ideal type, and it is useful in examining how meaning is applied to material. Weber sought to understand the different ways we classify the hierarchies of society; his thought is easily linked to architecture and craft through his use of the ideal type in cultural constructions.[82] It can be used to compare and analyse both a "general, suprahistorical phenomenon" like craft and a "historically unique occurrence"[83] such as the development of architectural woven wall hangings in Canada in the 1960s. First, it must be acknowledged that ideal types exist for the crafts, and that there are ideal types for each of the craft materials. This typology leads us back to Gottfried Semper and his 1860 division of craft into four categories of raw material: first, textile art – flexible, tough with high tensile strength and great *absolute* firmness; second, ceramic art – soft, readily formed (plastic), capable of hardening, lending itself to being molded and shaped into many forms, and, once hardened, holding its form permanently; third, tectonics (carpentry) – rod-shaped, elastic, and of predominantly *relative* firmness, that is resistant to forces exerted at right angles to its length; fourth, stereotomy (masonry) – firm, *densely aggregated*, resistant to crushing and buckling, and thus of considerable *reactive* firmness.[84] According to Semper's guidelines, almost all objects in decorative art collections and craft history fit these criteria. The textile products of Morris and Co., for instance, reflect the ideal types (embroidery, weaving, carpets, tapestries, upholstery fabrics) created from the first category of these raw materials.

Even the most radical of twentieth-century fibre experiments for architecture followed these ideal types. Frank Lloyd Wright's 1901 assertion that "our modern materials are these old materials in more plastic guise, rendered more so by the machine"[85] is echoed in the "Smart Textiles" now being developed by Muller and Bonnemaison in their "Centre for Cultural Technology and Innovation" at NSCAD. Wright himself never deviated from Semper's ideal textile type in his designs for the interiors of his buildings. The textile workshop established by the Bauhaus to harmonize with its architectural ideals was based entirely on weaving. Anni Albers wrote of the Bauhaus workshop that although "technique was acquired as needed, [the] play with materials produced amazing results, textiles striking in their novelty"[86] it remained rooted in the ideal type of weaving. Subsequent innovations in textiles have introduced problematic materials that challenge Semper's definition – how, for instance, to classify Jennifer Angus's monumental wall ornamentation that is composed entirely of exotic beetles, but exhibited in venues like the Textile Museum of Canada? Such innovations beg the question: Is this age of interdisciplinarity moving away from ideal types in the crafts? Can the same be said of architecture? Obviously, a discussion of how the craftsperson and architect employ materials today is worlds away from a similar discussion in 1908. Or is it?

Institutionalizing Materials

In 1908 the art world was responding to a startling new idea: immateriality. In *The Intangibilities of Form: Skill and Deskilling in Art after the Readymade*, John Roberts traces how the idea of immateriality and "revolutionary thinking about the social form of art beyond artisanal production of the conventional studio" led to the further dissociation of craft, or the artisanal, from the category of art.[87] Or, as the American fibre artist Warren Selig puts it: "Attachment to a medium rather than to an idea is a defining element of the crafts. In contrast, fine art subordinates materials to content."[88] Roberts examines the concept of skilled labour, a central theme in the manipulation of craft materials, and relates it to the emergence of the readymade, specifically the work of Marcel Duchamp. While many authors have related Duchamp's readymades to the dilemma of craft under twentieth-century modernism,[89] Roberts offers a fresh perspective by foregrounding the tension between materiality and immateriality. He asks "why deskilling in art after the readymade does not represent the absolute loss of artistic sensuousness." How is it that while the institutions of art had to shift to incorporate the new category of immaterial art and judgments about value and labour, craft remained marginal to these changes? How is it that architecture was developing into a "profession" at the top of the artistic hierarchy while the work of craft remained seemingly dormant as skill-based labour? Roberts suggests the following: "[The dominant framework of art] subordinates handcraft to technique ... The absence or presence of skill in art, therefore is not derivable from a model of handcraft as such, because art does not experience an incremental process of deskilling which leaves producers at a lower level of capacity than previously attained, otherwise we would only be able to designate certain kinds of handcrafted objects as art."[90] This leaves architecture in an interesting position. While architects are considered artistic and philosophical figures whose emphasis on the conceptual can take precedence over the material, they are also expected to produce a body of "real" physical buildings. While architects are far removed from their guild roles as carpenters or masons, an expectation remains that they will have enough material knowledge to direct engineers, carpenters, and others to carry out their plans. So, can Roberts's assertion that art subordinates handcraft to technique be equally applied to architecture, or does the relationship between craft and architecture – the relationship of the Allied Arts – exclude architecture from this discussion?

A long legacy of philosophers and critics have pondered the topic of art and craft and concluded that they were substantially opposed. Diderot in 1751 was careful to distinguish between the hand skills of the mechanical arts (crafts) and the emphasis on the mind in the liberal arts, creating a distance between fine arts and the notion of skill. It could be argued that ideal types were applied to the crafts long before the upset of the readymade determined that craft was not in a position to play within the institutions of art. The emphasis placed by Ruskin, Morris, and Marx on the need for skilled craftspeople to stand as moral anti-industry symbols contributed to the entrenchment of these ideal types, as did the craft materials that were bound up with the idea of truth to materials. Ideal types within art are constantly being created by art institutions (particularly by art schools that have a vested interest in promoting their programming as unique and cutting-edge). Postmodern art history explores the range of assumptions that accompany these ideal types, and postcolonial critiques serve to remind us of the dangers of identity biases.

It is ironic, therefore, that the many craft materials employed by artists to make political statements about classification and identity have escaped a postmodern reading. So many early feminist interventions in art history relied upon the easy links between craft materials and gender assumptions. Why is it that Judy Chicago's "Dinner Party" has not been more heavily critiqued as further entrenching the distance between the genius artist's idea and the hundreds of skilled hands who brought the idea to life through their manipulation of materials, thereby reinforcing the distance between skill and concept? Why are so many architecture programs devoid of craft content, whether in history or practical classes? Are these indications of alienation simply indicative of deep material biases against craft, or have craft materials been so separated from architectural and art education that they remain a non-issue within these programs?

If craft was left out of the post-readymade reframing of art and architecture as a result of the entrenchment of ideal types of skills and materials, how is it possible for craft now to enter the institutions of art and architecture as an equal player? And what happens to the materiality of craft in the process? Not many institutions are designed to cope with craft's materiality. Consider something as simple as insurance policies, which discourage the open display of fragile or rare objects. Many makers want to display their work to encourage interaction beyond the visual; however, it is difficult to insure such an exhibition in a traditional gallery space, and in public buildings security guards often make it their role to discourage physical encounters with works of art, which are frequently hung behind desks or barriers, or high on walls. Furthermore, visitors to galleries and museums are not habituated to interact with the material on display; the result is an almost comical dance between non-traditional artists who want viewers to touch, and their reluctant participants. At the Dalhousie University Art Gallery in Halifax, Nova Scotia, the maximalist artist Allyson Mitchell encountered this frustration when she displayed her piece "Big Trubs" (fig. 2.13). Apart from eager children who loved to hug the faux fur legs of Mitchell's sexy Bigfoot, visitors were so wary of breaking gallery rules that attendants were positioned nearby to encourage visitors to please touch. In the more anonymous and less protected spaces of public art, lobbies, passageways, and rest areas, on the other hand, excessive touching is sometimes an issue.

While it may appear that the debate over the introduction of craft objects into gallery spaces is close to being resolved, it is undeniable that for the economic value of much craft that is not the case, even in the work of internationally significant artists. Emily Carr stands as one of Canada's most famous artists and her dramatic paintings of British Columbia's west coast have become iconic symbols, but how many people are aware that she was a prolific producer of ceramics and hooked rugs? In fact, the sale of her ceramics was a main source of income and funded much of her painting.[91] Carr has not been excluded from the process of institutionalization; it's just that certain of her materials have been left out, thus affecting the valuation of those materials within art gallery collections and auction sales, and for private collectors. This privileging of art works determines the contemporary pricing of materials as well as the spaces dedicated to the exhibition of craft objects. It

Fig. 2.13
Allyson Mitchell, "Big Trubs," faux fur
sculpture, 2004.

is no surprise that the craftspeople who win competitions for public art commissions often underprice their labour, and frequently end up in debt after fulfilling the commission. Jack Sures, who created the enormous tiled ceramic façade on the Sturdy Stone building in Saskatoon, Saskatchewan, recalls that after the expense of materials, hired labour, and his own time he ended the project without realizing any profit.[92]

The Reception of Materials

All these subtle and overt material biases have an impact on the way the public views craft. Cultural Studies theorist Stuart Hall emphasizes that the reader's (viewer's) reception of a cultural object is never neutral, and that audiences are constantly interpreting cultural objects in relation to their own subjective positions.[93] This is a hugely important idea to craft because the materiality of craft is what makes it easily accessible to many audiences. Joyce Wieland's "Barren Ground Caribou" quilt in the Spadina subway station may have been intended as a reminder of the natural world for busy commuters, but the material itself – quilted textiles – makes as strong a statement as the visual narrative. As Wieland's biographer Jane Lind recounts, Wieland had a specific goal for "Barren Ground Caribou": "She imagined businessmen, carrying briefcases, walking past these caribou, and young children holding onto the hands of an adult, asking questions about the caribou as they walked past."[94]

Equally important is the idea that in recognizing the quilted nature of the work, business people, mothers, fathers, and children engage in reconciling that material with their own personal narratives involving quilting. The ideal types behind materials may hinder the institutionalization of craft (it is perceived as more difficult to exhibit quilts in public spaces, and they are not commonly shown in galleries); however, these ideal types create immediate and visceral responses in viewers – and therein lies the dilemma. While the popular reception of craft objects has been consistently positive and often political (consider the large number of successful craft projects initiated through President Roosevelt's Works Progress Administration during the New Deal, or public craft pieces commissioned during the Canadian federal government's one-percent art program from the 1960s to 1980s), critical reception of craft objects is often negative. Selection committees formed to determine the artworks for federal buildings seldom include craftspeople or critics supportive of craft, and archival documents of meetings make it clear that a derisive tone was often employed when assessing craft materials.[95]

It is clear that the inclusion of craft materials and techniques in architecture and public spaces serves a vital function. Not only does it provide viewers with an easily referenced set of visual processes, but it reinforces the idea that crafts belong within architecture and provide an ideal complement to the other visual arts. It is a lived reminder of the Allied Arts. But entrenched expectations that surround craft materials such as ceramics, textiles, wood, metal, and glass – and assumptions around form, scale, and time – remain strong.

3 SCALE AND FORM

Something is monumental only because it underscores the
smallness and vulnerability of those who experience it.
Arthur Danto[1]

Craft products are widely perceived as objects on a small scale. Multitudes
of craft fairs feature booths exhibiting objects of a moveable size, and on-line
markets for easily shipped crafts through fashionable sites like Etsy.com are
proliferating. This notion of small-scale works is also reinforced by homages
to craft that focus on the hand, as found in essays such as Octavio Paz's 1974
"In Praise of Hands" and in Richard Sennett's 2008 book *The Craftsman*,
whose cover features a seemingly wise hand gently cradling a small carved
object. An intimacy with the body is implicit in the domain of the crafts, and
the human body has historically dictated acceptable craft forms and scales.
But, as the struggles of twentieth-century studio craftspeople to break free of
these limitations demonstrate, this formulation is overly reductive. From Jack
Sures working on exploding the scale of the ceramic façade of the Sturdy
Stone building in Saskatoon to the free-standing textile walls being explored
at NSCAD University's Centre for Cultural Technology and Innovation, craft
materials are now being manipulated on a grand scale and in unique forms.

Architecture is the catalyst for this development. As craft moves toward
establishing itself as a legitimate partner in the grandeur and monumentality assumed by sculpture and painting, it is worth asking whether this project
has been successful. Do craft materials succeed on a large scale? Why were
many architectural attempts at collaboration with craftspeople met with
derision in postwar Canada? And what does the future hold now that new

technologies and attitudes enable craftspeople to think beyond traditional forms and sizes? In this chapter I explore theories of scale, from human scale to Le Corbusier's Le Modulor, to add a dimension to understanding how craft can be read within contemporary architecture. I shall dispell the myth that large-scale monumental works are safe from destruction, and investigate the financial constraints that affect the commissioning of craft works. As a metaphor for these discussions of scale, the case of Canada is useful on two levels. First, regional, or smaller-scale influences on architectural craft act as contrasts to national, or larger-scale desires for cohesive (and elusive) architectural and craft identities. Second, the scale of the country and its regional variations suggest the impossibility of reaching a truly national or global approach to crafts. We shall see that the discussion relates directly to the same issue in architecture.

Human Scale

Before entering a discussion of form and scale in relation to craft, it is worthwhile considering the social and cultural constraints that determine the basic concepts relating to the size and shape of objects. Western culture generally accepts that the Golden Ratio (or Divine Proportion), a complex mathematical formula popularized during the Renaissance, defines aesthetically pleasing and harmonious proportions in simple geometric figures like the rectangle. The accuracy and importance of the Golden Ratio have been exaggerated in fiction through books such as Dan Brown's *The Da Vinci Code*; however, it remains a basic formulation for a wide variety of artistic endeavours and is still taught in many architectural programs. Leonardo Da Vinci's 1497 drawing "Vitruvian Man" made the Golden Ratio famous in art. Showing a male figure in two superimposed positions, Da Vinci drew upon the Canon of Proportions described by Marcus Vitruvius Pollio in his treatise *De Architectura*, published around 25 BCE. According to Vitruvius, there exists a set of ideal human proportions based on the Golden Ratio, and he laid out the exact measurements, which were later illustrated by Da Vinci. For example, the length of a man's outspread arms is equal to his height, and the distance from the bottom of the chin to the top of the head is one-tenth of a man's height.[2] Although these ratios are not always precise, they established an aesthetic ideal that continues to dominate Western architecture and art. However, this ideal is fundamentally flawed in two ways. First, Vitruvius's calculations were based entirely on the ideal male form; and second, they assume that a universal standard exists.

The notion of an ideal standard appealed to the designer and architect Le Corbusier, who built upon Vitruvius's early calculations. In 1948 Le Corbusier published "Le Modulor," a scale of proportion that he described as "a range of harmonious measurements to suit the human scale, universally applicable to architecture and mechanical things."[3] The formal language he employed in his building designs relied on harmony through rational mathematics and was obviously gendered. In his groundbreaking large-scale apartment building "Unité d'Habitation" (1947–52) in Marseilles, France, Le Corbusier cast a version of "Le Modulor" in concrete. This image depicts a man with his body segmented according to the Golden Ratio. Historian Judi Loach argues that Le Corbusier was not necessarily interested in the specific mathematical calculations of "Le Modulor"[4] but rather was attracted by the idea of laws that could produce universally applicable aesthetics: "It is not necessarily a matter of calculation but rather the presence of a sovereign power; a law of infinite resonance, consonance, organisation … Rigour and exactness are the means behind achieving solutions, the cause behind character, the rationale behind harmony."[5] For Le Corbusier rationality was the source of aesthetics. In his 1925 essay "The Decorative Art of Today" he argued that good aesthetics are "the prerogative of proportion, which is a sensed mathematic."[6] What stood in direct opposition to this logical worldview was over-decoration, which was created through the crafts and perpetuated by a desire for "the flourish, the stain, the distracting din of colours and ornaments," elements that were "as disagreeable as mosquitoes."[7]

Le Corbusier was thinking on a monumental scale that would create universal standards for the greater social good (without questioning the very foundations of the Eurocentric notion of the universal). Although his plans to raze the historic buildings of central Paris and replace them with sixty-storey towers were never realized, it could be argued that he left many cities with a legacy of high-rise housing projects that were intended to equalize through standardization but instead led to social problems as the impossibility of applying universal standards across racial, social, and economic lines became evident. Le Corbusier's faith in rationality was a product of the age of progress, one of whose maxims was "bigger is better." In this view, studio craftspeople were at times considered obsolete, for the scale of their production was necessarily limited to the physical speed and capacity of the human body.[8] However, the notion of human scale, which refers both to the scale of production and to the size of finished objects, was – and remains – a driving force behind the continuing success of the crafts.

In the 1950s economics professor and social anarchist Leopold Kohr developed a theory of human scale in contradistinction to what he termed the "cult of bigness" that was the result of postwar notions of progress.[9] Kohr proposed a return to human scale, referring to the limits of natural forms of growth and the problems of overgrowth: "Though highly beneficial up to a certain point, beyond it, it not only becomes life's chief complexity; it becomes nature's principal tool by which it leads its organism to obsolescence and destruction."[10] Society's unchecked growth, he argued in his book *The Breakdown of Nations* (1957), would lead to obliteration. Kohr's theory of human scale ran counter to the imperative of progress, and in that respect it can be compared to the studio crafts themselves. He pointed out that limitations exist around human scale: one or two metres is the extent of humans' reach, stride, and height; human attention has a span of only seconds or minutes; lifespan is limited; human life depends upon defined pressure and temperature systems. Architecture and craft both necessarily apply some of these considerations to the scale and form of objects. For instance, the finger-to-handle ratio in a ceramic mug and its ability to buffer unprotected skin from hot liquid are fundamental considerations. The height, thickness, direction, and velocity of the swing of a doorway are chief factors in its selection for a built environment. The ability of woven fabric to retain heat, and the weight of the fabric, whether draped on the human body or hanging from a rod, is determined by the choice of fibres and woven structures. The key point in all such examples is that the fields of craft and architecture are built upon assumptions about "acceptable" scales and forms. As with architecture, ergonomics plays a fundamental role in making and using crafts, and the idea of a sensory connection with an artist through his or her materials retains its romantic appeal. The thumbprint on a mug handle (when not mass-produced of course) serves as a physical and metaphorical reminder of the manipulation of materials.

Categories for Craft

In his 2007 book *A Theory of Craft*, Howard Risatti puts forward strict guidelines for defining forms and scales that reinforce assumptions about craft dimensions and materials. Risatti posits three possible sets, or categorizations, for craft: containers, covers, and supports.[11] These sets are based broadly on functional, or utilitarian, craft forms such as bowls for containers, quilts for covers, and chairs for supports: however Risatti notes that "a fourth [set] might be shelters, which would include architecture."[12] Even though H.W. Janson had in 1962 argued in his *History of Art*, "architecture is, almost by definition, an Applied Art," Risatti resists creating this fourth set because, while craft and architecture are "related by the idea of applied function, they are not the same."[13] In his view, the difference is related to scale; craft is limited to objects "that can be picked up and moved about and are also of a size that doesn't dwarf the human body."[14] A product of architecture, he argues, cannot be considered an "object," although he does not go into this distinction in relation to the idea of buildings as objects. In this sense, the dualism that Risatti creates between craft as creating portable objects and architecture as creating non-objects can be related to the principles of two key philosophers of architecture – John Ruskin and Martin Heidegger.

Ruskin had argued that the portability of a crafted object reduced it to a mere decorative art, rather than fine art. In his 1859 lecture "Modern Manufacture and Design," he forcefully asserted: "Portable art – independent of place – is for the most part ignoble art"; and he implored his listeners always to think of craft in relation to architecture, or to a fixed place.[15] Ruskin's views contributed to the Arts and Crafts Movement's position that craft was a fundamental component in architectural design and a necessary element in the creation of harmonious buildings and interiors; it was assumed that certain craft objects such as stained glass windows would be created on a large scale. Risatti finds that stained glass is a troubling material in relation to his sets, as are "tapestries … mosaics, and ceramic tile."[16] These large-scale craft objects Risatti writes, do not "possess a sense of objecthood. By sense of objecthood I mean a sense of thingness, of self-sufficiency."[17] This conceptualization of self-sufficiency diverges from Ruskin's notion of considering craft works as part of a greater whole; it can be linked to the studio craft movement and its desire to shift craft as being the provision of merely decorative accoutrement to craft as being the creation of one-of-a-kind art objects.

Heidegger's assertion that building and dwelling are not "architectural ideas" but "art … as a technique of construction,"[18] parallels Risatti's point that architecture is not an object. For Heidegger, building and dwelling are poetic concepts mired in language. Building is dwelling, dwelling is "the manner in which mortals are on the earth," and "building as dwelling unfolds into the buildings that cultivate growing things."[19] To reduce this greater philosophical realm to mere "objecthood" or "thingness" is therefore to detract from human potential itself. Just as Risatti neatly places craft into sets based on utilitarian function and resists the fourth set that unites craft and architecture, Heidegger rejects essentializing buildings into mere objects. Ruskin, Heidegger, and Risatti approach the role of craft within architecture in very different ways, but all acknowledge its importance while simultaneously reinforcing commonly held assumptions about acceptable scales and forms.

Domestic Scale

The crafts have always relied upon a science of materials to determine form and scale, and in this respect architecture and craft are again closely connected. Historically both craft and architecture have been dependent upon the availability and properties of local materials and scientifically determined according to the principles of human scale. The pyramids, the great mosques, and the cathedrals were considered wonders of the world because they broke the previously accepted boundaries of scale and form as craftspeople responded to the need to manipulate their materials on a grand scale. The advent of the industrial revolution, on the other hand, contributed to the entrenchment of crafts within domestic environments, and the gendering of non-tool or machine-produced crafts. Craft became aligned with domesticity, intimacy, hobby, and the feminine.[20]

Public sculptures often immortalize craft objects as belonging to the feminine and domestic realm. In a recent example, Barbara Paterson's epic bronze sculpture "Famous Five" depicts Canada's leading suffragettes celebrating the 1929 decision of the Privy Council of England that declared women were "persons."[21] Apart from the political resonance of this figurative sculpture, it is significant for the way it portrays women in a parlour scene from this period (fig. 3.1). Large-scale chairs and a table set the stage for teacups and saucers, as Henrietta Muir Edwards, one of the "Famous Five" suffragettes, toasts the group's success by raising her teacup.[22] The social expectations of the time for proper ladies (and the strict temperance of the group's leader Nellie McClung) are captured in the cups and saucers, allowing viewers to read these comfortable, usually ceramic, forms on several levels. My observation of the public interacting with the sculpture made it clear that the double-sized cups and saucers were a source of great interest. Children pretended to lift and drink from them, and the handles of the teacups were rubbed to a shine more

Above Fig. 3.1
Barbara Paterson, "Famous Five," bronze, 1999. Detail showing Louise McKinney (R), and Hentriette Muir Edwards (L) toasting with her tea cup. Olympic Square, Calgary.

Left Fig. 3.2
Barbara Paterson, "Famous Five." Detail of tea cup with rubbed handle.

than any other area of the sculpture through repeated touching (fig. 3.2). The odd juxtaposition of bronze imitations of fine porcelain on a monumental scale and in a public space continues to elicit strong reactions.

Although feminist discourses relating to craft production are not as heated today as they have been, it cannot be denied that a masculine imperative exists in the impulse to expand the scale of craft within architecture. Specifically, in Canada in the late 1960s and early 1970s when the federal government's one-percent art funding program for federal buildings was instituted, the majority of these buildings were designed in the stark modernist style – bigger was better, and the architecture was distinctly stripped-down, un-ornamented. Critics such as Anita Aarons emphatically wrote of the need to humanize these buildings through the introduction of recognizable and comforting craft materials, and contributed to the increased use of tapestries and ceramics to soften the overwhelmingly large and sterile corridors of public buildings. Conversely, the opportunity for craftspeople to work on this new scale and develop new forms suited to modern architecture was perceived as inventive in relation to twentieth-century studio craft traditions. This idea has not gone away. In 2007 the philosopher Arthur Danto explained: "Most objects of ceramic art are small relative to their users – cups, ewers, vases, figurines. But visionary ceramics reverses this relationship of scale: it overpowers and diminishes – but at the same time somehow exalts."[23] He acknowledges, however, that this formula is inherently gendered: "American artists eager to produce work that was 'plastic, mysterious and sublime' had to force a division between art – understood as heroic painting – and craft. Scale was one formal way of enforcing the distinction ... And, not coincidentally, a lot of the machismo that emerged in the idea of the 'real artist' was an effort to distance the artist from women, from decorativity in general, and from craft-work in particular."[24]

One of Canada's most highly regarded architectural artists, Jordi Bonet, winner of the Royal Architectural Institute of Canada's "Allied Arts" medal in 1965, began his ceramics career on the domestic scale. In 1957 he established a small workshop in the kitchen of his house in Montreal where he would "fire tiles [vases, plates, and lamps] in a one cubic foot bake oven."[25] From the outset Bonet was interested in the architectural potential of ceramics, but following a 1958 visit with Salvador Dali in Spain he returned to Quebec determined to explore the psychological and emotional possibilities of large-scale ceramic tile murals.[26] The same year, he met Montreal interior decorator Claude Hinton, who supported Bonet's ceramic explorations by selecting his vases, lamps, and plates for his interiors. Not only were Bonet's designs exceptional, but the fact that he could produce ceramic forms with only one arm (Bonet had lost his right arm as a child[27]) made his work all that more remarkable. Hinton's promotion of Bonet's domestic-scale objects led to a growing demand for his work. Soon Bonet employed two salespeople and decided to leave domestic utilitarian pottery for architectural mural work. Bonet's decision to change scale and form in his work was driven by his "ambition of covering the walls of public and private buildings and making his work accessible to the greatest number of people" (fig. 3.3).[28]

Fig. 3.3
Jordi Bonet, detail of "Citius, Altius, Fortius"
(22 x 2.3 m), aluminum and concrete, 1976.
Pie-ɪx Metro Station, Montreal.

The intimacy and human scale of Bonet's domestic ceramic objects may have allowed him to communicate his emotional thoughts to individual users, but for the artist this was not enough. Architectural commissions placed prominently in public spaces would allow him to enter into psychological exchanges with a far wider audience, an imperative no doubt encouraged by his visit with Dali. To undertake these large-scale commissions, which were "pouring in"[29] partly thanks to the popularity of his domestic ceramics, Bonet moved his home and studio to a larger building in Montreal. By the early 1960s he had a dozen people working with him on commissions.[30] Bonet's wife, Huguette Bouchard-Bonet, attributes his success with sculptural ceramics to his respect for the craft of ceramics and his understanding that clay was an accessible material with a rich history: "Jordi Bonet dreamed of an authentic public art like that of the cathedrals in the Middle Ages. He wanted to build for everybody, everywhere, he said."[31] Furthermore,

Bonet's success was due to his willingness to collaborate with architects, engineers, and clients: "He knew how to incorporate and integrate his work with the physical and human environment."[32] But it must be noted that Bonet was also renowned as a charismatic, strongly masculine figure, with the ability to move ceramics out of its domestic confines: "[in his] collusion with Eros … a mutilated hero, he burns with one inexhaustible desire – the desire for freedom."[33]

An interesting dynamic emerged in the Canadian art scene, where strong-willed women like Aarons and tapestry weaver Mariette Rousseau-Vermette led the way alongside men like Bonet in achieving a new relationship for craft within architecture, while established male critics like Robert Fulford responded negatively to these overtures. Aarons's first *Allied Arts Catalogue*, designed to introduce architects to talented Canadian artists working on a large scale, was initiated as an experiment by Aarons and the Royal Architectural Institute of Canada, but it was an important document in that it brought together for the first time images of art that had been executed in collaboration with architecture. Many of Canada's leading artists, including Rousseau-Vermette, Charlotte Lindgren, Harold Town, and Bonet were included, each with a full-page of black and white illustrations of their work. Robert Fulford was not impressed with the *Allied Arts Catalogue*. In a February 1967 review column for the *Toronto Daily Star* newspaper he called it "appalling."[34] Fulford was so offended by the "slick, highly accomplished junk contained in the *Allied Arts Catalogue*"[35] that he was driven to suggest that the entire concept of artists collaborating with architects be scrapped. Instead, he proposed, architects and their clients should simply purchase art for buildings after they were completed: "More and more painters today work on a mural scale anyway, and more and more sculptors aim for grandeur in the sculpture they make privately."[36] Fulford's proposition not only negated Aarons's passionate view that architects and artists needed to increase collaborations but it completely debased the crafts. Although painters and sculptors may have been working on a large scale, many craftspeople relied upon securing architectural commissions to begin transitioning away from domestic-sized objects. Such commissions granted them funds to pay for assistants, larger studio spaces, and greater quantities of materials. Although Fulford's objections were rooted in masculine modernist discourses, they do raise the question of how successful Canadian craftspeople were in responding to the demand that they integrate their materials and methods into these enormous buildings?

Commission Controversies

The records of juror debates over public art commissions during the federal one-percent art program are restricted by Public Works Canada. However Anita Aarons's monthly "Allied Arts" column in *Journal RAIC* (later *Architecture Canada*) clearly indicates problems related to the role of the selection committee in determining the success of craft submissions. Architectural historian Janet Wright maintains that when James A. Langford, chief architect of the Department of Public Works, instituted the fine arts program, there was much resistance from both within and outside the government. This opposition was based on fears that such artistic "frills" would jeopardize the image of the Department of Public Works, particularly if the public did not like what they paid for – or staged increasingly likely public protests.[37] After all, according to Wright, the department had worked hard to place "itself comfortably within the mainstream of established architectural tastes and it rarely assumed a leadership role."[38]

The committee was formed of a rotating group of jurors (usually six) selected from prominent art galleries across the country.[39] Interestingly, no architects sat on the committee. Aarons was concerned that the lack of input from architects and the institutional focus of the jurors would result in too much power falling into the hands of the "artist-advisors" who often were hired as intermediaries between the jurors and the architects.[40] These artist-advisors were supposed to work on the ground securing maquettes and submissions for specific building commissions from artists they deemed suitable. The difficulty with this formula was that artist-advisors were almost always selected from the inner circle of Canadian art, and were not familiar with the crafts. A more insidious problem was made public by Aarons: "Regrettably for at least two known projects, the artist-advisor saw fit to allow himself a lion's share of the commission – in neither case did the results warrant such audacity."[41] Although Aarons did not link the two directly in her article making the claim of artist-advisors' dipping too deeply in the commission pool, she illustrated her arguments with the controversial piece called "Nootka Whaling Scene" completed by Lionel Thomas, the art advisor for the Royal British Columbia Museum in Victoria.

When Lionel Thomas, an associate professor of Fine Art at the University of British Columbia, was asked to serve as the artist-advisor in the museum project in 1965, he began by inviting 120 "important artists, designers and sculptors who reside in BC." to submit proposals for the new museum,

Fig. 3.4
Lionel Thomas, carved exterior doors for the Royal British Columbia Museum.

writing, "I believe I have covered the field."[42] And A.E. Webb, deputy minister of Public Works agreed with Thomas that a "sufficient number of mature artists of proven ability and known to the sub-committee" existed to commission works through invitation.[43] However, Thomas neglected to open up the commissioning process to a public competition. The selection committee for the Royal BC Museum was seeking many types of artwork, ranging from large-scale sculptures and murals in the entrance hall, and ornamented exterior doors, to "small sculptures, lamps, ceramic ashtrays, various size ceramic pots, medallions and lettering for Lounge areas, entrance foyers and offices."[44] The problem with having an associate professor of sculpture overseeing the monumental commissioning process was twofold for the crafts. First, craftspeople were conspicuously absent from Thomas's circle of "artists of proven ability." Second, as the above list of commissions suggests, his vision of the crafts remained small-scale. In the end, twenty-eight BC artists were hired to work on the museum; however, it was Thomas himself who received the largest commissions for the project, namely the carvings on all the large exterior doors (fig. 3.4) and the "Nootka Whaling Scene" sculpture for the front entrance hall – both projects for which skilled First Nations crafts-people existed.[45]

The architecture of the Royal BC Museum itself was remarkably ornamental, featuring tall archways framing the building, a decorative diamond pattern on the façade, and tall, thin columns reflecting the ornamental shallow pond in front of the archives. The building and Thomas's carved doors mirror architectural historian Harold Kalman's assertion that West Coast architecture was unique in Canada in maintaining a decorative tradition even at the height of International Style modernism. Furthermore, Thomas's use of native British Columbian woods for his doors connects them to their physical surroundings in a grove of tall, spectacular trees. The carved doors provided a dramatic natural and social history of British Columbia and they remain aesthetically pleasing and popular to this day. It was his depiction of the Nootka whaling scene that became a public issue.

When it was revealed that Thomas would receive the large sum of $80,000 for the commission, outrage erupted. The critics of his sculpture came from many backgrounds. Museum consultant George Moore described the work as "tedious, inaccurate, unimaginative, confused, dead and far, far too expensive." Don Abbott, the museum's curator of archaeology, and Charles Guiget, the curator of zoology stated publicly that they disliked the carving. Philip Ward, brought in as a consultant from the British Museum, said: "The display turned the museum into a shoddy tourist trap. It is a sad case of mistaken identity. It does not resemble a whaling scene at all … It resembles ancient Egyptians rescuing the bloated bodies of camels at the Suez canal."[46] Buried in the *Times Colonist* article were the poignant comments of Henry Hunt, the renowned First Nations carver, who criticized the figures in the canoe as not accurately depicting West Coast Aboriginal peoples. Hunt had not been one of Thomas's 120 "important artists, designers and sculptors who reside in BC." In fact the only Aboriginal involvement in the Royal BC Museum was on the part of the two carvers Thomas hired to execute his design of the canoe. "It's an authentic whaling canoe," Thomas argued; "I paid two Indians $12,000 to carve it."[47] Public indignation increased when it was learned that because of the over-expenditure on the art budget the museum could not afford to install a system for humidity control. On 28 May 1968 the *Victoria Daily Colonist* newspaper ran the headline "Museum Sculptor on Strike": "Lionel Thomas, the provincial museum sculptor whose carving of an Indian whaling scene has been under fire from numerous critics, made his first reply Monday night. He's going on strike until the 'meddling' ceases."[48] Fairly or unfairly, Thomas came to represent the abuse of the new one-percent art programs that perpetuated the nepotism of Canada's already small art community. The incident enraged Anita Aarons, who championed greater inclusion of craftspeople and craft materials. No public voice supported a greater presence for First Nations artists in the programs.

When the Department of Public Works' fine art program was launched, the Canadian Craftsman's Association, one of Canada's national craft organizations, immediately responded by encouraging craftspeople to take part in the program. In their national magazine, *Craftsman/L'Artisan*, the association listed every federal commission secured by a craftsperson, and also spread the word about how the program worked. In a 1972 article titled "Art in Public Buildings," the magazine reminded its readers: "As a Canadian craftsman, you can become involved in the federal Department of Public Works' fine art program. Artwork in federal buildings is not confined to murals and paintings, but includes such design elements as mosaics, frescoes, tapestries, stained glass, ceramics and wall hangings."[49] The article told craftspeople not to apply directly to the Department of Public Works, and to avoid the selection committee: "The consulting architect for the project is the man you want to see."[50] The reason for this advice was that, "naturally an architect is going to propose an artist whose work is known to him and whose work he thinks will complement the interior or exterior of his building."[51] As well, it was imperative that architects be able to see beyond craft materials as small-scale interior design elements and view them instead as large-scale artworks.

Craftspeople had mixed success with architects. Those who received large commissions were perceived as fundamentally shifting the public's understanding of craft, not only in terms of scale and form, but also in terms of economic value. As *SW Magazine* pointed out in 1969: "You can buy a ceramic ashtray, hand-shaped to resemble a maple leaf, for as low as 49 cents, and place-mats from a back-parlour loom for a few dollars a set. But when the builders of Toronto's Olympia Square wanted a mural for their walls, they paid ceramist Jordi Bonet $50,000 for his two 52 ft. by 16 ft. panels."[52]

Jack Sures

In the 1968 "Terms of Reference for an Advisory Committee on Fine Art Works for New Building Projects by the Department of Public Works," a definition of "Fine Artwork" was established: "Fine artwork shall be defined as those elements of a building design including murals, sculptures, ornamental surface treatment, mosaics, frescoes, tapestries, paintings, fountains, special lighting installations, etc., which are conceived and executed by professional artists."[53] It is obvious from the literature about the one-percent fine art program that a concerted effort was being made to include craftspeople and crafts. Aarons's lobbying through the Royal Architectural Institute of Canada was raising the profile of craft, with positive results. But craftspeople faced new challenges once they were selected for these enormous commissions. The "Standard Form of Agreement Between the Department of Public Works and Artists" made it clear that artists were responsible for all costs incurred for the creation of their works once they had accepted to complete a piece in a building.[54] For craftspeople who were manipulating craft materials to such large scales for the first time, this level of responsibility was daunting. The federal government's standard agreement was similar to those issued by provincial and federal governments: across the board craftspeople were responsible not only for the costs incurred for creating and installing the artworks but for guaranteeing the materials would not be damaged over the subsequent ten years.

When Sures took on the project of completing a 2,900-square-foot exterior ceramic tile mural for the Sturdy Stone building in Saskatoon, Saskatchewan, he did not anticipate that it would end up costing him money to produce. "I'm sorry I did it," he candidly states. "I worked fourteen months without pay"[55] (figs. 3.5, 3.6, 3.7). The Sturdy Stone building, named after two former Saskatchewan premiers, is a spectacular ode to Saskatchewan ceramics, featuring clay works on almost every floor. Initially the architects intended to "hire French Canadians to put bathroom tiles on the outside of the building, but someone on the Saskatchewan Arts Board said no way, we have lots of good Saskatchewan ceramists."[56] Sures had completed his first piece of public ceramics in 1964 for the University of Manitoba, a clay mural that was placed in the lobby of the progressive modernist Faculty of Architecture building designed by Smith Carter and Parkin in 1959. "It was pretty awful, but I made $300.00 and that was big money at the time."[57] When he was invited to complete the western exterior of the Sturdy Stone Centre, the Saskatchewan government's centrepiece in Saskatoon, the opportunity to work on such a prestigious project and on this large a scale appealed to him. Constructed in the shape of a trapezoid, devoid of its ceramic murals the Sturdy Stone Centre could have been accused of adopting a prison-like form of brute modernism. Instead, it was transformed through the work of six Saskatchewan ceramists into one of Canada's strongest regional architectural and craft statements.

Sures soon determined he could not complete the mural without more help, and realized his mistake: "I had to pay my labourers good wages, and in order to pay my helpers I ended up donating equipment to the University [of Saskatchewan] for 20% of their value as a tax write off. They garnished my wages for back taxes."[58] The reason Sures required additional help was that the first process he attempted for building the mural failed. His design was described in the official Sturdy Stone Centre publication as a "low relief circular motif made up of alternating bands radiating out from the centre of the circle. The mural is the artist's expression of a flower and is designed to complement the exterior architecture."[59] In order to achieve the alternating bands, Sures extruded a long ribbon of clay, but after completing half the mural he realized he had too many gaps in the piece. After rethinking his approach, he switched and used block pieces, which was "a scary process, counting pieces in twenty-three different shapes, 1200 of them for the outside circle alone."[60] In addition to the money lost switching processes, Sures hired contractors to install the piece as he stood on the scaffolding and directed them. He completed the piece in 1978, and by the time the work was installed in the summer of 1979, his enthusiasm for the project was eroded: "I should have listened to Don Wright (professor emeritus of Ceramics, University of Saskatchewan), who told me 'it's great to do these big commissions if you only lose $1000.00.'"[61] Sures went on to complete other large-scale ceramic murals, most notably for the Canadian Museum of Civilization in Gatineau, Quebec, but he was careful to ensure that his future contracts included provisions to adequately cover his costs.

Of course Sures would not have known what his expenses would be for this scale of work had he not undertaken the Sturdy Stone commission in the first place. Slowly craftspeople and artists were awakening to the problems of submitting estimates of expenses for projects on a large sale. The fact that they were often forced to work with unionized labour during the installation process brought expenses sometimes unanticipated in preliminary budgets. Furthermore, artworks installed by unionized labour were often guaranteed for a shorter period of time than the ten years of artist responsibility expected by the federal art works program. Nobuo Kubota, a sculptor who completed a piece for the south dining room of the Trans-Canada Training Institute building for the Ministry of Transport in Cornwall, Ontario, suggested changes to

Left Fig. 3.5
Worker installing the Sturdy Stone Centre mural, 1979.

Above Fig. 3.6
Finishing a single stoneware tile (unfired) for the Sturdy
Stone Centre, 1977–79.

Fig. 3.7
The Sturdy Stone Centre with exterior scaffolding and completed Jack Sures mural, 1979.

this agreement: "It is too vague and general in its present form. Specifically, where there are sub-trades involved, my guarantee can only be as good as their guarantee."[62] In 1978, thirteen years after its inception, changes were finally made to the agreement between the Department of Public Works and the Artist. However, despite these changes, agreements between artists and clients often neglected the issue of the moral rights of the artist.

Carole Sabiston

British Columbian textile artist Carole Sabiston was inspired by the idea of craft working within architecture, and romantically described the importance of craft in warming brute modern buildings: "At first [my] pieces were convenient lap size … but the growing feeling that there must be something more was incessant … Then the realization came! With the return to large-scale architecture in public buildings, my desire was to do as our mediaeval ancestors had done by creating colourful mammoth tapestries to give visual and physical warmth to the austere castle interiors."[63] Sabiston began her architectural commissions with the Skyline Hotel chain, completing tapestries for their buildings in Ottawa, Toronto, and London Heathrow. Her colourful fabric collages were inspired by her background in designing costumes for theatre productions, which led to her thinking "of all things as vignettes or scenes … public art as theatre, the creation of an environment that is light-filled and kinetic."[64] Her work in the theatre also gave her experience in creating collaboratively, and provided her with an understanding of how her artwork related to stage lighting, theatre design, and actors moving about in the space. As a result she adapted her forms and expanded their scale. Soon architects took notice of her collaborative abilities and she began working directly with architects, including John Parkin, Moshe Safdie, and Tom Moore, on a number of proposals and projects.[65]

Sabiston's textiles are composed of multiple layers with fabric and netting sewn as collages, and often feature metallic textiles that react to light and create ephemeral surfaces. Among her most popular architectural commissions are her depictions of the "Four Seasons" and ten banners of classic works of literature at Munro's Books in Victoria, British Columbia (fig. 3.8). These large-scale banners provide counterpoints to the neo-classical interior of the historic building housing this famous bookstore. The white of the accentu-

Fig. 3.8
Carole Sabiston, "Four Seasons" banners, fabric, textile. Munro's Books, Victoria.

ated columns with their ornate capitals and the consistently white colour palette throughout the store highlight the banners, which float above the top shelf-line and cover every wall in the store. Although their forms retain links to traditional tapestries and wall hangings (the "Four Seasons" have a rounded top that suggests windows or archways), their size and colour-filled surfaces befit Sabiston's desire to "give visual and physical warmth" to a space.

Sabiston's ability to work on a large scale led to the 1986 commission to complete a huge sunburst tapestry to be placed centre-stage during the opening ceremonies of Expo '86 in Vancouver. This design was to be based on the flag of British Columbia, and Sabiston was flown back and forth for meetings: "I made many maquettes, all moveable so the rays moved up and down."[66] Her dramatic design was executed by the same people who completed the tents for Expo '67, and Sabiston was soon left out of the process of production. She did not receive a ticket for the opening ceremonies, and the program, which featured a drawing of her design, credited the design to a man. Sabiston was indignant: "When I called the producer she claimed the initial idea of the sunburst was done by a man."[67] Following Expo '86 the sunburst was destroyed along with the other stage sets, leading Sabiston to question her moral rights. Her experience with Expo '86 was not the only negative one. Her four large panels for the Bayshore Hotel (each 3×7.3 m) in Vancouver were moved from the lobby to an area behind the elevators, and one panel went missing. "Now all four of my major works in Vancouver are gone," states Sabiston; she stills gets notes from travellers saying they miss her works.[68] Despite these unfortunate experiences, many of Sabiston's commissions for other locations remain, and she has won prestigious awards for her experimental works that pushed the boundaries of scale. In 1987 she won the Saidye Bronfman Award for Excellence in the Crafts, and in 1992 she was awarded the Order of British Columbia.

Destruction

Sabiston's experiences with the destruction and removal of her work offer a cautionary note that large scale offers no guarantee of permanence or monumentality for artworks. Scale does not assure public valuation of a work, nor does it deter from the destruction of art. In the words of art historian Annie Gérin: "If public art can be seen as an attempt to petrify accepted notions of collective identity in a given place … it also becomes a site where the homogeneity or legitimacy of these representations is constantly challenged and reframed."[69] What may have been celebrated at the moment of its unveiling will always be subject to the multitude of its viewers' personal aesthetics and changing socio-political currents. In this, public art and public craft are exactly the same. Painted murals and bronze sculptures are equally as vulnerable to vandalism as textile wall hangings and ceramic murals; however, the Canadian public has had far more exposure to paintings and sculptures and is trained to read them as acceptable forms of art, with a restricted palette of materials and scales. Haydn Llewellyn Davies blurred the line between craft and sculpture materials in his 1975 commission "Homage" for the Lambton Community College in Sarnia, Ontario.

"Homage" was a large outdoor sculpture constructed in laminated red cedar shapes carved by the artist (fig. 3.9). Davies was working in advertising when he submitted his proposal for "Homage" and much to his surprise he was selected to complete the sculpture. Davies spoke of his work for the new college building in terms similar to those used about the crafts: "I felt immediately that it was a marvellous piece of architecture, all striated concrete and glass, but it was cold. I wanted to humanize it, so the wood idea came to me easily."[70] For years "Homage" stood on the Lambton campus, "reminiscent of Stonehenge"[71] in its form. Sadly, in the summer of 2005, without any communication with the artist, bulldozers tore down "Homage"; the college administration claimed that its rotting wood made it a "safety hazard."[72] Davies was recovering from a serious heart attack when he learned of the destruction of his artwork, but his son Bryan Davies travelled to Lambton College where he inspected and photographed the remains of the piece. One of the best-publicized outcries over the destruction of public art in Canada ensued. Davies determined that his father's sculpture was not rotten and that the damage could have been repaired as it was only superficial.[73] In 2006 Davies sued the college for more than a million dollars, for "breach of

Fig. 3.9
Haydn Llewellyn Davies, "Homage," laminated red cedar sculpture, 1975.

contract, violation to moral rights, and 'intentional infliction of moral distress.'[74] On behalf of his father, he created a website, "Homage2Homage," which features a video clip of the destroyed sculpture with quotes about the work superimposed on top of the images. Set to a jazz soundtrack, "Homage2Homage" makes a strong statement about the vulnerability of artworks, regardless of their scale.[75] Although the lawsuit has not been settled and Haydn Davies passed away in 2008, the controversy remains in the public eye. The 2B Theatre Company in Halifax mounted a play by Anthony Black named *Homage*[76] based on the story.

What is so disheartening about the unapologetic destruction of Sabiston's and Davies' artworks is that it runs counter to cultural beliefs around monumentally sized art. When governments and institutions invest large amounts of money in public art, longevity is assumed. Daily interaction with these pieces leads viewers to create a relationship with a piece – whether the relationship is based on positive, negative, or disinterested feelings. Guiliana Bruno creates an analogy between a viewer's fleeting engagement with public art and discarded garments: "As part of an aesthetic collection that speaks of its wearer's taste, the discarded garment enacts recollection, recalling for us the person who inhabited its surface – the lively body that animated it."[77] Both artists and viewers anthropomorphize public artworks. Sabiston referred to her desire to "go see my babies" when she visited her tapestries at the Bayshore Hotel in Vancouver.[78] Rousseau-Vermette called her enormous woven curtain for the Eisenhower Theater in Washington's Kennedy Center for the Arts her "unwieldy child."[79] On a personal note, my father, Andrew Alfoldy, completed three cotton batiks for the BC liquor store in Creston, British Columbia, in 1982. These large wall hangings depicting swans were stretched across as a frieze. When I visited the store to document them in August 2009 they were gone. My father had not been contacted about their removal, but the employees in the store openly expressed their disappointment that they had been taken down. "I feel like my old friends have been taken away," said one woman. "Those swans were always there to greet me when I got to work."[80]

Intimacy

This process of anthropomorphizing speaks to the question of impact – whether personal or collective. Size may determine how much awe is inspired

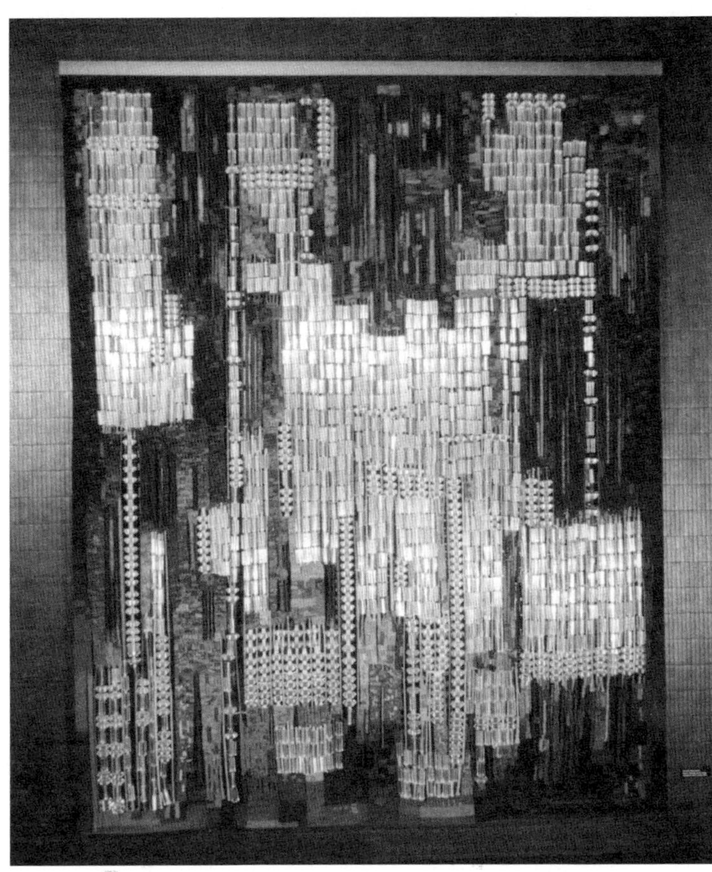

Fig. 3.10
Micheline Beauchemin, "A-B 1"
(4.3 x 3.3 m), woven materials,
acrylic fibres, transparent acrylic
beads, 1968.

in viewers, but daily interaction with public works of a more modest scale can lead to another form of influence through daily intimacy. Arthur Coleman Danto writes that scale contributes to "feelings of awe and wonder," a sentiment shared by Aarons, who promoted monumental craft for its metaphysical capacity. The crafts occupy a unique position in relation to eliciting wonder. In addition, the popularity of craft materials as hobbies means that great numbers of people have some level of familiarity with crafts, which can act as both a positive and a negative in terms of the public's acceptance of large-scale craft. This familiarity is an asset because recognition contributes to interest and to excitement about an object. In my observations of Micheline Beauchemin's wall hanging at the Macdonald Block of the Ontario Provincial Government building in Toronto, observers' sense of familiarity became evident (fig. 3.10). Beauchemin's piece is composed of shimmering acrylic fibres and beads in rich blues, greens, and silvers, shot through with red. It is an undeniably beautiful piece, and its aesthetic strength contributes to the positive reaction of the public; but what caused the most comment was familiarity with both the materials and the techniques of construction. Despite the fact this large work (4.3 × 3.3 m) hangs rather high in an elegant white marble stairwell, in my few minutes of observation, two people attempted to reach up and feel the piece, each mentioning that they had made woven wall hangings themselves.[81]

In contrast, even a mild understanding of craft processes can elicit severe criticism on the part of observers. Gathie Falk's 1979 "Beautiful B.C. Multiple-Purpose Thermal Blanket," a truly monumental quilt, hangs in the Credit Union Central of British Columbia main building in Vancouver designed by Walkey/Olsen Architects. Falk's "blanket" is composed of nine quilted canvas panels, each featuring a spring afternoon scene at the painter's home, with bright red tulips and other spring flowers interspersed with domestic scenes. While observing, I noted a group of three women openly touching the piece, which hangs low to the ground, commenting on its "poor quilting," and deriding it for having ripples of "displaced stuffing" on some of the quilted blocks (fig. 3.11).[82] The massive scale of Falk's piece suits the solidity and size of the building, and serves to connect the architecture to its surroundings, as the building is awkwardly situated on a small side street among townhouses and condominiums on Vancouver's Granville Island. The women made no comment, however, on the way Falk's quilted work interjects a strong domestic statement into the impersonal red brick lobby of the typical late-1980s office building. The fact that this piece is so enormous that it required insulation for quilt batting remained beyond the understanding of domestic-scale quilting that these observers used as their point of reference. They certainly did not pay attention to Falk's challenges with sewing on this scale, which she describes: "Sewing together all the squares on the sewing machine was so difficult that I thought instead of making the material move through the sewing machine, maybe I should move the sewing machine along the floor … So I got a dolly to put the machine on until the needle broke and then I couldn't find another to replace it. I was very close to despair with that, just because it was so hard to move stitch by tiny stitch, trying to move this enormous canvas that was very heavy with its four coats of undercoat, plus paint."[83]

These comments are paradoxical, given that the women observers made no remark on the colossal scale of this quilt; nor did they consider their technical criticism in light of the ironic inversion of quilting undertaken by Gathie Falk.

Fig. 3.11
Gathie Falk, "Beautiful B.C. Multiple-
Purpose Thermal Blanket" (5.5 x 4.9 m),
canvas, fibreglass, 1979.

Empty Narratives

Falk's "Thermal Blanket," remarked curator Art Perry in a review of the work, "is not meant as a narrative but more as a composite image of time and place."[84] Indeed, narrative plays a central role in any discussion of the impact of architectural craft. The narrative can be read as a form of material or technical narrative; the public may relate more to the craft materials in relation to the viewers' lives than to the visual or surface image of the entire piece, as evidenced by the criticism of Falk's quilt. Narrative in craft also draws in multi-sensory experience. Viewers' intimacy with craft materials may lead them to assume a more permissive space between themselves and public craft, leading them to touch (or even vandalize) public murals and sculptures. Personal narrative informs their understanding of the materials even if domestic forms are challenged through dramatic shifts in scale.

While many craftspeople use abstraction to avoid literal narratives or surface readings of their works, craft materials tend to invert any interpretation of disinterested concepts. For example, Sures' exterior clay mural for the Sturdy Stone Centre in Saskatoon was purposefully composed of a background of flat brown tiles with a raised concentric ring of brown tiles in the centre. This simple composition was not intended to be read as pure abstraction, but rather as a tribute to the power of Saskatchewan's clay artists, and the popularity of simple brown glazes during the late 1970s. However, in researching Sures' Sturdy Stone Centre mural it became evident that this abstracted motif has been accorded numerous literal interpretations, ranging from a rippling wheat field and flowers to a mandala. When artists do use their craft materials to form literal or personal narratives, as happened with Falk's "Beautiful B.C. Multiple-Purpose Thermal Blanket," their stories are sometimes obscured by their choice of materials. Worse still, critics may dismiss as empty or meaningless craftspeople's attempts to move away from the constraints of material or form and into large-scale abstracted or pictorial work.

Danto may have praised visionary ceramics, which he described as eliciting awe through the explosion of scale and an understanding of the sublime (Danto uses Immanuel Kant's formulation of the sublime, or the connection between wonder and astonishment), but other critics have argued that it is not simply enough for craft to move into the same realm as painting or sculpture through an increase of scale or a rethinking of forms. Robert Fulford called such early efforts of Canadian craftspeople "stillborn." To be fair to Fulford, he did not place all the blame for this at the feet of craftspeople. He argued that the process involved in applying for, winning, and completing an architectural commission was itself flawed, as "in the process of submitting sketches, or altering this detail or that, the work of artists becomes less and less interesting."[85] Craft critic Glenn Adamson shifts the blame back onto the craftsperson.

In his 2007 book *Thinking through Craft*, Adamson uses the architectural critic Kenneth Frampton to frame his ideas about craft's relationship with architecture, and focuses on the concept of means and ends. In the postwar industrial economy, Adamson argues, craft and architecture faced similar tensions between stripped-down modernist design and modern culture: "It was the same dilemma that had existed in different forms at the Bauhaus, and arguably even in the Arts and Crafts movement: the fundamental incompatability of autonomous design values and the realities of economic exigency."[86] Craftspeople, therefore, were financially inconvenient in terms of modern architecture, and rather than rethinking their materials and forms in order to become once again indispensable to the architect, they moved further away. Adamson refers to Frampton for his "writings on the tectonic, and his championing of architecture as a unique form of craft-based knowledge [which has] the real potential to serve as a corrective to the post-post modern architectural environment in which we find ourselves, with its 'Bilbao effects' on the one hand and complete mall-like standardization on the other."[87] Craft, in this view, stops being "a discrete set of techniques" and becomes "a way of being within society," in a way reminiscent of Heidegger's philosophical interpretation of building as a spiritual activity.[88] According to Adamson, architecture affords craft the unique opportunity to both respect "the qualities of particular disciplines and transcend … their self-assigned limits. It is a set of ideas that seem overdue."[89] Form and scale are among these self-assigned limits; however, rising above them is not enough. To Adamson many of the highest-profile craftspeople do not challenge the limits by grappling with the role of craft in a post-modern, cross-disciplinary world. Instead they return to comfortable ideas of narrative contained in craft materials and decoration, arguing: "If contemporary art cognoscenti still have a tendency to regard 'craft' with suspicion, who can blame them?"[90] It is an unfortunate reflection on the contemporary situation that, almost forty years after Fulford's critique of the crafts illustrated in Aarons's *Allied Arts Catalogue*, Adamson is able to apply the same criticism to the field.

Expo '67

Despite such pessimism, breakthroughs in the crafts have taken place and many of them have resulted from the challenges of working within architecture. Expo '67, the Montreal World Fair, offered Canadian craftspeople unprecedented opportunities to work on a large scale, shatter expectations around domestic forms, and show their work on an international stage. Crafts were highlighted in many of the ninety pavilions, and Canadian craft played an important role in provincial and federal buildings. Most significant was Moncrieff Williamson's national exhibition of craft titled "Canadian Fine Craft," held in the Canadian pavilion. The sixty-nine pieces on display ranged from the traditional, like an early Sures bowl of heavy brown stoneware, to the architectural, most notably Lindgren's "Winter Tree," a wood and lead

Fig. 3.12
Charlotte Lindgren, "Winter Tree"
(148 x 73 cm), wool, lead wire, 1967.

wire hanging composed of a complex single woven form that emerges from a tight circular base and becomes a series of loose threads suggesting the branches of a tree (fig. 3.12).[91] The large scale of many pieces, including Lindgren's, and the dramatic new forms that were unveiled, led to the acceptance of crafts alongside the other fine arts. The Canadian Pavilion housed simultaneous exhibitions on painting, sculpture, drawing, printmaking, and crafts, and while some critics expressed surprise at the inclusion of crafts at this international venue, others praised the exhibition for showing work of "sufficiently high quality to rank as art."[92] Craftspeople like Lindgren, who were successfully working with architects and pushing the boundaries of crafts, were the driving force behind this sea change in the way craft was being exhibited.

Canadian Fine Crafts at Expo '67 was not the only major exhibition at the time to feature crafts alongside the other fine arts. The Centennial Commission's "Perspective '67" at the Art Gallery of Ontario presented fine crafts, painting, sculpture, and graphic arts of Canadians between the ages of eighteen and thirty-five. It was no surprise that Williamson served as a member of the exhibition's national jury, or that Lindgren took the top prize for crafts in the exhibition. Dorothy Todd Henaut's article "1967 – The Moment of Truth for Canadian Crafts" in *artscanada* magazine credited the inclusion of crafts within fine art exhibitions as an indication of "the rapid evolution in attitude."[93] While Henaut did not highlight the new relationship with architecture that many craftspeople were building, her article featured an image of Lindgren's "Winter Tree," implicitly making this connection.

Contemporary analyses of the craft objects shown at Expo '67 have disappointingly glossed over the relationship between these pieces and architecture. Instead, exhibitions like the Confederation Centre Art Gallery's 2004 "From Our Land" have essentialized the craft shown at Expo '67 as symbolic of "utopian idealism [of] the craft revival realized through their small-scale, regionalized, utilitarian craft production."[94] It is also disturbing to see crafts equated with a nostalgic sense of the romanticized past by dint of their inherent materiality and comforting forms. This attitude is obvious in curator Lee Plested's statement: "The tourist audience of Expo '67 was interested in exoticizing the rural craftsman, while the artisans themselves were invested in replicating the myth in their work: it imbued their mastery of a craft with the effect of un-alienated labour."[95] Nothing could be further from the truth. For artists like Sures and Lindgren the exploration of ceramics and textiles was intimately linked to architecture, and intended to push the boundaries of material, form, and scale rather than making "lifestyle" statements through the crafts. For Sures, a resident of Regina, and Lindgren, whose home was in Halifax, the rural ideal simply did not apply. Furthermore, the buildings that featured their work were located in major cities like Ottawa and Winnipeg. It is clear that their artwork was not about regional specificity; it was about achieving new levels of professional production for craft in Canada, and architectural commissions were among the most important vehicles for this process.

This idea paralleled the goals of architecture at Expo '67. As Kalman expresses it: "Although in architectural terms Expo was intended to demonstrate Canada's international stature, many of the Canadian buildings ironically promoted expressionism and architectural distinctiveness, largely at the expense of the International Style."[96] Ironically, the crafts at Expo '67 had the same tendency, the only difference being that there was no International Style in the crafts to rally against; nor did a distinctly Canadian style of craft emerge, within or outside architecture. Aarons used her "Allied Arts" columns in *Architecture Canada* to reinforce the professionalization of craft through architecture, and Expo '67 provided her with excellent fodder. In June 1967 she dedicated her column to "The Artists and Expo." On the positive side she noted: "Architect, painter, sculptor, designer, film maker and lighting expert trespass so thoroughly on common territory that arbitrary divisions are useful but not always true."[97] This idea of cross-disciplinary exchange was relatively new in Canadian art writing, and Aarons championed the "conceptual architectural designer" as encapsulating this ideal.

For Aarons the Quebec pavilion and Moshe Safdie's cutting-edge apartment project "Habitat" surpassed all other Canadian efforts in establishing exciting new forms for craft and art, and the reason was simple: "This is indeed the spirit of this Canadian enterprise in Quebec – excitement and aesthetic pleasure rate higher than commercial profit."[98] "Habitat" featured an apartment decorated completely in the best of Canadian craft and design (fig. 3.13). It included a large tapestry by Rousseau-Vermette (which was purchased by the photographer Yousuf Karsh), and her husband Claude Vermette did the ceramic tile floors.[99] Quebec's provincial pavilion featured works such as Rousseau-Vermette and Micheline Beauchemin's woven tapestries, which challenged ideas of form and scale. Kalman suggests that Quebec's vibrant expressionistic architecture was politically motivated by the Quiet Revolution of the 1960s: "French Canadian architects may have been seeking a new national expression that was distinct from the International Style mainstream of Ontario and corporate Montreal."[100]

Textiles

Quebec had long been recognized as the centre for Canadian developments in tapestry.[101] The concept of breaking down boundaries between disciplines had long existed in Quebec, and the fact that Canada did not have

Fig. 3.13
Habitat, interior view, 1967.

an entrenched system of tapestry making allowed for freedom of expression. Quebec was the site of Canada's first tapestry weaving workshop, at the Ecole des Beaux-Arts de Québec, established in 1949.[102] Helen Duffy, in her introduction to the seminal exhibition of Canadian tapestry at the Barbican Centre in London, England, in 1982, writes that Walter Gropius's urging of his students at the Bauhaus in the 1920s to start from zero in order to "shed the 'dead weight' of an accumulated heritage" was naturally present in Canada, so Quebec's efforts to start a tapestry weaving workshop "injected new life into an industry which had, in Europe, reached an aesthetic impasse."[103] To Duffy, 1949 marked the beginning of "'the modern fibre movement,' La Tapisserie Nouvelle, in this country."[104] In 1959 the National Gallery of Canada exhibited ten of Rousseau-Vermette's tapestries, and nine hooked tapestries by Beauchemin. In 1961 the Musée des Beaux Arts in

Montreal held an exhibition titled "Textiles into 3D," which showcased Rousseau-Vermette and Beauchemin's "tapestries and luminous sculptures."[105] Naturally then, Quebec fibre artists like Rousseau-Vermette and Beauchemin would impress Aarons with their forward-thinking creation of large-scale tapestries, or flexible walls.

It is no surprise that today's efforts to bridge remaining gaps between craft and architecture rely heavily on woven textiles. Carole Collet of London's Central Saint Martins College of Art and Design believes that, just as the textile industry played a major role in the industrial revolution, it will lead the way in our technological revolution.[106] For Collet the new emphasis is on sustainability and the creation of organic, low-impact textiles. For many others today's textiles naturally align themselves with architecture both through their shared interest in developing environmentally sound green techniques, materials, and spaces, and through what is being termed responsive textile environments. As Sarah Bonnemaison and Christine Macy of Dalhousie University report: "Many designers, artists and architects are creating objects and environments that combine these new textiles with software, robotics and sensors. Whether their focus is clothing or immersive environments, their aim is to make textiles that interact with their users not only in visual or tactile terms, or even by being mobile, but which use digital interfaces to respond in all of these ways."[107] The challenge that once lay in manipulating textiles on a large scale has become almost irrelevant today, as new technologies allow for the production of works of an unprecedented size.

Not only have these developments shifted paradigms of scale but the very idea of what textiles are in relation to the human body or architectural spaces is changing. NSCAD University's Centre for Cultural Technology and Innovation's project "Architectural Applications of Electronic Textiles," headed by Bonnemaison and Robin Muller, is working toward the development of "smart" textiles that will be interwoven with lights and sensors to create "textiles responsive to sound, movement, sunlight and touch, and provide prototypes for curtains, free-standing walls, theatre backdrops and hung ceilings. The potential is limitless."[108] Similar projects are active across North America, the United Kingdom, and Europe, and an almost "Holy Grail" attitude of expectation exists in the hope that one of these textile labs will develop a truly new type of architectural craft.

What is interesting is that international efforts to develop responsive textile environments rely largely on traditional forms of the craft like curtains and walls. This reliance is related to the fact that architecture demands certain forms and scales of textiles for practical reasons. An excellent example is Rousseau-Vermette's innovative three-dimensional acoustic ceiling tapestry for Arthur Erickson's Roy Thomson Hall in Toronto, which received international praise when the hall was opened in 1982 (see fig. 2.4). The journal *Concrete Quarterly* described the practical aspects of the ceiling in detail: "The tapestry appears to hover between the ceiling and the seats in a sunburst pattern of suspended cylinders covered in wool, many of which are linked by heavy wool membranes which effect most of the sound absorption. These elements, or banners, radiate from two concentric rings of light fixtures connected by mirror-finish stainless steel rods like the spokes of a bicycle wheel ... Colours are white, cream, red, purple and burgundy with light silver-grey to complement the warm greys of the sandblasted concrete elements of the auditorium. To vary the reverberation time, different groupings of banners can be fully retracted so that the appearance of the tapestry changes with variations in the acoustics."[109] Every element of Rousseau-Vermette's design was worked out in close collaboration with the architect and the sound engineers, from the shape of her forms and types of wool to the colour palette. Rather than resenting this level of involvement she embraced it, arguing, "the architect should be your friend and involved from the concept stage."[110] Rousseau-Vermette presented her drawings to the architectural team from the beginning, and she created detailed maquettes at every stage of the design process.

It could be argued that the new responsive textiles are forcing this high level of collaboration and involving architects in textiles at an unprecedented level. It seems quite natural that Rousseau-Vermette was one of the first Canadian textile artists to begin working with fibre optics in her pieces. It became a successful and innovative practice because she was "willing to listen, to be flexible, to understand that the first drawings and designs presented to the client are done in the spirit of the building and the piece, not a finished statement."[111] Gottfried Semper explored the fluid interchange between textiles and architecture in his nineteenth-century writings that argued that textiles gave rise to various forms of architecture. Specifically, Semper claimed that woven textiles were the basis for archetypal patterns of wall coverings well before civilization had developed timber-framed or masonry buildings. Semper's theory has not been well received in the architectural world. In describing a 2004 design for a railway station in Worb, Switzerland, which was based on Semper's theory of textile patterns in architecture, *Architectural Review* called his philosophy a "wacky idea (based on no real evidence)."[112]

Wacky or not, Semper's views on textiles and architecture are enjoying a renaissance, largely through the efforts of responsive textile labs in the United Kingdom and North America. Semper's theory and new approaches to craft within architecture together remind us to question the forms we take for granted, and to think of scale in new ways. Much rests on the hope that craft will work with technology in enabling new architectural tools and materials to evolve; however, efforts so far have not always been successful. A certain sameness persists in the fibre optics employed in curtains and hanging walls, and we are only now entering a post-euphoric phase regarding the implications of computers as tools for the crafts.

It is significant that to date most criticisms of the efforts resulting from the integration of new technologies into craft practice have had to do not with form, scale, or materials but with ornamentation. Glenn Adamson argues that the longevity of the debate over decoration is related to "perceptions about craft as a cultural phenomenon" and the "late-capitalist character" of popular craft decorations such as the glass work of Dale Chihuly, which Adamson describes as "hedonism not conceptualism."[113] Craft it seems, despite efforts to rethink scale and form in relation to architecture, has once again become the victim of ornament.

4 ORNAMENT

I am interested in how the pair ornament/structure has throughout
the history of Western culture had an acritical relationship with
the pair feminine/masculine and in the ramifications of this for
architecture as cultural production.
Jennifer Bloomer[1]

At the corner of Nelson and Burrard streets in Vancouver is a striking expanse
of highly decorative ceramic tiles (fig. 4.1). As one approaches, the green and
blue geometric design that dazzles through its deep colour and repetitive pattern grows larger until it reveals itself to be an enormous ornamental mosaic
covering the lower level of a towering building. The BC Electric Building,
constructed between 1955 and 1957 and now a condominium, is a twenty-two-storey high-rise. The fact that it is built in the classic modernist steel and
curtain-wall style makes it remarkable that artist B.C. Binning's ceramic mural
formed an integral part of the design. Architect Ned Pratt, assisted by Ron
Thom, worked closely with Binning to realize the artist's vision of a mosaic
that abstractly referenced the natural beauty and climate of Vancouver:
green for the rainforest, blue for the waterways, and black for the mountain
and frequently grey skies.[2] Binning, a professor of Fine Art at the University
of British Columbia, was a dedicated modernist who built his career on abstract
painting and had undertaken several public commissions. It is noteworthy
that his most enduring public artwork remains metres of porcelain mosaic,
a bold statement on the importance of ornament in Canadian architecture.

In this chapter I explore the tense relationship between ornament and architecture in postwar Canada, looking first at the Eurocentric assumption that
minimal decoration equalled progressive rationalism. I continue by placing
Canadian craft's concern with decoration in the context of E.H. Gombrich's
sense of ordering provided by ornamentation. This contextualization allows

us to trace how regional and national differences are articulated through decoration, and how Fine Art theorists and writers conflated craft with ornamentation and gender, leading to moments of marginalization within fine arts and architectural discourses. However, as I shall propose, ornament and craft were never separated from architecture, and during the postwar period they remained Allied Arts in Canada.

The term "ornament" is a double-edged sword. On the one hand craftspeople shy away from using it because of its long and damning history in relation to craft. On the other hand, architects rarely think of their buildings in terms of ornamentation, with its allusions to frivolity and the feminine. I hope to demonstrate that, while the term is rarely employed within Canadian craft and architecture, ornament remains central to the Allied Arts. The myth that ornament died out with the introduction of early twentieth-century modernism is intricately linked to the fate of the crafts, which were also seen as suffering near-death under the reign of the modernists. Architectural his-

Fig. 4.1
B.C. Binning, porcelain mosaic mural, 1955–57. BC Electric Building, Vancouver.

torians such as Harold Kalman, Janet Wright, and Alan Gowans have argued that the myth is untrue in the Canadian context. While Kalman states that "'Modernism' (the 'ism' affirms it as a doctrine) reached Canada tentatively in the 1930s and became firmly entrenched in the 1950s,"[3] it never became the dogmatic, unornamented International Style. Vancouver, home of the BC Electric Building, is acknowledged as the place where modernism first developed in Canada and, as Kalman notes, Binning was the "leading participant in the acceptance of the International Style and the development of an early and important regional variant, the West Coast style."[4]

Kalman's emphasis on regional variation is central to understanding how Canada avoided a reductionist attitude toward ornament within architecture, and helps explain why the BC Electric Building remains festooned with Binning's colourful porcelain mosaic, one of the most celebrated pieces of public craft in the country. While Binning was a devoted formal abstractionist, he was equally passionate about celebrating the natural beauty of his province. Kalman argues that this observance of regional uniqueness through architectural decoration went beyond British Columbia and informed national architecture as a whole: "Many [architects] chose to deviate from international modernism in order to express a regional character and a personal vision."[5] In realizing their vision, architects often needed to collaborate with craftspeople, as it was craft's attention to material details that would complete a building's distinctive statement, and Canadians were seeking to make these types of assertions.

The Psychology of Ornament

Ornament is a visual necessity and a critical interpretive tool. It opens up the possibility of play, engendering moments of surprise and delight in otherwise quite serious and bland public spaces. In postwar Canadian society, neutrality became an important tool in negotiating the complex, ideologically fraught multicultural ideal, and as a result many government buildings are purposefully dispassionate in their decorative elements. It is far safer to construct an international-style minimalist statement than one that draws upon regional or cultural specificities, and this applies not only to architectural design but also to modes of ornamentation. The result has often been an underutilization of the decorative to make strong Canadian statements. Perhaps that underutilization elsewhere explains why B.C. Binning's overtly ornamental homage to British Columbia has become one of Vancouver's most popular public art projects, carefully preserved and promoted as representing a uniquely local style. But Canada is not alone in its general neglect of ornament and craft within architecture; it simply reflects the trend away from the decorative in the twentieth century. While the great majority of postwar buildings either completely ignore ornament, accidentally create it, or apply craft objects as ornamental afterthoughts, the most enduring and beloved architecture in Canada has embraced the decorative as an essential part of the design: Ottawa's Parliament buildings with their post-war stone carvings, Toronto's Massey College, Saskatoon's Sturdy Stone Centre, and Vancouver's BC Electric Building are excellent examples.

Despite theoretical and practical shifts away from the use of ornament, writers have commented for centuries on the close associations between ornament and emotional well-being. Writer and poet Karin Cope, in speaking of art and literature, asserts that cultural spaces are potentially places of negotiation between individual beings and their surrounding environments, and as such are mediators in the relationship between play and reality. Art, she states, is a manifestation of play.[6] But since many art critics, curators, artists, and art historians see play as antithetical to the project of creating serious art, the desire to distinguish between serious and non-serious art becomes important in terms of elevating craft in relation to architecture. Ornament can be whimsical, frivolous, and too playful, according to modernist dogma, jeopardizing the seriousness of art as a whole. But key writers and thinkers on ornament find this accusation unfair, as it overlooks the deep-seated human desire for decoration. One of the most famous texts on ornament, Gombrich's *The Sense of Order: A Study in the Psychology of Decorative Art* (1979), is based on the notion that a human being is simply an organism that "searches and scans the environment ... and must, as it were, plot the message it receives against that elementary expectation of regularity which underlies ... the sense of order."[7] Ornament provides this sense of order or, as Gombrich argues, "the world which man has made for himself is, as a rule, a world of simple geometric shapes" reflecting "our tendency to regard order as the mark of an ordering mind."[8]

This analysis rings true in relation to Canada's organized program of government building projects that was launched in 1965. Not only were the buildings themselves designed to reflect the federal structure of the country but the committee determined the minimal and cautious use of ornament, to be regulated as carefully, and one might say in as orderly a manner, as pos-

Fig. 4.2
Merton Chambers, plasticized
illuminated batik, 1968.

sible. In her book *Crown Assets: The Architecture of the Department of Public Works 1867–1967*, Janet Wright offers a rationale for this concern for conformity and regulation: "The majority of federal buildings were erected on a modest and economical scale but they too were built to project a suitably dignified architectural image that would reflect creditably on the state."[9] Gombrich stresses the ethical aspects of this economy of style, taking the strongly moral, almost religious tone employed in discussions of ornament: "Ornament is dangerous precisely because it dazzles us and tempts the mind to submit without proper reflection."[10]

This criticism of lack of reflection, or lack of seriousness, has been directed equally at overly decorative craft objects. In his book *Thinking through Craft*, Glenn Adamson deplores the blown glass Dale Chihuly chandelier that hangs in the lobby of London's V&A Museum as "hedonistic" for its complete submission to decorative beauty and lack of critical content.[11] When Canadian art critic Robert Fulford panned Anita Aarons's *Allied Arts Catalogue* in 1967, he was essentially levying the same charge, calling the featured works by craftspeople "stillborn art" for their lack of criticality, or seriousness. The objects shown, such as Merton Chambers's bright batiks (fig. 4.2), defied the sober and rational through the playfulness of their materials and designs. The fact that these craft works were attempts to revive and expand upon historic craft techniques had no significance for Fulford, whose dismissive attitude simply reinforced the idea that "old-fashioned virtuosity – supreme skill in craft – has yet to shake off the taint of naive literalism and soulless artificiality."[12] The outspoken Aarons worked tirelessly to demonstrate that Canadian crafts for architecture were based upon concepts not on skill alone; however, she was frustrated in these attempts because architects and craftspeople continued to be educated in divergent ways – architects rarely hearing anything positive about ornament and craftspeople seldom learning about architecture.

While Canadian craftspeople and architects may have found themselves isolated from each other during the postwar period, art historians and critics still debate ornament as a central forces that unites these two areas. For example, art historians continue to analyse Gombrich's rooting of ornament in biological heritage, and deconstruct his tendency to conflate ornament, decoration, and pattern.[13] In a study on Gombrich, Isabelle Frank notes the difficulties the psychologist faced in seeking to understand and categorize ornament, confirming that changes to these schema are rare and difficult to achieve.[14] According to Gombrich and Frank's notion of set representations for ornament, creating a new and uniquely "Canadian" form of ornament becomes almost impossible; to craftspeople and designers, on the other hand, combining or rethinking historical or natural schema in innovative ways remains an intriguing possibility. But if architects are not taught to read ornamental schema, and craft students are equally deficient in the language of decoration, the problem is deeper than a lack of communication between architects and craftspeople; it becomes recognizable as part of a greater social attitude.

There was another attitude behind the distaste for decorative craft in postwar Canadian architecture – an abhorrence of excess. As Gombrich points out: "Not only the splendours of kings and princes, but also the power of the sacred has been universally proclaimed by pomp and circumstance."[15] Federal, provincial, and municipal governments had to be careful to shy away from associations with the monarchy and the church while simultaneously demonstrating rationality. It was equally damning for corporations to be seen to promote immoderation in their decorative schemes. But it can be difficult to make ornament appear rational. Ornament theorist Brent Brolin supposes that this is because the visual nature of embellishment relates more to feeling than to the intellect. "[Architectural ornament] has no relation to the pseudo-

moral, pseudo-rational principles of design ... The quality of an ornament –
is it well done or not? – should be determined by what you feel when you see
it, not whether or not it fits some intellectual construct."[16] In the midst of this
postwar impulse to control and order the national character of public spaces,
it was not surprising that flickers of the need to express a deeper psychological longing through ornament should emerge.

The Metaphysics of Ornament

In her monthly columns for the Royal Architectural Institute of Canada's
magazine, Aarons emphasized the mysterious nature of art. For her, public
art commissions were not simply decorative objects designed to break up
space. She felt that large-scale artworks had an obligation to offer the
public reflective moments in their everyday lives, and that the use of ornament
as "metaphysical beguilement"[17] was key to achieving a symbiotic relationship between the artist and the viewer. In an effort to encourage craftspeople
to consider the deeper meaning of the decorative, Aarons dedicated columns
to themes such as "Signs, Signals, Symbols and Traditions."[18] She argued that
contemporary Canadian art was devoid of totems and traditional forms, being
left instead with sterile artifacts. This absence of reference, she determined,
distinguished craft from art: "Mere function has replaced ritual use. Decoration is now idle and meaningless."[19] She was concerned that the modern world
no longer attached significance to historic ornament, thus rendering meaningful decoration obsolete. As a result, she wrote: "The archaeologist of
tomorrow will find more truth and excitement in the symbols, torn from the
earth, of today's children's toys, the TV antennae, or the giant steel girders
of the power lines straddling the countryside."[20] Aarons found the cleaving
of ornament from its deeper metaphysical roots troubling, and she described
the dramatic "clumsy" images of contemporary art as "'awe'ful, *ie* full of awe
rather than charming, graceful and beguilingly decorative." Furthermore, the
more Canadian artists became removed from the significance of symbols,
the more they separated art from architecture. "Artist and architect serve their
separate gods. Outmoded, out of practice and out of context, the inclusion of
art merely as a decorative element is as sacrilegious as a black mass."[21]

Over the next five years Aarons used her writings to urge artists and craftspeople to reintroduce deeper conceptual meaning to their materials, forms, and

surfaces through eloquent ornamental schema. She curated the exhibitions "Crafts for Architecture" (1967) and "Art for Architecture: The Wall" (1969), published two Allied Arts catalogues (1966, 1968), and dedicated her monthly columns for the *Journal RAIC* (later *Architecture Canada*) to an effort to demonstrate that meaningful decoration was being achieved by some Canadian craftspeople. She clearly laid out the elements required for a successful ornament: a consideration of the relationship between light and space; the creation of a certain mood or ambience; the suggestion of metaphysical possibilities; and the conveyance of profound meaning. She dismissed pure decoration for its meaningless: "Art is not interior decoration or punctuation for an unresolved space. It should have presence."[22] Although she denigrated the wholly decorative, she acknowledged the emotional and aesthetic impact of minor decorative details such as grilles, wall treatments, and door handles – as long as they were effectively integrated into the larger vision of the artist executing these details.[23] The inability to combine the decorative with the conceptual was a sign of amateurism to Aarons, the "albatross" that weighed down much of Canadian craft. In her determination of what was "primitive" decoration (both in terms of cultural aesthetic and unrefined approach) Aarons expressed the Eurocentric attitudes prevalent in 1960s Canada. She dismissed crafts that exhibited a "sentimental desire to preserve Canadiana" and waved aside "the indigenous art of the Eskimo and Indian, who are sadly without reason for the artefacts they produce."[24]

In Aarons's search for artworks that built community through the conceptual and metaphysical, the attempt to create a Canadian identity through Canadiana or Indigenous ornament was too limiting. She was not interested in determining easily identifiable "Canadian" decorative motifs; rather, she was seeking to establish the country's craftspeople as capable of producing universally significant ornament.

Nationalism

Any discussion of a particularly Canadian form of ornament is made difficult by the diversity of national and identity politics within the country. But Canada is not unique in its inability to reconcile ornament and nationalism. For centuries art historians, critics, and architects such as Owen Jones, August Schmarsow, Heinrich Wolflin, Eugène-Emmanuel Viollet-le-Duc, and Alois

Riegl have put forward ornamental theories with both subtle and overt nationalistic overtones. In his remarkable compendium *The Grammar of Ornament*, published in 1856, Owen Jones wrote one of the most famous passages on the global appeal of ornament: "From the universal testimony of travellers it would appear, that there is scarcely a people, in however early a stage of civilisation, with whom the desire for ornament is not a strong instinct. The desire is absent in none, and it grows and increases with all in the ratio of their progress in civilisation. Man appears everywhere impressed with the beauties of Nature which surround him, and seeks to imitate the extent of his power the works of the Creator."[25]

Jones highlighted three enduring characteristics of ornament: first, despite its universality, not all ornament is considered equal, and "improves" according to Western prerogatives of progress; second, all ornament finds its roots in nature; third, ornament is created in response to, and seeks an understanding of, higher powers. On the basis of these qualities, philosophers and critics have argued that any attempts to create a nationally specific form of ornament must first acknowledge wider ranges of influences. This idea is repeated and amplified in the majority of writings on ornament, which are built upon Eurocentric assumptions that while "savage" or "primitive" ornament provided some basis for designs, artists of the European enlightenment propelled these ideas into the modern age. In the nineteenth century John Ruskin and William Morris's musings on good decoration in relation to the morality of handicraft further conflated morality and craft; a society needed to hold proper moral standards in order to advance either in decoration or in the crafts. The corollary was also true. "The pursuit of art without reference to natural form," Ruskin stated when speaking of the need to study the human figure as the basis of all good ornament, can only lead to "degradation of temper and intellect."[26]

For Ruskin, any style of ornament was necessarily composed of "characteristic or moral elements" that reflected a society's character.[27] Of course not all writers were as overtly moralistic or nationalistic as Ruskin, who regarded the Gothic Revival style as the pinnacle of enlightened ornament and craft. In his efforts to promote this style, he did achieve a sophisticated analysis of the difficulty of assigning a specific decorative style to a nation, arguing that within every country and period all buildings differ, and that viewers are forced to interpret greater and lesser degrees of national styles. He spoke in particular about "Gothicness – the character which, according as it is found more or less in a building, makes it more or less Gothic."[28] Following Ruskin, if such a thing as a truly Canadian form of ornament exists it would necessarily have to be referred to in terms of its "Canadianness."

Adolf Loos

As modernism took hold in the first part of the twentieth century, debates about decoration and ornament focused on the need to reduce ornament in an effort to streamline industrial designs and achieve an international form of decoration, as espoused by Adolf Loos and Le Corbusier. This would not be the universally appealing ornament described by Jones, but rather a specific decorative style established by a European artist. In 1908 Loos composed "Ornament and Crime," his famous diatribe against ornament in which, presupposing a disturbing hierarchy of national and cultural characteristics, he recommended a new universal rule for the decorative – that it be completely abolished. Loos began his essay with this idea: "The human embryo in the womb passes through all the evolutionary stages of the animal kingdom. When man is born, his sensory impressions are like those of a newborn puppy. His childhood takes him through all the metamorphoses of human history. At 2 he sees with the eyes of a Papuan, at 4 with those of an ancient Teuton, at 6 with those of Socrates, at 8 with those of Voltaire. When he is 8 he becomes aware of violet, the colour discovered by the eighteenth century, because before that the violet was blue and the purple-snail red. The physicist points today to colours in the solar spectrum which already have a name but the knowledge of which is reserved for the men of the future."[29]

According to Loos, then, enlightenment belongs to European models, and the future belongs to science. Irrational, passionate ornament no longer has a place in this world, and serves only to cause "damage and devastation … in aesthetic development." He continues: "The speed of cultural evolution is reduced by the stragglers."[30] Who are the stragglers? Non-European peoples, peasant folk cultures in Europe (Loos speaks condescendingly of the "Slovak peasant woman who embroiders her lace"[31]), and craftspeople. Not only are the crafts emblematic of ornament and confused national pride but craftspeople are portrayed as beyond help. Loos stresses that his essay is directed toward the aristocrat, "who stands at the pinnacle of mankind" and controls the purse strings of the nation, ultimately dictating the level of ornamentation that craftspeople produce for the marketplace.[32] Yes, it is a passionate appeal to rid the world of the scourge of ornament. But more significantly, given the socio-political context of 1908 Austria where Loos composed his thoughts, it is a call to craftspeople and consumers to recognize the dangers of nationalistic decoration. It is a waste of time and labour, and obscures larger political and social issues through the demanding focus on detailed work.

Yet the craftsperson is at the heart of Loos's article. He emphasizes the economic interests of craftspeople: "Even greater is the damage done by ornament to the nation that produces it. Since ornament is no longer a natural product of our culture, so that it is a phenomenon either of backwardness or degeneration, the work of the ornamentor is no longer adequately remunerated."[33] Consistent with Loos's imperative of progress, he warns that in an increasingly industrialized world there is no way craftspeople can be paid for the time it takes to create intricate decoration, and therefore it becomes superfluous. Furthermore, the peasant folk crafts he identifies as stragglers represent a dangerous fractioning of nationalistic sentiments, in opposition to the goal of universal aesthetics.

Gender and Ornament

In our postmodern era the idea of a universal form of decoration points up the Eurocentric nature of such a proposal, which assumed that a European architect or designer would determine the dominant style. Despite such a dubious perspectives and the excessive nature of Loos's anti-ornament position, by the end of the Second World War the modernist vision of reduced ornament had taken hold, in opposition to the late nineteenth-century celebration and study of good decoration represented by such institutions as London's V&A Museum.[34] It was during this period that scholarship relating to ornament, previously the domain of male scholars seeking a scientific approach to art, became overtly linked to the feminization of art. This development came about in part through the rejection of the British Arts and Crafts Movement – and Ruskin and Morris – as being outdated, overly fussy, and too feminine. In Canada Donald Buchanan, the head of the National Gallery of Canada's Industrial Design Department, established in 1947, and chair of the National Industrial Design Committee, denied the crafts a role in either industrial design or architecture, arguing that the future belonged to the modern, simplified materials of "aluminum sheets and magnesium rods, plywood and laminated wood, chemical, plastics and cellulose compounds, the new techniques of design."[35] Buchanan's anti-craft position was part of his effort to elevate Canadian design on the international stage, where limited ornamentation was synonymous with good design.

Canada's national craft organization, the Canadian Handicrafts Guild, founded in 1906 by Alice Peck and May Phillips, was so fundamentally a female organization, both in its approach to the crafts and in its membership, that it was doubly marginalized in any thinking about architecture. Indeed, the guild, whose mandate was founded upon philosophies from the British Arts and Crafts Movement, was set up to counteract developments within contemporary design and architecture. As historian Joy Parr points out: "Younger Canadian Modernists, such as the architect Humphrey Carver, saw the English Arts and Crafts as a feminizing error, a design doctrine about workshop production which too soon isolated 'itself from the vigorous real world' and 'declined into a reactionary and sentimental spinsterhood.'"[36]

The guild was well aware of the negative sentiment it elicited. J. Murray Gibbon, wartime president of the guild, had been "an Oxford student in the heyday of the English Arts and Crafts Movement"[37] and he tried to coax Canadian art institutions into working with the guild by appealing to Arts and Crafts ideals, emphasizing the importance of educating artists, craftspeople, and architects in the elements of good ornament. He approached the venerable Royal Canadian Academy in 1943 and argued that the small size of the Canadian market, Canada's abundance of raw materials, and the potential for postwar growth made the crafts an ideal area of inclusion within the institution. Gibbon's appeal fell upon deaf ears, as did the guild's call for the establishment of a Handicraft Office at the National Gallery of Canada to work alongside Buchanan's initiatives in regard to industrial design.[38] Not only was this rejection a blow to the efforts of craft supporters to encourage the relationship between craftspeople and architects but it reflected the lowly position occupied by any materials so obviously connected to gendered ideas of ornament.

The gender bias was pronounced. Employing terms reminiscent of Carver's insulting use of "spinsterhood" to malign craft, Deane H. Russell, the federal secretary of the Interdepartmental Committee on Canadian Handicrafts, presented a report in 1941 on "Hand Arts and Crafts in Canada" to the International Conference on Food and Agriculture in Virginia. He chastised the "craft revival's potential to 'glorify without qualifying, what our grandmothers made.'"[39] While anglophone Canada was bitterly chipping the crafts apart from modern architecture and design, for a brief time things were quite different in Quebec.

Ornament in Quebec

When the École du Meuble was formed from the cabinetry department of Montreal's École Technique in 1935 it established a refreshing new perspective on the importance of decoration and the decorative arts in Québec. Previously the École des Beaux-Arts, established in 1923, had adhered to a rigid hierarchy that separated craft from fine art and architecture, but with the advent of the École du Meuble "the economic possibilities that craft and design created for emerging artists" were acknowledged.[40] Alena M. Buis, in an article "The Practical Side of Decorating: Paul-Émile Borduas at the École du meuble," traces how one of Québec's most famous abstract painters started out working in close association with the decorative. Borduas was hired in 1937 as the École du Meuble's professor of Drawing, Decoration and Documentation and taught classes with titles such as "Decorative Composition," which stressed colour theory, symmetry, and design.[41] Under the leadership of Jean-Marie Gauvreau the school paid great respect to the decorative history contained in Québécois vernacular furniture, textiles, and architecture.[42] As Buis comments: "While teaching at the École du Meuble, Borduas was physically and theoretically situated in an environment that encouraged and valorized craft production." As a result he began working with architecture professor Marcel Parizeau to renovate and furnish his home, which was a "combination of modernist and traditional elements."[43] In relation to the distinct divide between craft, fine art, and architecture in Canada's art schools, universities, and art societies, this was a radical approach by a modernist artist. Rather than rejecting the decorative nature of craft, Borduas surrounded himself with its possibilities. He even went as far as allowing one of his paintings, "Number 28 (1942)," to be reproduced as a silk-screened furnishing fabric, sold for $5.00 a yard, available in three colours, and "ideal for making lampshades, dresses, slipcovers, scarves and curtains" (fig. 4.3).[44]

Unfortunately, this close liaison between the decorative and the modernist abstract agendas was to be short-lived. In 1948 Borduas was one of sixteen artists (the *Automatistes*) who published their famous "Refus global," or

Une coopérative d'art

Des artistes canadiens partagent avec nous la beauté qu'on ne croyait accessible qu'aux riches

Stanley Cosgrove travaillant à l'esquisse que lui suggéra sa toile, "Les arbres", reproduite sur la page ci-contre. Photos Bert Beaver.

Robert LaPalme, le caricaturiste renommé, auteur de plusieurs séries de dessins sur la médecine, la guerre et la mode à travers les âges.

Sa collection de peintures canadiennes donna à Peter Freygood, l'animateur de Canadart, l'idée de réunir des artistes en coopérative et de faire partager par tous le plaisir qu'on éprouve à vivre avec de belles choses. Il n'était pas question de reproductions des oeuvres de ces peintres ni de bibelots, ce qui serait encore du luxe pour la plupart, mais d'objets utiles et indispensables. Pourquoi pas des tissus dessinés par ces peintres? Tissu d'ameublement pour draperies et housses, tissus pour robes, jupes, écharpes et abat-jour.

La plupart des grandes filatures ont toujours prétendu que l'acheteur exige certains motifs décoratifs et pas d'autres et se sont instituées juge et partie du goût féminin au Canada. Canadart, au contraire, n'impose aucune restriction à l'artiste; c'est lui qui choisit les éléments de son dessin et l'exécute sujet à l'approbation de sa femme, car les membres actuels de l'équipe d'artistes sont mariés. La femme de l'artiste pourrait-elle s'enthousiasmer pour des draperies ou des housses qui lui déplairaient et qu'elle serait fort probablement condamnée à voir dans sa propre maison tous les jours de sa vie?

Le dessin terminé, il est imprimé au pochoir dans les ateliers de l'entreprise à Verdun. Quatre peintres, déjà, ont vu leurs dessins imprimés et en vente chez Henry Morgan Co. Ltd, à Montréal et chez Robert Simpson Limited à Toronto. Le tissu à draperies et à housses est un lourd croisé qui tombe en beaux plis; lavable, il ne se fane pas à la lumière. Le prix en est de $5.00 la verge. Chaque dessin est imprimé en trois couleurs différentes afin qu'il se prête à l'harmonie préférée de l'acheteur.

Les artistes de Canadart reçoivent une royauté sur chaque verge de tissu vendu. Par conséquent, ils sont dédommagés pour autant que le public acheteur apprécie ou non leur oeuvre. C'est le système de la vente d'un livre. Si l'on n'avait pas aimé *Bonheur d'occasion* ou *Les Plouffe*, ces romans ne se seraient pas vendus.

Canadart réunit d'abord quatre artistes: Stanley Cosgrove, d'ascendance française et irlandaise, dirige un atelier de peinture et de fresque à l'Ecole des Beaux-Arts de Montréal. La plupart des galeries d'art canadiennes possèdent de ses oeuvres. Il a étudié l'art et la technique de la fresque sous Orozco, le grand artiste mexicain. Robert LaPalme, caricaturiste renommé au journal *Le Canada*, auteur de plusieurs séries de dessins sur la guerre, la médecine, la mode à travers les âges. Maurice Raymond, chef de section d'arts décoratifs aux Beaux-Arts de Montréal. Ses toiles figurent dans la plupart de nos musées. Pendant que Cosgrove étudiait au Mexique, Raymond, lui, obtenait une bourse pour les Etats-Unis où il séjourna durant un an. Paul-Emile Borduas, un des plus grands représentants de la peinture non-figurative au Canada et dont les oeuvres apparaissent dans nos galeries d'art. Depuis, Jeanne Rhéaume, peintre montréalais bien connu, gagnante du prix du Salon du printemps, et Campbell Tinning, un autre Canadien, ont formé un groupe auquel s'ajoutera d'autres peintres.

A la fabrique: Peter Freygood, Maurice Raymond, Cosgrove et Robert LaPalme surveillent l'impression d'un dessin au pochoir.

Above and opposite Fig. 4.3
"Paul-Émile Borduas watching his wife and daughter hang curtains made from his printed fabric" (opposite, bottom), La Revue Moderne, vol. 32, no. 3 (July 1950), 10–11.

Voici la toile de Cosgrove qui inspira au peintre le motif de ses draperies. Ce même dessin est imprimé en trois couleurs de fond.

Maurice Raymond, dans son atelier, achevant son premier motif pour Canadart: des coqs sur une route. Photo Studio Louis-Philippe.

Un dessin de Robert LaPalme et son tissu d'ameublement qui représente une de nos légendes les mieux connues "La chasse-galerie".

Paul-Emile Borduas, sa femme et une de leurs filles mettent en place des draperies dont le dessin a été tiré d'une gouache de l'artiste.

"Total Refusal," an anti-establishment manifesto that completely rejected what they considered to be the outdated and antiquated ideas of Québécois society.[45] These artists, including Borduas, were influenced by the writings of Surrealists like André Breton, who insisted on pure aesthetics that disregarded everyday utility. Therefore, not only did Borduas find himself rejecting the celebratory stance of Gauvreau and the École du Meuble toward traditional Québécois handicrafts but he distanced himself from decoration, reacting angrily to an April 1950 article in *Canadian Homes and Gardens* that "declared Borduas as one of four Canadian artists united in the belief that art should be extended to the practical side of decorating."[46] Following the publication of the "Refus Global," the École du Meuble fired Borduas, thus officially ending one of Canada's most promising collaborations between decoration, abstract painting, and architectural interiors.

Clement Greenberg

This breakdown of the relationship between abstraction and decoration was purposefully effected throughout the fine art world for one simple reason – nothing is more decorative than an abstract canvas. To extend the analogy further, non-figurative ornament derived from natural sources could be called the original abstract art. For example, one of the most famous ornamental motifs – the Greek egg and dart – is so ubiquitously abstract that it not only graces the capitals of columns and pediments around the world but is used without comment in fabric designs, stationery, and a wide range of home decoration supplies at big box retailers like Home Depot and Walmart. Yet, because of its close associations with architecture and historical ornament, the egg and dart is not read as abstract art. It was precisely this separation of the artistic from the decorative that art critics like Clement Greenberg were seeking during the 1940s when they realized the precarious position abstract art occupied vis à vis the decorative. Craft historian Elissa Auther believes that Greenberg's push to separate abstraction from decoration "derives from the opposition of art to craft,"[47] thus reinforcing traditional artistic hierarchies and damaging craft's relationship to architecture.

In his staunch support of American Abstract Expressionism, Greenberg made it a priority to dismiss the decorative, and in turn the crafts. He did this "by transcending the decorative, or in his words by 'using the decorative against itself.'"[48] Ironically, his central critique was the very thing celebrated by ornament theorists of the nineteenth century – the static conventions of ornament. To Greenberg the fact that all decorative motifs relied upon a language derived from natural sources was limiting and prevented originality. Another factor in his rejection of ornament (and craft) was that it was simply too easy to read; or as Auther states, he resisted "the idea of an easy embrace of modern art facilitated through décor and the idea that art and life could be reconciled."[49] This stance was a direct critique of earlier artistic movements such as art nouveau, and especially William Morris's central tenet of the Arts and Crafts movement that "the complete work of applied art, the true unit of the art, is a building with all its due ornament and furniture."[50] In Greenberg's conceptualization of ornament, applied art was nothing more than skilled labour, a view reflecting the modernist perception that "related modes of ornamentation or surface adornment are perceived as lacking meaning."[51] Greenberg, like his contemporaneous Canadian modernists Carver and Buchanan, then went on to associate decorative crafts with femininity, the final and most damning tactic in the process of marginalization.

This attempt at marginalization was not as easy as one would assume. As previously mentioned, Canadian architecture never fully adopted the International Style of architecture, which reflected the philosophical position of Greenberg. Rather, as Kalman argues, Canadian architecture was developing along the lines of "Critical Regionalism," which "combin[ed] an attempt to develop a modern and regional vernacular language, an intensive integration of the building with its site, honesty and sense of craft in the use of materials, a sophisticated structural sensibility, and, most importantly, a respect for the regional cultural and psychological context of the work."[52] Attention to ornamented details, no matter how subtle, played a central role in the vision of Canadian architecture described by Kalman, a role that would have disturbed Greenberg's vision of pure, unornamented spaces by introducing regional concerns.

Auther, for her part, criticizes Greenberg's derogatory position that women and crafts merely represent aspects of popular culture: "To Greenberg, artists who exhibited nothing more than good taste, promoting in art an attractive decorative look, were derivative and essentially feminine, a characterization that conflates the decorative with mass culture, ornament and femininity."[53] Greenberg's aversion to kitsch easily extrapolates onto the female hobbyist crafter, stereotyping craft and further isolating it from the professional artistic ideals of modern art. As Glenn Adamson states: "Such amateur pursuits constitute their own worlds of reference … easily dismissed from the outside. Yet the disdain goes both ways. The amateur mindset implies a complete indifference to the self-critical values of the avant-garde."[54] This antithetical relationship deeply damaged the Allied Arts, as did the resulting stereotypes of the indifferent artist and architect, and the uncritical female craft hobbyist. Influential critics like Greenberg drove home the opposition to ornament within schools of architecture in postwar Canada, embedding a resistance that is visually obvious in the dramatic move away from ornamented public buildings during the 1940s. It is particularly interesting, then, that Canada's highest-profile public buildings, the federal Parliament Buildings in Ottawa, not only continued with a highly ornamental building campaign, but made the bold move of hiring a woman to oversee its progress.

Eleanor Milne

Ottawa's Parliament Buildings provide a fascinating exception to the rule of the sober and rational denial of ornament in postwar Canada. Built in the Gothic Revival style, they intentionally reflect both the nation's links to Britain and the religious allusions to morality bound up in this style. The original Parliament Buildings were completed in 1859 but burned to the ground in 1916. The only portion left standing was the Parliamentary library, which the architects Jean-Omer Marchand and John Andrew Pearson used as the basis for their 1916 designs for the reconstruction of the buildings. Marchand and Pearson maintained the Gothic Revival style, using Tyndall stone from Manitoba for the interiors and corridors of the buildings and Nepean sandstone for the exteriors. The carving blocks used for decorating the building were Indiana limestone.[55] Given the remarkable speed of rebuilding (the Parliament Buildings reopened in 1920) the architects purposefully left the stone uncarved in large sections of the buildings. Pearson was concerned about consistency in the decoration, and in 1916 he oversaw the hiring of John Bonnor as the Dominion Carver. This position was subsequently held by Walter G. Allen (1917–24), Cléophas Soucy (1924–29 and 1936–49), Coeur de Lion MacArthy (1936–49), and William Oosterhoff (1949–61), until Eleanor Milne was hired in 1961.[56] By 1938 the majority of exterior carvings had been completed. These carvings covered a variety of decorative schemes, with Cléophas Soucy's gargoyles attracting popular attention.

When Milne began as the Dominion Carver she focused her attention on the interior ornamentation and also made it a priority to change her official title to Dominion Sculptor. Between 1961 and 1993 she completed a remarkable number of carvings and stained glass windows, and even restored the linen ceiling of the House of Commons. Milne was forced to adhere to the Gothic style in all of her work, and her designs and carvings had to contain symbols of Canadian history. She never signed her work out of concern for its public nature and the group effort required to bring her designs to life.[57] As a result of the restrictions placed on her stylistic choices, a specific form of ornamentation emerged in her work, but it was astonishingly contemporary, given the Gothic emphasis of the architecture. Milne was able to fuse the aesthetics of early twentieth-century monumental sculpture with the realistic ornament of the Gothic Revival, and she often pushed the boundaries in terms of Canadian themes.

Although it was noteworthy that a woman had been hired as Dominion Sculptor, Milne was following in the footsteps of women who had established themselves within the field of monumental sculpture. In Canada Frances Loring and Florence Wyle were recognized as outstanding memorial makers, and had been hired to complete large-scale sculptures for prominent Canadian buildings, including seven bronzes and a bronze plaque for the Canadian War Records Department in 1918 and a marble sculpture for the Great Library at Toronto's Osgoode Hall in 1928.[58] Loring and Wyle befriended Eleanor Milne, who in 1950 was inspired to go on to study a more modernist form of sculpture with Ivan Mestrovic at the University of Syracuse.[59] Mestrovic was known for his flattened, geometric surfaces, some of which bear a striking similarity to the streamlined angles of the Art Deco movement. Milne's own work began referencing this style, an influence that informs some of the more flattened planes found in her carvings for Ottawa's Parliament Buildings.

Although she could never abandon realism in her work, Milne enjoyed playing with traditional ideas of the symbols and decorations of Canadian national identity. Her epic "History of Canada Frieze" (fig. 4.4), which occupies the rotunda of the second floor of the House of Commons lobby, was executed on a dramatic scale (1.4 × 37 m). Milne started the project only after completing eight months of study for the images and narrative, and the work was executed between 1962 and 1975.[60] She resisted incorporating stereotypical decorative elements such as maple leaves, beavers, and canoes, opting instead for a combination of easily readable symbols and deeper philosophical statements. She also determined to use a more challenging history

Fig. 4.4

R. Eleanor Milne, "Set 1: The First Inhabitants of the North American Continent," History of Canada Frieze, detail (2.9 x 3.5 m), high-relief carved Indiana limestone. House of Commons Lobby, Parliament Buildings, Ottawa.

of the nation. In Milne's realistic approach to Canada's history, bored monarchs and exhausted explorers are bound in with the social injustices behind the founding of the country. Milne boldly depicted the 1755 expulsion of the Acadians, and featured Aboriginal peoples as the strongest and most positive social elements in the frieze. Her choices caused considerable dissension: "The depiction of the Native population and [non-Native] people being friends with the Natives on an equal level was important to me [but] this was a major point of contention."[61]

In the course of our several interviews in 1998, Milne willingly discussed the politics of her choices of subject matter, media, and ornamental style, but she refused to enter a conversation about gender, concerned that a feminist revisioning of her artistic contributions would be too reductive. Although she would recount amusing anecdotes that touched on gender – including one about the day Pierre Elliott Trudeau teased her about wearing a skirt while carving up on the scaffolding in the House of Commons lobby – she resisted easy categorization as a female artist. To Milne, gender was inconsequential, given the restrictions of working within the Gothic style and leading a group of entirely male assistants. Certainly, when viewing her carvings it would be impossible to identify them as gendered; however, the fact that she was the country's first female Dominion Sculptor raises certain questions related to ornament and architecture.

First, Milne's desire to address issues of social inequity and social stratification through the narrative of her carvings introduced an entirely new approach to public sculpture and carving in the Parliament Buildings. Prior to Milne, the carvings had been uniformly celebratory in their approach to Canadian leaders and shining moments, most of which were explicitly male-driven. Second, Milne's education in a number of media, including stained glass, led to her working on diverse projects for the Parliament Buildings, including the completion of twelve stained glass windows and the restoration of a linen ceiling. While gender may not have been a factor in the selection of Milne to complete these works, gender certainly played a role in the materials she was introduced to as a student at the School of Art and Design, Montreal Museum of Fine Arts (1944–46). Third, Milne's dedication to having her title changed from Dominion Carver to Dominion Sculptor represented her awareness of the need to professionalize her position. The craft-emphasis of the title of Dominion Carver had been upsetting to Milne, who saw herself as a designer and the generator of concepts."[62]

Here we return to the distinction Adamson and Greenberg made between ornament, craft, and concept. Milne was justifiably concerned that being titled a carver rather than a sculptor would detract from an appreciation of the conceptual and philosophical ideas at the heart of her stone carvings and stained glass, reducing them to mere ornament. Despite her concerns, Milne established herself as a leading figure in the creation of uniquely Canadian decorative schemes, and it could be argued that greater numbers of Canadians and non-Canadians are toured past her carvings and stained glass windows than any other public craft objects in the country.

The Language of Ornament

The great contradiction in the use of ornament in Canadian public spaces is that the desire to establish a uniquely national identity for the country depends upon not imitating historical styles borrowed from other cultures or nations; however, *all* ornament depends upon previous conventions. In Gombrich's *The Sense of Order* the author demonstrates the origins of popular decorative motifs, most famously the classical ideal in Western art, pointing out that "the aesthetic ideal of restraint is inextricably interwoven with classical tradition."[63] Despite Canada's promotion of the multicultural ideal, as seen in Milne's tribute to the Acadian and First Nations populations in her

"History of Canada Frieze," the majority of public buildings in the country pay homage to classical ideals, using fundamentally Eurocentric ornamental schemes that are often replicated through the objects that decorate the interiors. Even International Style modernist buildings and postmodern approaches rely upon classical ideals of the Golden Ratio, or witty references to columns, friezes, and cornices.

Ornament theorist James Trilling puts forth the argument that ornament is a form of language built upon conventions. Although Trilling and Brent C. Brolin both argue that ornament is now acceptable once again, the problem according to Trilling "is that few people remember the language of ornament well enough to enjoy it, let alone use it correctly."[64] This gap in knowledge becomes a particular problem in the Canadian context, where craftspeople are trained to think in terms of craft as fine art, not craft as subservient to architecture or in service to the language of ornament. One would be hard-pressed to find an emerging craft talent conversant in traditional conventions of ornament and willing to remain anonymous in the decoration of a building. Although it is frustrating that so many examples of public craft are objects seemingly applied to building surfaces as afterthoughts, the placement of authored objects on walls demonstrates the desire that craft be perceived as fine art. This wish for a new status is part and parcel of the revival of craft, which is bound up in the supposition that the demise of craft paralleled that of ornament. But this is a mistaken notion.

The idea that the birth of modernism led to the death of ornament and craft is much too neat and also patently false, as Trilling acknowledges: "Ever since Loos replaced traditional ornament with the natural play of colours in his building stones, the evolution of decorative art has been linked to the eclipse of craftsmanship."[65] Trilling disagrees with this simplistic formula, adding, "This is far, very far, from being the whole story."[66] But the idea has nevertheless been damaging to the relationship of craft to architecture. Blame has been squarely placed upon Loos's article "Ornament and Crime," but it must be noted that Loos was concerned primarily with the inefficient economics of craft. Nowhere in his article does he mention abolishing craft; he speaks rather of the low wages of the woodcarver, the embroideress, and the lacemaker and notes the inequity of the situation: "The ornamentor has to work twenty hours to achieve the income earned by the modern worker in eight … If I pay as much for a smooth cigarette case as for an ornamented one, the difference in the working time belongs to the worker."[67]

It could be argued that Loos made an important contribution to the development of the studio craft movement in that he believed all makers should receive proper wages for their labour. Although he was espousing the end of ornament, his position as an architect and designer made him sensitive to the need for professional craftspeople to support the very objects and interiors he was designing. In the Western craft model this concern for equity foreshadowed the growth of art-school trained craftspeople who perceived themselves not as artisans fulfilling architectural commissions based on other people's designs, but rather as self-sufficient artist-designer-craftspeople who controlled the entire process of production from concept to final sale. This is a tenuous argument if one reads Loos as a staunch adherent of industrial production, as craft modes of manufacture simply do not fit into this model; however, Loos's vision of craft makers earning greater wage parity for simplified handcrafted objects was relatively groundbreaking.

No matter which way one interprets Loos's essay, the fact remains that his style of simplified building became the norm, with the result that many craftspeople and traditional artisans found themselves operating outside the realm of architecture. But viewed through a different lens, the simplified style of modernist architecture also led to some exciting developments within the crafts.

The Bauhaus

The Bauhaus (1919–39) has long been considered a historic leader in the unification of craft and architecture. When Walter Gropius composed his 1919 "Manifesto of the Staatliche Bauhaus in Weimar," he put out a call to all artists: "Architects, sculptors, painters, we all must return to the crafts! For art is not a 'profession.' There is no essential difference between the artist and the craftsman. The artist is an exalted craftsman … But proficiency in a craft is essential to every artist."[68] The Bauhaus curriculum was established according to the model of the ancient craft guilds, yet it soon emerged that a gendered, hierarchical vision of the crafts had replaced this initial utopian vision. Gropius had read William Morris and was influenced by several of Morris's key ideals for the crafts, including the need to have craft and architecture work closely together to achieve harmonious buildings; however, in the influential 1938 Museum of Modern Art exhibition "Bauhaus 1919–1928," this relationship was downplayed. In Alexander Dorner's introductory essay to the catalogue, "The Background of the Bauhaus," he stressed the anachronism of Morris's perspective: "A retrogressive Romantic, [he] would have nothing to do with machine production ... He strove, rather, for a revival of medieval handicrafts. But with the means of mass production developed in the industrial revolution, and with the new mass demand, his concentration on the obsolescent techniques of handicraft brought about one of the very things he was trying to prevent – the isolation of the individual artist-craftsman able to produce handmade objects only for a select few."[69]

It was central to this revisionist exhibition about the Bauhaus to cast a negative light on Morris and his "outmoded" ideas, thereby effectively erasing the important role that crafts had first played at the institution. The exhibition championed the streamlined, simplified Bauhaus design aesthetic, in a decision closely influenced by a fear of the feminine decorative suggested by certain materials and designs. Sigrid Wortmann Weltge, in her book *Women's Work: Textile Art from the Bauhaus*, makes the case that after the initial exuberance toward the crafts, by 1923 "the emphasis was on artistic expression, on individual pieces, reflecting the instruction and design philosophies of the painters."[70] Women were channelled into the Weaving Workshop, and the results of early collaborations between all departments and the weavers, most notably objects like Marcel Breuer and Gunta Stolzl's "Africa Chair" of 1921, for which Stolzl used the frame as her loom, gave way to polished, designed objects like Breuer's 1925 Wassily chair, featuring stainless steel and undecorated black leather. The Bauhaus ethos of efficient, unornamented design could be read as an afterthought, a reconsideration of decoration that wrote out the many contributions of women working in the Weaving Workshop.

Given the constant revising of the history of the Bauhaus, it could also be argued that the institution played a fundamental role in how North American architects and craftspeople came to view ornament during the postwar era. Alfred J. Barr, director of the Museum of Modern Art in 1938, opened the "Bauhaus 1919–1928" exhibition by noting the importance of returning "American Bauhaus students [and] after the revolution of 1933 ... Bauhaus and ex Bauhaus masters who suffered from the new government's illusion that modern furniture, flat-roofed architecture and abstract painting were degenerate or Bolshevistic."[71] The inference that Nazi Germany embraced ornament indicates that once again, the aesthetics of simplified ornamentation were being manipulated for nationalistic purposes.

Kalman argues that the manifestation of the Bauhaus influence through the International Style was slow to take hold in Canada because Canadian architects "were generally sceptical or negative towards it."[72] He quotes the influential architect Percy Nobbs as writing in 1930: "The architectural realists of Europe may have an enormous influence for good on our future work, that is, if we keep our heads, accept so much of their doctrine as will help us, and solve our own problems in our own way, with a weather eye on our climate."[73]

Despite initial reluctance, the International Style had by the 1950s taken hold in Canada; however, architects "showed less respect for it and its variants than their counterparts in other countries."[74] The Bauhaus continues to have an impact on the work of Canadian craftspeople and architects, and directly contributed to a significant change of direction in the work of Ian Johnston, a Canadian architect who abandoned the discipline for ceramics after spending time at the Dessau Bauhaus in the early 1990s. Johnston received his architecture degree from Carleton University and travelled to the Dessau Bauhaus on the advice of a friend in 1989. During the heady days after the fall of the Berlin Wall, he found himself surrounded by the rich history and intense contemporary political realities of the Bauhaus. While at the Bauhaus Academy Johnston helped to develop interdisciplinary workshops based on the timely theme of urban renewal and public intervention, a process that introduced him to a wide array of makers and materials.[75] Once he returned to Canada in 1996, it was easy for Johnston to make the transition from architecture to ceramics for, in his own words: "I am most interested in the very idea of material … architecture was a poor profession – creating legal documents for a living and dealing with contractors and clients. The creative applications of architecture were too minimal."[76]

After settling in Nelson, British Columbia, Johnston and his partner, Stephanie Fischer, a fellow architect he had met at the Bauhaus Academy, began experimenting with ceramics. After Fischer took an evening class in clay they developed functional vase forms based on industrial slip-cast designs that echoed the streamlined modern aesthetic of the Bauhaus. "We walked in with our eyes closed," Johnston says of the initial approach they took to ceramics, but he was soon thinking of the material of clay in literal architectural terms. "I caught onto the idea of little houses that kids draw, whimsical in nature. I wanted to give this idea grace and sophistication." Johnston's houses began playfully, starting with amorphous, curvilinear

Fig. 4.5
Ian Johnston, "Coming Together, Flying Apart," detail (38 x 79 x 31 cm), porcelain, larch, 2003.

walls and foundations that joyfully revealed the plasticity of clay. Whereas Johnston and Fischer's vase designs were purposely undecorated, stressing clear lines and minimal glazing, Johnston's houses used thin porcelain walls and dramatic shadowing resulting from the negative window spaces cut to create decorative spaces. His 2003 wall-mounted piece "Coming Together Flying Apart" (fig. 4.5) is a dramatic assemblage of broken porcelain house façades delicately combined using almost violent insertions of larch wood. Any potential playfulness in this work is countered by the suggested aggression of the shooting sticks of wood. Nevertheless, "Coming Together Flying Apart" remains strongly narrative about the role of architecture in our daily lives. Johnston describes his series of porcelain houses, titled "Leftover and Under," as a statement on reuse, and the fate of seven years of his ceramic work that was reassembled for these pieces.[77] The ornamental effect of the windows that dot the exterior of each broken house is part of a larger statement on the inversion of the traditional role of crafts as architectural addenda: "Windows are an element of architecture supported by the structure and façade of a building. They shape a perspective of the world both literally and figuratively. In this work, the windows are transformed from void to be supported to that which supports."[78]

The power of Johnston's work lies in its easy interplay between architecture, sculpture, and ceramics, as well as its ability to operate both as a decorative wall sculpture and an uncomfortably anti-ornamental political statement. There is something poetic about a Canadian architect with Bauhaus experience turning to a career in ceramics. It both parallels and resists the legacy of Bauhaus ornamentation as embodied by its masters and students who immigrated to North America following 1933.

Less Is More

Following Adolf Loos's vision of simplicity in architecture and design, his admirer and Bauhaus instructor Ludwig Mies van der Rohe generated the aphorism "Less Is More." Van der Rohe became famous for his contributions to modern International-Style architecture that emphasized simplicity and the use of modern materials and which, like Loos, relied upon the inherent richness of materials themselves to supply ornament. On 1 July 1967, in celebration of Canada's centennial and maturation into a sophisticated architectural nation, van der Rohe's Toronto-Dominion Office Tower was opened on King Street West in Toronto. The leading modernist architectural firm of John B. Parkin and Associates was responsible for the six office towers that formed the complex (completed in 1991), but it was van der Rohe's presence as chief consultant that made the buildings famous: "With the Toronto-Dominion Centre, Mies realized an architecture of movement, and yet at the same time, through proportional relations among parts and whole and through the restrained use of fine materials, this is also an architecture of repose."[79] This restraint in terms of materials was reflected in the enormous number of simplified, geometric lines and the dark coloration of the structures. Occupying over three acres in downtown Toronto, the buildings can confuse visitors, but through the use of greened commons, they succeed in avoiding a cavernous effect of wind tunnels and austere in-between spaces. In what must be one of the most ironic juxtapositions of public art and architecture in Canada, Joe Fafard's seven realistic bronze cows – "The Pasture" – sit regally in the midst of this tribute to the power of the international movement in architecture (fig. 4.6). If less is indeed more, then the cows work well in this context because they are highlighted by the austerity of the surrounding buildings.

Surprisingly, a high number of textiles are displayed in the buildings that make up the Toronto-Dominion Centre complex; nevertheless, they are treated as distinctly decorative in the spaces they occupy. Hoping to learn more about these textile wall hangings, I looked for plaques and information on the artists and pieces in the lobbies of the six buildings. While most of the works were authored and had accompanying plaques, little or no information was available about the works themselves. My queries about the artworks to the concierges on duty in each lobby elicited a range of reactions, from complete disinterest to surprise over the presence of the pieces that hung behind them every day. I was told property managers could not be contacted without advance appointments, and that no published information was available to the public. Was this perhaps simply an extension of van der Rohe's "Less is more"? What was more disturbing was the assumption that these textile wall hangings – each one obviously a sophisticated work both conceptually and technically – served only a decorative role in terms of the architecture. There is nothing new about this idea, but the glaring gap

Fig. 4.6
Joe Fafard, detail from "The Pasture," bronze, 1985.

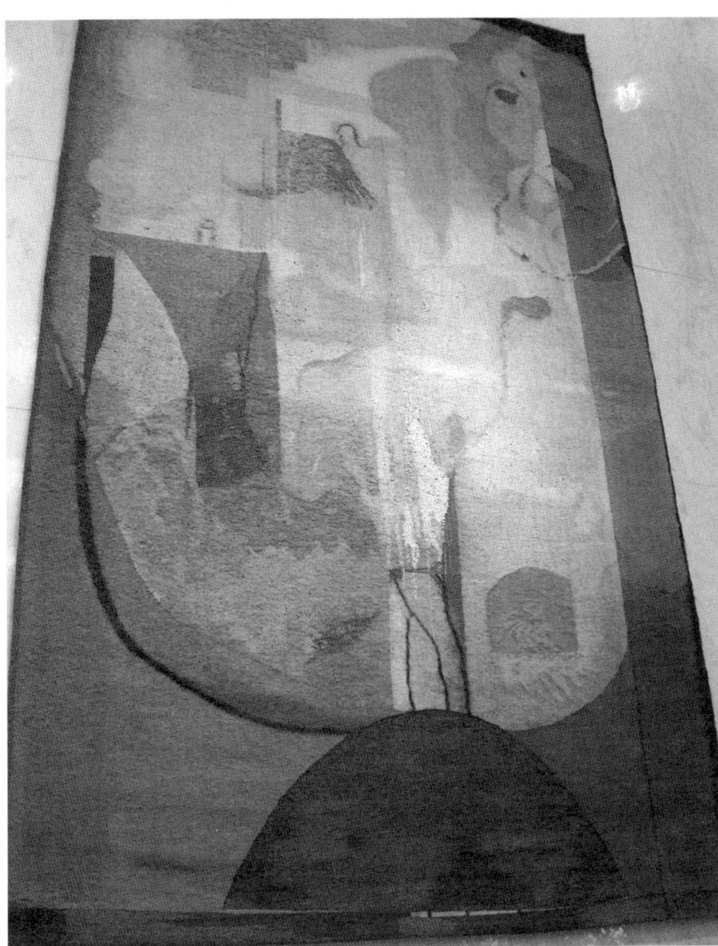

Fig. 4.7
Tamara Jaworska, "Quartet Modern," single panel detail, Gobelin tapestry, 1974.

between the revered buildings and the dismissed textiles was dismaying. The on-line version of *fibre quarterly* magazine addressed this issue in its Winter 2007 publication "Who Made That? A Question about Public (Textile) Art in Canada." This article carefully lists the textile artists whose work hangs in the Toronto-Dominion Centre buildings,[80] but the anonymous author of the article had encountered similar frustrations when researching the pieces: "Information about these artists has not been found and the obvious source of it, building management, often considers [it] nothing more then [sic] decoration if they notice it at all. This is unfortunately indicative of attitudes about public art in general."[81]

Tamara Jaworska's Gobelin tapestries "Quartet Modern" (fig. 4.7) are among the most striking series of wall hangings at the Toronto-Dominion Centre. Located in the First Canadian Place building on King St. West, these colourful, dynamic and movement-filled pieces are hung in prime locations, and complement the subdued marbled lobby that re-creates the feeling of an art gallery space. John E. Vollmer describes the tapestries' ornamental properties as more important than any other of their characteristics: "Surface is an adventure of tactile delight. These large-scale tapestries are not merely background decoration to be admired; they are expressions that command our attention, demanding reaction."[82] This reaction is largely a response to the vibrant composition of the works, which attests to the artist's sophistication and professionalism. Fafard's cows and Jaworska's tapestries provide nationally and regionally specific artworks that contrast with the International Style of the buildings, which is "independent from issues of use, geography and context."[83] It is unfortunate that the generalized architecture of the Toronto-Dominion Centre buildings, in combination with a lack of labelling of individual artworks, reinforces the idea that it is the role of craft merely to provide ornamental moments in otherwise minimalist spaces.

Not all craftspeople are content to have their work situated as ornamental "afterthoughts" in modernist built spaces. Ruth Chambers, professor of Ceramics at the University of Regina, is known for her delicate, feminine, and ornamental incursions into classic "white cube" art gallery spaces that serve as understated challenges rather than decorative accoutrements. She began questioning the unadorned spaces of contemporary art galleries in her 2007 installation "Untitled (arched doorways)" at the MacKenzie Art Gallery (Regina) exhibition "Mobile Structures: Dialogues between Ceramic and Architecture in Canadian Art." As Chambers explains: "What I decided to address/redress here was what is predominantly absent from the architecture of most modern gallery sites; a sense of ornament, decoration, history, and consequently, among other things, nostalgia, desire and imagination and the liminal."[84] This piece, composed of high-fired porcelain paper clay slip, presented columns and arches "densely emblazoned with tracery, words and leafy devices [to] reconfigure the modernist space of the MacKenzie Art Gallery such that it calls to mind the foliate embellishments of a medieval cathedral"[85] (fig. 4.8). Amy Gogarty, in her essay for the "Mobile Structures" exhibition, describes how Chambers's decorative intervention into the gallery space startles the viewer: "The temporal shift provoked by the interjection of such a contrasting style is palpable and disorienting."[86] This is exactly the reaction Chambers desires: "These installations are intended to intervene into contemporary architecture with the intent of inserting a different kind of aesthetic into spaces that are usually unornamented and designed to be quite neutral.

Fig. 4.8
Ruth Chambers, "Temporary Adornment (for Patkau)," porcelain installation, 2008.

I am interested in changing these spaces, either subtlety or more assertively, with playful, decorative, idiosyncratic and material-based forms."[87]

In 2008 Chambers was invited to create an installation at the Canadian Clay and Glass Gallery in Waterloo, Ontario. She was inspired by the architecture of the gallery, completed in 1996 by the award-winning husband and wife firm Patkau Architects, which Chambers read as continuing the white cube history of galleries. John and Patricia Patkau, on the other hand, interpreted their designs for the Canadian Clay and Glass Gallery as moving away from the white cube, a sentiment also expressed by the architectural historian and critic Kenneth Frampton in his 2006 book *Patkau Architects*: "The Clay and Glass Gallery explicitly announces the emerging importance of expressive construction in the Patkau practice, not only in relatively small-scale joints – brackets, hinges, pivots, etc. – but also in the articulation of larger components ... This elaboration served to deliberately distance the museum from the received ideal of the art gallery removed from everyday life."[88] Patkau architects, based in Vancouver, had constructed the Air Canada International Arrivals Lounge at the Vancouver International Airport, where their attention to detail and use of local materials reflect the influence of the Pacific Northwest coast landscape and culture on their work. However, the West Coast style evident in the Vancouver International Airport did not translate readily into the Canadian Clay and Glass Gallery, despite the Patkaus' statement that "the museum interiors are strongly connected to the outside world"[89] through skylights and windows. Certainly the gallery makes an expressive statement through its use of materials, notably the warm, golden wood frames around windows set into umber bricks; however, the reinforced concrete used in the gallery spaces conjures up the stark minimalist gallery spaces viewers are accustomed to occupying.

It was these concrete walls and floors that led Ruth Chambers to create "Temporary Adornment (for Patkau)" in 2008 (fig. 4.8) in an attempt to "contest the rather heavy, masculine, inorganic qualities of the design of the space and to assert the value of ornament and imagination."[90] Installed in the Keith and Winifred Shantz Gallery, Chambers's work uses fragile porcelain components and her trademark foliage-based ornament to create columns and arches suspended in space. Contrasting with the weight and mass of the material of concrete that dominates the gallery, "Temporary Adornment (for Patkau)" highlights the divide that still exists between masculine modern built environments and feminine ornamentation, despite the Patkaus' genuine desire to express care for the gallery viewer through attention to details. Those particulars, as the ornateness of Chambers's work reveals, still remain forms of minimal ornamentation. Although her columns and arches are heavily decorated, she keeps them entirely white in order to create a quiet space for viewers to consider the legacy of gendered modern built spaces.[91] Her work also inspires reflection on the enduring inheritance of "Less is more."

Less Is a Bore

The peppering of textile statements throughout van der Rohe's Toronto-Dominion Centre operates as a reminder that "Less is more" is almost impossible to achieve. Certainly the Eurocentric imperative of simplification demanded that architecture, craft, design, and art headed away from ornamentation; but in addition to the impossibility of entirely stripping the decorative from objects, another problem became apparent – complete individual control. In order to achieve the picture-perfect simplified modernism espoused by architects like van der Rohe one individual needed to keep control over the entire project. After the single artist's vision had been completely rendered into three-dimensional reality, it then became necessary to prevent inhabitants from cluttering these spaces. Famous gossip reverberates around architects like Frank Lloyd Wright, who is said to have visited the homes he designed (in their entirety, from the buildings, furniture, textiles, and lighting down to the gowns to be worn by the ladies in residence) and shown anger at the presence of books on the bedside tables in the master bedrooms.[92] Whether these rumours are true does not matter. What is important is a recognition of the need for vigilance on the part of the individual architect, if he or she is to preserve the simplified vision. The introduction of handcrafted objects exhibiting the artistic vision and decorative elements of another creator becomes problematic – these pieces must not only be approved by the architect but must fit into his or her own personal aesthetic.

After decades of modernism's dogma of strict simplicity, the architect Robert Venturi penned his famous book *Complexity and Contradiction in Architecture* in 1966. Commonly referred to as his "gentle manifesto," Venturi's book questioned the lack of room for the vision of others in modern architecture, ushering in the era of postmodern architectural expression in the process. While Venturi expressed his admiration for the elegant works of high modernist architects like van der Rohe, he observed: "The doctrine 'less is more' bemoans complexity and justifies exclusion for expressive purposes."[93] Venturi was critical of the increasingly severe limitations imposed by the concept of simplicity, and pointed out the dangerous proximity between the ideas of simplicity, oversimplification, and exclusion. His book spawned the famous axiom "Less is a bore," which appeared in this passage: "The building becomes a diagram of an oversimplified program for living – an abstract theory of either-or. Where simplicity cannot work, simpleness results. Blatant simplification means bland architecture. Less is a bore."[94]

It could be argued that this alternative axiom might have ushered in new opportunities for ornament and created a more positive environment for craftspeople, in that their ideas and objects would no longer be looked upon as cluttering clean, simplified spaces. But to think that is overly optimistic. The reality is that while Venturi's *Complexity and Contradiction in Architecture* was published only a year after the Canadian federal government had instituted its one-percent public building art works program, decades of resistance to ornamentation had created an entrenched attitude. Within this attitude were varying degrees of tolerance not only of ornament but of decorative handcrafted objects. There was also the thorny issue of how postmodern architecture was interpreted by Canadian architects. Kalman describes postmodern architecture as "a turn to the physical context and to buildings from the past, from which they gleaned a new-old architectural vocabulary"[95] that opened up the possibilities for architects to pay homage to the regional and cultural specifics of the country. However, some architects, notably John C. Parkin (not related to John B. Parkin of the Toronto-Dominion Centre), lamented the historical pastiche unleashed by postmodernism as "'foggy chaos' and 'digressions which I just don't think are going to last.'"[96]

Yes Is More

While architects argued over the role of postmodernism in their designs, there appeared to be less debate among craftspeople. Perhaps this is because craft, which has always been perceived as more eclectic, was eager to adapt historicism and the decorative impulse (which some critics might argue was never absent from the craft movement in Canada). However, just as the space between "Less is more" and "Less is a bore" was occupied by a range of positions among architects, curators, interior designers, and clients, Canada's craftspeople held differing views on the proper aesthetics of good architectural crafts. Their position had largely to do with the background and training of the individual artist. In her research on Scandinavian modernism in Canadian design, Rachel Gotlieb has observed particularly that while "in the 1980s Modernism was increasingly undermined by historicism, whimsy and ornament," in Canada the strong presence of Scandinavian émigré designers led to a longer entrenchment of simplified designs.[97]

Danish-born weaver and designer Suzanne Swannie brought a sophisticated analysis of good ornament to textiles. Trained in the studio of John and Kirsten Becker near Copenhagen, she had moved to Sweden in 1965 to complete a diploma at the Texitilinstitutet, before undertaking a contract to teach handweaving in Newfoundland in 1967.[98] When she arrived in Newfoundland, Swannie was surprised by the lack of opportunity afforded to industrial designers. As Gotlieb describes the situation: "Since the setting was Canada, the infrastructure for art and industry were and remain miniscule in scope: professional versatility and entrepreneurialism were and remain the key resources available to a textile artist."[99] Swannie proved her adaptability by morphing her industrial design training into one-of-a-kind textile objects that interpreted Canada's landscape as well as personal narratives. She achieved this through subdued and careful coloration of wools, abstracted patterns, and strongly composed surfaces.

But another side approach emerged in Swannie's artwork, one that pushed the simplified aesthetic of Scanadinavian modernism toward the rational geometry of architecture. For her 1986 Master of Fine Art exhibition at the Nova Scotia College of Art and Design, Swannie completed "Repassage," a witty take on gender in the service of architecture. "Repassage" translates literally as "ironing," and suggests the mundane repetitive actions of women within architectural spaces – the daily maintenance of drapery, fabrics, and interiors. Swannie's interpretation consisted of hundreds of diaphanous fabric pieces installed piece by piece and woven on the wall. A grid was laid out in exact detail and drawn with thread, then Swannie spent two days installing the work with great precision. Although the work was minimalist, with its intense layering of fabric pieces and the beautiful casting of shadows, its quiet whiteness became overtly ornamental. In 1992 Swannie took the ideas behind the

Fig. 4.9
Suzanne Swannie, with Andrew Terris,
"Untitled," fibre and steel, 1992. Mount
Saint Vincent University, Halifax.

temporary gallery-based "Repassage" and reinterpreted them into a permanent architectural installation. Mount Saint Vincent University's new library stairwell leading to the E. Margaret Fulton Communication Centre provided ample natural light through large windows and a high, wide open space (fig. 4.9). Swannie moved the pieces off the wall of the art gallery and positioned them on a geometrical structure created by Andrew Terris. The undulating geometry of this large-scale untitled sculpture subtly references architectural icons like Buckminster Fuller's geodesic domes, where triangular elements support large surfaces. The white fabric held taut between each metal grid reminds viewers of the intersection of textiles and architecture, and demonstrates the success of Swannie's restrained ornamentation.

It is evident from her work, as well as her conversation, that Swannie loves architecture and considers it the basis for much of her art. She is inspired by working with architects like Brian MacKay-Lyons, and admires their ideas for future sustainability. Swannie is a fan of Bjarke Ingels, the Danish architect whose popular lecture "Three Warp-speed Architecture Tales" is featured on the internet at TED talks. For her, Ingels's energetic approach to solving problems through architecture symbolizes the future. His manifesto is "Yes is more," a witty play on van der Rohe's "Less is more" and Venturi's "Less is a bore," which he has published in the form of a 130-metre-long cartoon strip (now available in comic book form). Rather than thinking of architecture in terms of a need for simplicity or limitation, or a postmodern acceptance of anything-goes, Ingels speaks of "architectural alchemy," which can reconstruct the cities of the future while simultaneously making sustainability sexy and fun.

Good ornament is central to the designs created by Ingels's architectural firm, BIG (Bjarke Ingels Group), founded in 2006. The firm's buildings themselves, including the Danish pavilion at the 2010 Expo in Shanghai, rely on simple but decorative forms, like the looping, shell-like structure of the pavilion, which allowed visitors to ride one of the 1,500 available bicycles to give a truly "Danish" experience. In the centre of the building was a water pool featuring the famous "Little Mermaid" sculpture, transported outside Copenhagen's harbour for the first time. As the pavilion demonstrateed, BIG is interested in how architecture and its ornamental motifs can offer visitors strong impressions of a country, or a culture. Swannie's untitled sculpture for Mount Saint Vincent University approaches aesthetics in a similar manner, if on a much smaller scale. Encapsulated in this simple geometric form are messages about what it means to adapt from one culture to another, to work as a woman in the buildings and galleries of Canada, and to reconsider ornament not only as it is perceived in the moment of creation but as it applies within contemporary architectural spaces.

Throughout the postwar period craftspeople have had to overcome the challenges of imbuing their materials with conceptual seriousness while promoting ornament as a positive contributor to elegant and sophisticated architectural spaces. Often, despite the social stigmas surrounding ornament and the decorative, they have succeeded. But the greater challenge of identity, and what a work on public display means to a city, a region and the country, remains.

5 IDENTITIES

Communities are to be distinguished, not by their falsity/genuineness, but by the style in which they are imagined.
Benedict Anderson[1]

Is there such a thing as a distinctively Canadian form of architectural craft? In addressing this controversial question, this chapter looks first at the identity of craft within postwar Canadian architecture; and second, at national as opposed to regional or local identities in specific allied arts initiatives. Problems relating to definitions of identity arose from the outset in this research project. When contacting representatives of public institutions that house art collections, I had difficulty explaining the parameters of architectural craft commissions. Did these only include traditional craft materials like clay, glass, fibre, wood, and metal? Would non-utilitarian forms be included? What scale of object would be acknowledged as a public commission rather than simply something of the scale of a teapot for use in the staff kitchen? Soon the limits of "craft" widened to include projects like the Parliament Buildings, where Canada's Dominion Sculptor Eleanor Milne carved stone and designed stained glass from 1961 to 1995.[2]

The virtual impossibility of declaring an absolute definition for craft is compounded by seeking at the same time to delineate craft within a specifically Canadian context. Therefore the goal of this chapter is not to declare any definitions, but to explore the nuances of identity as contained in specific architectural craft examples. As with craft, it is impossible to provide a clean, concise definition of "Canadian" architecture; however, it certainly does exist. As architectural historian Harold Kalman argues: "Some curmudgeons have wrongly argued that [Canadian architecture] does not exist. It is true that much that was built in Canada was derivative, closely related to sources in Europe and the United States. But that did not prevent the development of a uniquely Canadian character."[3] Ironically, a sense of national identity begins to emerge once one discards any pretense of pinning down Canadian Allied Arts.

Monumental Identities

Public craft serves a nationalistic role. At the same time, as art historian Annie Gérin comments, it is important to resist an overly nationalistic reading of public art: "In the Canadian context … art has often been studied in terms of its contribution to identity formation and nationalism"[4] rather than in relation to its aesthetics. While this caveat may be particularly true for Canadian art, when any artwork is viewed outside the space of the art gallery, it invites a reading of its relationship to the local, regional, and national cultures. The messages that monuments provide depend both on how individuals are educated to read them and on the way they occupy public spaces.

In a round-table on democracy and civic dialogue, Timothy J. Stanley noted: "The problem is that not everyone enters democratic spaces under the same conditions. In Canada and the United States, public memory (the widespread historical representations of movies, TV shows, newspapers, popular fiction, public monuments, and school textbooks) makes it appear as if certain people belong in certain spaces while others do not."[5] While Stanley's formulation problematizes viewers' experience of encountering messages, that experience becomes further complicated if the materials or forms are not easily read. In the North American context, a marble or bronze figurative statue is clearly identified as a public monument, whereas a giant quilted acrylic painting like Gathie Falk's "Beautiful B.C. Multiple-Purpose Thermal Blanket" hanging in the Credit Union Building in Vancouver, is not. Furthermore, in Canada, where European settler history has provided the standard narrative, the preponderance of Aboriginal craft objects installed as national monuments – like carved wooden totem poles – often glosses over the difficult and tragic relationship between First Nations peoples and their crafts, and the colonizers. Despite these enormous challenges, efforts at creating monumental forms of public craft have been undertaken in Canada, commemorating local, regional, and national relationships.

But what grants an object monumental status? According to John Ruskin: "The acts of a nation may be triumphant by its good fortune; and its words mighty by the genius of a few of its children: but its art, only by the general gifts and common sympathies of the race."[6] So what are Canada's common sympathies? I begin by highlighting two themes relating to the Allied Arts as they reflect national and regional identities: first, governmental attempts at creating "Canadian" forms of public art and second, aboriginal craft.

Architectural Identity in Postwar Canada

Before entering into a discussion of craft commissions for buildings, it is helpful to understand how Canadian architecture was conceptualized in the postwar period. Harold Kalman's definitive text *A Concise History of Canadian Architecture* does an excellent job of placing postwar architecture in context. He observes that modernism, "coincident with the postwar economic boom ... caused massive changes in the appearance of Canadian cities."[7] These changes resulted in a move away from previous historical influences such as the Gothic Revival toward the straight lines, curtain walls, and sparing use of ornament that marked modern International Style architecture. What differentiated Canadian architecture from that of other countries, in Kalman's view, was a reluctance to fully embrace the International Style; architects continued to be influenced by local materials and cultures, and strong regional styles developed, including the West Coast Style and Prairie Regionalism. Kalman acknowledges that throughout the postwar period Canadian architecture drew heavily on First Nations influences.

Following the World Wars, the influx of new and improved materials such as concrete and aluminum, in combination with an emphasis on clean, open spaces, created new orders of architecture around the world, and Canada was not immune to these trends. In Canada the International Style's tendency to develop a new relationship between interior and exterior spaces (which can be traced back in western arts and crafts history to Gustav Stickley's open-plan Craftsman bungalows and Frank Lloyd Wright's Prairie Style houses) was a subject of great interest. A distinctly West Coast form of architecture began to emerge in the late 1940s and early 1950s through a series of private homes in Vancouver like the Porter house (1948) and the Bobak house (1950).[8] *Western Homes and Living* magazine described the innovative close association between interior and exterior in this style of house: "The new portion is basically different from the old ... It's the floor-to-ceiling plate glass windows that make the difference. The leafy walnut just outside the window appears to be reaching right into the room ... The planting box and green outdoors set the atmosphere for the rest of the room."[9] The integration of Canadian flora and fauna naturally led to the incorporation of natural materials within these buildings, and by extension, to the crafts, like ceramics composed of locally dug clays and glazes, and textiles dyed with local lichens and flowers.[10] However, architects employed a cautionary tone in regard to this trend to bring the outdoors indoors. These houses could potentially lose the rigour of contemporary architecture if they fell prey to the whims of the housewives who occupied them: "Most of the women who worry over this problem ... don't stop to realize ... that the life expectancy of their furniture is only one sixth of the life expectancy of the house."[11]

It was rare to find public buildings that emphasized the integration of nature, and by extension crafts employing natural materials, to the same extent as domestic homes. One notable exception is the University of Toronto's Massey College by architect Ron Thom, completed in 1963. Thom had been actively involved in the development of West Coast Regionalism, and his D.H. Copp Residence (1951) was one of Vancouver's influential modern homes. Vincent Massey, the first Canadian-born governor general, envisioned that the college should, "in its form, reflect the life which will go on inside it and should possess certain qualities – dignity, grace, beauty and warmth."[12] Thom's elegant design still remains contemporary, with its square forms and avoidance of over-ornamentation; however, the brick and Indiana limestone is given a natural finish through his use of wood, plaster, and bronze. These exterior surfaces hint at the high level of craftsmanship contained inside the various college buildings and rooms, which highlight craft objects ranging from pottery, calligraphy, furnishings, silverware, and stained glass to stone carvings. Dramatic yet subtle, the seamless integration of the crafts into Thom's architectural vision was so successful this building received excellent critical and popular reviews and in 1989 was designated a historic building by the Toronto Historical Board.[13]

Thom commissioned many craftspeople, including his friend the potter John Reeve, to furnish Massey College. "I was pleased to receive the commission, because he was such an outstanding architect," says Reeve, who produced vases and decorative plates for the dining hall, as well as six massive lamps for the common room (fig. 5.1).[14] Carefully placed around the

Fig. 5.1
John Reeve, Massey College table lamps (109 x 56 cm), glazed stoneware, early 1960s.

sofas and coffee tables, Reeve's lamps reflect the same aesthetic as is captured by Thom's furniture and lighting designs. These monumental glazed stoneware lamps stand over a metre in height and present an Asian ceramic aesthetic through their subtle brown glaze and simple, faceted finish. The Asian influence is not surprising, given Reeve's work at the pottery of Bernard Leach in St Ives, Cornwall, from 1958 to 1961 (and again in 1966).[15] Reeve's relationship with Thom enabled craftsperson and architect to create an important collaboration, one that continues today as the lights remain in use in the common room. Kalman argues that Massey College anticipated Late Modernism through its uniting of Western and Central Canadian architectural styles and its reintroduction of traditional qualities that had been thoroughly modernized.[16] Vincent Massey had specifically requested that Thom create a space that embodied "certain qualities – dignity, grace, beauty and warmth,"[17] and the handcrafted finishes and objects successfully met that challenge.

Despite the success of Thom's Massey College, by the mid-1960s Canadian architects were being accused of creating inhospitable environments. Anita Aarons decried 1960s Canadian public architecture as "functional, inorganic, antiseptic and colorless," fully dependent upon art for any signs of humanity.[18] In 1961 the Structurists, a movement of artists related to the Prairies, published a special edition of their magazine, *The Structurist*, on the topic of "Art in Architecture." The editor, Eli Bornstein, who had created "Structurist Relief" commissions for the University of Saskatchewan's Arts Building in Saskatoon and the Winnipeg Airport,[19] wrote in his foreword to the issue: "There is a general agreement … that very little, if any, significant integration of art in architecture exists today." He firmly laid the blame on the "established" fashions in architecture and argued: "Only by forthright enquiry into our values and by critical appraisal of our creations … can we begin to move toward an environment of beauty that will realize our highest aspirations as they have never been realized by man before."[20]

Bornstein's "Structurist" reliefs played off the square, simplified angles of modern buildings, and used various elevations of rectangles and squares projecting from the wall in primary colours to achieve artworks that thoughtfully responded to contemporary architecture (fig. 5.2). However, even Bornstein was frustrated by what he perceived as the tightening restrictions around what constituted an appropriate modern style of architecture. The Royal Architectural Institute of Canada was aware of the negative reactions provoked by some minimalist buildings, and as early as 1958 began an intensive public relations campaign, acknowledging: "In Canada architecture has been exposed to radical influences from abroad. The profession in this country has been gauging the significance of new developments and trends in relation to [its] fellow citizens."[21] In 1960 the RAIC published a booklet entitled "The Architect Looks at Public Relations," which outlined strategies for architects to educate the public into understanding this new aesthetic. The booklet encouraged architects to give interviews to newspapers and to radio and television stations in order to publicize the use of new materials and make it clear to the public that the new styles of architecture were intended to "improve the lot of their fellow Canadians."[22]

Architecture was a growing field – from 1,300 architects in Canada in 1940 to 2,200 in 1960[23] – and architects were coming to understand that cultivating good relationships with artists and integrating art objects into new buildings constituted an important tool in their public relations campaign. In 1959 the Royal Architectural Institute started its "Sculptors' Register" to introduce architects and artists,[24] complementing its "Allied Arts" awards, which continued to be popular annual events at the national meetings, as well

Fig. 5.2
Eli Bornstein, "Structurist Relief in Fifteen Parts," enamel on aluminum, 1962.

as excellent publicity. It was one thing for the national architectural organization to develop initiatives for working with artists; however, when the federal government stepped in to take control, these relationships became a completely different game.

Department of Public Works

The most significant effort to create a nationally recognized infrastructure for Canada's public art was, as mentioned earlier, the federal Department of Public Works's one-percent art program, which lasted from 1965 to 1978. During this time Public Works Canada commissioned 235 major works of art, at a cost of approximately $3.6 million dollars.[25] This program, which ensured that one-percent of new federal building expenditures would be dedicated to art works for their interior and exterior spaces, had the objective of integrating "art works within the architectural elements of [buildings,] enhancing the spaces in which they are located and at the same time allowing the works to stand as statements of the artists in their own rights."[26] This was a fraught process from the start. The innovative program was the idea of James A. Langford, chief architect of the Department of Public Works, who took up this position in 1963 at the age of thirty-five, "the youngest ever appointed."[27] Langford's vision for using art to enhance architecture created exciting opportunities for craftspeople and artists, but as architectural historian Janet Wright argues, certain departments were "reluctant to increase the cost of buildings by such frills, particularly if they might not like what they paid for."[28] At the beginning of the program architects suggested artists to advisory committees that oversaw a national jurying competition for large commissions, but problems were soon encountered with architects who either refused to suggest names or argued that there were no suitable art works for their buildings.[29]

Some architects felt strongly that their buildings were "complete in themselves, without artwork."[30] By 1971 Arthur Laing, minister of Public Works, was compelled to issue the following statement: "It was recognized that there could be problems in what forms of art might be used, since in no other field of human endeavour does there seem to be such diverse opinion. Bearing this in mind, the department felt that the selection of artwork should be the responsibility of the designing architect who was commissioned for the particular building. In addition, an independent jury of Canadians, actively engaged in fine artwork, was set up to pass judgement on the architect's proposal."[31] The first advisory committee, established in 1968, was composed of a who's who of Canadians in the arts, including Guy Viau, deputy director of the National Gallery of Canada and Dorothy Cameron, advisor on art to the Canada Council.[32] Aarons immediately identified a major problem with the makeup of this committee – no architects were involved. She applauded Public Works for its efforts to revamp the selection process but warned: "The architect-designer has once again lost a valuable initiative – this time, the right to hire and fire his own artist. In public buildings fair trial has found the architect, for whatever reasons, along with other 'trusted advisors' (some of whom are well known if not esteemed artists) to be lacking in stewardship."[33] Aarons also noted that in at least two cases these artist-advisors took the lion's share of the resulting commissions, unfairly preventing a larger number of artists from participating. In her first "Allied Arts" column (January 1965) for the

Royal Architectural Institute of Canada's *Journal*, she made it clear that her most significant concern about this new federal program was its bureaucracy: "It requires a nobler attitude than forced legislation, resulting in more 'art work' by compulsion and less sensitivity [to succeed]."[34]

From the perspective of the crafts there was yet another problem. None of the committee members were active supporters of the crafts and, as archival documents prove, they were often hesitant to spend large amounts of money on craft commissions that either fell outside their knowledge area, or employed unusual materials like textiles and clay.[35] Furthermore, the one-percent nature of the program created difficulties for smaller, often more rural, building projects. K.C. Stanley, the chief architect at Public Works Canada and chairman of the advisory committee on art, acknowledged that smaller, less expensive buildings like rural post offices suffered under this formulation, because, "You can't commission art for $250.00."[36]

Successes

Despite the obstacles faced by the one-percent art program, it succeeded in creating the most intensive collaborations between architects and artists that Canada had ever witnessed. The program was an inherently nationalistic project, initiated in time for Canada's centenary and the Montreal World's Fair, Expo '67, and its goal was to raise standards of public art across the nation. In some cases it certainly worked. To counteract a barrage of complaints, some Canadians felt compelled to write in support of the artwork springing up in their communities. In 1977 Alan Gregson, dean of the Mohawk College of Applied Arts and Technology in Hamilton, Ontario, praised the newly opened Holland Landing post office: "Many people are noticing that the quality of the building has been enriched by the installation of an area of stained glass. It appears to me to be a most appropriate contemporary design; not only is it esthetically pleasing, but it also invites the viewer's mental involvement in its interpretation. I find it to be a challenging, and therefore, satisfying piece of functional art."[37] Of course it must be remembered that Gregson was dean of a school offering courses in art, craft, and design, and so his views did not necessarily reflect those of the majority of Canadians.

Kay Kritzwiser, art critic for the *Globe and Mail*, was an enthusiastic supporter of the program, which she felt succeeded best in the city of Ottawa, where the majority of new federal buildings and art works were constructed.

After her November 1973 visit to explore the city's new art she wrote: "I came away ready to trumpet my proud delight. For stunning twentieth-century art in public places no other city in Canada can hold a candle to Ottawa."[38] Of all the new architecture her favourite was the $32 million External Affairs Department building, named the Lester B. Pearson Building. From the custom-built burgundy furniture and Robert Hedrick's cast bronze set of four double doors to Arthur Handy's steel sculpture in the cafeteria, Kritzwiser praised the talents of Canada's top contemporary artists.[39]

Among the works at the Lester B. Pearson Building that Kritzwiser admired was a pair of popular and successful ceramic murals by Gathie Falk, one of Canada's leading multimedia and performance artists. Titled "Veneration of the White Collar Worker Nos. 1 & 2," (or "Veneration of the White Collar Worker" and "Veneration of the Blue Collar Worker"), each mural consisted of twenty-four ceramic squares in a trompe l'oeil effect of a man's dress shirt (one side with white shirts and the other with blue) complete with pocket and tie (fig. 5.3). These murals were placed back to back and situated toward the centre of the cafeteria where they could watch over the workers dressed in matching attire. In the catalogue for Falk's retrospective exhibition author Robin Laurence brings an interesting analysis: "Even as the ordinary office workers are here venerated and monumentalized ... it's possible to perceive a little nudge of satire on the conformity, the static hierarchies of bureaucracies. And for the persistently ghoulish, it's also possible to see the work as a kind of burial place, a vault, a tomb with rows and rows of commemorative plaques."[40] How ironic, then, that Falk's satirical commentary was itself lampooned in an *Ottawa Citizen* cartoon shortly after it was unveiled in 1973 (fig. 5.4).

Voices of Complaint

The cartoon for Falk's "Veneration of the White Collar Worker Nos. 1 & 2" was only one in a long string of media complaints about the federal one-percent program and its attendant art works, which were echoed by letters sent in from concerned members of the public. The Library and Archives Canada files on the program are filled with letters that refer to specific art-works in such terms as "monstrosities," "freak sculpture," and "insanity," and complain about the cost to taxpayers.[41] An interesting complaint came from Listowel, Ontario, regarding a textile (string) wall piece by Reg Holmes.

Fig. 5.3
Gathie Falk, "Veneration of the White Collar Worker" (2.8 x 8.4 m), ceramic mural, 1973. Department of Foreign Affairs and International Trade, Ottawa.

Fig. 5.4
Ottawa Citizen, cartoon of Gathie Falk's "Veneration of the White Collar Worker Nos. 1 & 2," 1973.

The complainant was apparently less concerned by the artwork than by the fact that it hid "the beautiful woodwork on either side of the entrance lobby" which had been paid for by the "taxpayers of this country."[42]

Archival files on the one-percent art program contain letters from prominent politicians who objected to what they saw as questionable art works within their ridings. One Nova Scotia politician complained that until the steel sculpture that had "rusted over the winter [with] rust … run down onto the concrete base" was removed he could not consider officially opening the building.[43] Ralph Stewart, chairman of the Commons Committee on Broadcasting and Assistance to the Arts, went one step further, publicly insulting Robert Murray's sculpture "Tundra," which was unveiled at the Department of National Defence Headquarters in 1972 (moved in 2006 to Carleton

Fig. 5.5
Robert Murray, "Haida," steel and painted epoxy, 1973. Department of Foreign Affairs
and International Trade, Ottawa.

University). "Junk, hoaxes and monstrous," he exclaimed, adding that it "should be removed or covered up."[44] Stewart was chastised by Wayne Howell of the *Toronto Star* who, in his 1973 article "If It's Inoffensive, It's Got to Be Great Canadian Art," asked whether members of Parliament could suggest "legislation that clearly states what forms of art they find acceptable and inoffensive."[45] It was as if Aarons's worst fears about bureaucratization had come true.

Although not considered craft, two art works need to be singled out here for the overt hatred directed at them by members of the public: Robert Murray's "Haida" (Ottawa) and John Nugent's "No. 1 Northern" (Winnipeg). What these pieces have in common, apart from the verbal, written, and physical abuses they received, is that they are both large-scale abstract steel sculptures. Robert Murray's "Haida," a steel sculpture painted epoxy blue, was positioned in front of the Lester B. Pearson Building (Department of External Affairs) in Ottawa in 1974 (fig. 5.5); John Nugent's "No. 1 Northern" was mounted in front of the Canadian Grain Commission Building in 1976 and was made of steel painted epoxy yellow (fig. 5.6). As their titles suggest, both works make metaphorical references to larger

Fig. 5.6
John Nugent, "No. 1 Northern," steel and epoxy, 1976. Canadian Grain Commission
Building, Winnipeg.

themes, leading one to wonder if realistic representations of these subjects
would have invoked equally negative responses.

The one-percent program selection committee had expressed strong approval for Murray's "Haida": it had "the scale and power needed to enhance
the surrounding architecture and yet maintain its own dignity and freedom.
The blue curved sculpture, in this case, was designed with lyrical, flowing lines
that contrast with the strong horizontal lines of the building."[46] The public
disagreed. As an outraged taxpayer wrote (somewhat prophetically) from
Rocky Mountain House, Alberta: "This sculpture is a monstrosity. It is atro-
cious. Put your house in order or soon it won't be yours to put in order."[47]
While controversy surrounded "Haida," art critics such as Kritzwiser praised
the piece, which she described as "all curve and soaring rectangles" and decried
the attacks. Kritzwiser got political when she asked of its critics: "Is there
anything more square than a square editor with his eye on the taxpayers'
money? Yes, a square politician from Hoedownsville with an eye for a headline
quote."[48] Murray remained relatively philosophical about the controversy,
admitting that some of the more slanderous statements had "rankled" him.

But, he added: "When … disinterested souls are suddenly confronted by contemporary works at sidewalk level, it is bound to cause a few rumbles."[49]

John Nugent's "No. 1 Northern" met with an even darker reaction. According to Robert Epp, curator of the University of Manitoba's Gallery 111, "No. 1 Northern" is a "beautiful piece with a sad story."[50] While the national papers did not give it as much negative attention, rumours swirled that it simply disappeared one night and no one claimed to know who was responsible. In the early 1990s the artist asked for the public's help in finding the piece. It was said to have been found in the city scrapyard cut up in pieces in the salvage area.[51] In 1997, more than a decade after its removal, it was restored in front of the Canadian Grain Commission Building. The federal government's "Cultural Property Inventory" tells a very different story: "This piece was removed about 1976 by order of the Minister because of complaints from the people working in the facility, and the general public, that the piece was ugly and meaningless. There were also charges that the piece was dangerous in the winter because someone might walk into it and injure themselves."[52] The story of "No. 1 Northern" is an account of a most extreme negative reaction toward a piece of art, but there were many instances of damage – some accidental, some intentional vandalism.

Not only did the media and members of the public voice complaints about the art works but artists involved in the program also faced difficulties. Shortly after Falk installed "Veneration of the White Collar Worker" and "Veneration of the Blue Collar Worker," the glaze began to craze and large sections began lifting off the clay. On 5 October 1973 Dr N. Stolow, director of the Canadian Conservation Institute wrote to H.G. Cole, program manager of the Public Works Fine Art Program, outlining his concerns with Falk's piece: "While Miss Falk has indicated that a certain amount of crazing was intended, we are terribly concerned about those spots where the coating seems to be lifting right off the clay."[53] Falk flew to Ottawa in November to examine and repair her pieces and was dismayed at what she discovered. While there had been a certain amount of natural crazing in the glaze, the majority of the damage had been caused by employees who were eating in the cafeteria scraping their chairs against the ceramic surface of the mural. Falk immediately saw what had happened: "The chairs are placed about two feet from the murals. When a person pulls back his chair to leave he often rams right into the murals. The murals are ceramic. The ties are totally vulnerable: three of them have already broken within four months." Falk wrote suggesting that the chairs be removed from behind the tables closest to the mural and that a low fence be put up to prevent future damage. She concluded with a damning comment: "Perhaps this sets a precedent for mistreating an artwork through neglect."[54]

Given the angry responses from some members of the public, members of the Fine Art Advisory Committee were likely not surprised that employees showed such a lack of respect for Falk's ceramic sculpture. The *Ottawa Citizen* cartoon lampooning Falk's "Veneration of the White Collar Worker Nos. 1 & 2" (mislabelled "Homage to the White Collar Worker") depicted an elderly woman standing confused in front of the collage of ceramic dress shirts, asking a government representative, "Would you have size sixteen and a half in short sleeve, please?" The seemingly downtrodden man in uniform is holding a scroll indicating that Falk's piece cost the taxpayers $15,000 (fig. 5.4). The message is clear – such conceptual art statements were wasted on the public. Further, a gender and age bias was made clear, as the cartoon suggests that elderly women were the ones who were not impressed. One of the high-profile artists who benefited from the federal art works program wrote disdainfully that the placement of "large works of sculpture on public sites is bound to stir-up the old ladies."[55]

Although those who registered their objections came from a wide spectrum of the Canadian public, administrators of the program, such as K.C. Stanley, director, Resources, Design, Construction, Department of Public Works, put on a brave face in response to the increasing wave of criticism. In a 1974 interview he stated: "We expect criticism. It means the art work is having an effect on people."[56] However, the department had been wary of negative public reactions from the inception of the program. As Janet Wright comments in *Crown Assets*: "It also left the government open to criticism from the public as to what constitutes good art and whether public funds should be spent on such extravagances."[57] That same year the decision was made to add two members of the general public to the advisory committee to assist in selecting pieces that would have a greater public appeal. As well, the Department of Public Works agreed to raise the amount of money spent on publicity devoted to promoting new commissions.[58] Soon irate letter writers were pointing their finger at the Minister of Public Works, Liberal Jean-Eudes Dubé. In an angry letter of January 1974, a writer from Prince George, British Columbia, coined the term "Dubé's Folly."[59] Dubé responded to these critics by increasing publicity efforts. Shortly before losing his position as minister of Public Works he was followed by the media when he headed out on the street in front of Murray's controversial "Haida" sculpture to solicit public opinions on the federal art works program. The *Ottawa Citizen* promoted this stunt, writing: "His office announced Friday that Mr. Dubé, with a tape recorder and microphone, will interview people passing in front of the Lester B. Pearson building on Sussex Street at noon Monday."[60] Unfortunately, no recordings from his intervention are available to researchers today.

Some interesting sub-themes emerge from the type of criticism levelled at the art works commissioned by the federal government. Certainly, based on the location of the writers of the most vitriolic letters against the program, a rural-urban divide is evident. By far the majority came from residents of smaller communities, including Salmon Arm, Rocky Mountain House, and Prince George. Remarkably, most of the letters were sent from the western provinces of British Columbia and Alberta. Given the high level of antipathy toward Pierre Elliott Trudeau's liberal government, in power throughout the one-percent art program, it could be speculated that the prominently positioned, often abstract art works became symbols in small communities of federalism and the Liberal government, thus invoking such a high level of written criticism. It was in Salmon Arm, British Columbia, after all, that Trudeau famously gave the finger to a group of protesters shouting anti-French slogans.

Another issue that was identified through the deliberations of the selections committees was the level of commitment to regional identities. Although many advisory committee members were from central Canada, discussions were held around the need to commission artists who represented the country's diverse populations. In Grand Forks, British Columbia, for instance, K.L. Chang, architect of the Government of Canada Building for the town, recommended that Doukhobor art be sought out for the building, as it would reflect the strong presence of this community in the area.[61] The Advisory Committee for the post office in Clementsport, Nova Scotia, was presented with two maquettes by the folk artist Joseph Sleep, whose accompanying letter stated: "I want to Paint a country Picture on the top all houses in Four colors … a ball and a cow and wolF and Flowers and a cat."[62] Paul Hébert, the architect of the post office, supported Sleep, who eventually won the competition. Hébert was eloquent in his reasons for selecting Sleep as the artist: "The proximity of Clementsport to Digby immediately reminds one of the primitive art which until a few years ago was created locally by the late Maud Lewis. With this in mind it would seem fitting to retain for the work of art on this project such a person as Mr. Joseph Sleep, who I trust would come up with an interesting presentation for this work."[63] In 1969 Papineau, Gérin-Lajoie, Le Blanc, the architectural firm responsible for the Frobisher

Bay Academic and Occupational School, initiated a carving competition to determine the winning artist for the project. Quite understandably, there was a lack of response from within the Inuit community.[64]

Aboriginal Craft

In his seminal text from 1983, *Imagined Communities*, Benedict Anderson argues that in the eighteenth century the eclipse of religious modes of thought by the impulse toward nationalism gave rise to the very idea of the nation:[65] "It is the magic of nationalism to turn chance into destiny."[66] The European settlement of Canada may be seen as a case in point: the country needed symbols that espoused a national destiny, rather than symbols that recalled a narrative of accidental discoveries and lingering resentment. Objects of Aboriginal art and craft could ideally fulfil the cultural requirements of nationalism, offering evidence of the "civilizing" values of European conquest and the benevolent leadership that permitted the survival of indigenous traditions.

Of course the lived reality was very different from any idealistic nationalistic message. By the time Queen Victoria and Prince Albert opened London's Great Exhibition of 1851, Aboriginal crafts had become widely read as "Canadian"; however, they were regarded as ethnographic specimens rather than accomplished craft objects. As Robert Ellis, editor of the official catalogues of the Great Exhibition proudly but condescendingly noted: "A number of native curiosities adds to the value of this collection,"[67] which included "Indian and Negro bones and baskets"[68] from Nova Scotia. His observation clearly served to reinforce the low rank of these cultural groups within the hierarchy of the British Commonwealth. Ellis lavished praise upon Canada's natural resources and was impressed by "the excellent qualities of this timber for useful and ornamental purposes [as] illustrated in the specimens of furniture exhibited."[69] Indeed, furniture and sleigh makers were well represented in the exhibition, and sleighs were singled out as a uniquely Canadian form of transportation and entertainment.

Shortly after that Great Exhibition, Canada instituted the Indian Act of 1876, which placed severe restrictions on Native cultural production. As artist and curator Gerald R. McMaster points out: "In the years from the 1870's to the 1950's there were rapid changes and developments in the relationship between the Euro-Canadian and the Native Canadian: social, political, economical and cultural. In those 80 years the Indian people had to survive overwhelming changes, moving for better or worse from a dependence upon land and sea, and their own resources, to an economic base similar to that established by the Europeans, which brought with it commercial attitudes founded upon possession, profit and achievement, and which ruthlessly undermined Aboriginal customs and values."[70] McMaster raises an important point for the discussion of the relationship between craft and architecture – the traditional ritual and cultural values of Aboriginal crafts rendered them inappropriate candidates for the establishment of permanent, monumental buildings by the national and regional governments. The result was a lack of Aboriginal art objects in "official" buildings or monuments and the increasing use of these artworks in museum or tourist displays. Nevertheless, Kalman argues, First Nations architecture remains fundamental to understanding the complete story of Canadian buildings: "Within the space of only a few centuries, Canadian architecture has evolved full circle … Conservation and Post-Modernism come together in a number of recent buildings whose forms and materials are directly inspired by – and may even replicate – buildings of the past."[71] Here, Kalman is referring to overtly Aboriginal structures such as the First Nations House of Learning at the University of British Columbia (Larry McFarland Architects, 1991–92). Whether or not one believes that Aboriginal building styles have influenced Canadian architecture as a whole, it is undeniable that Aboriginal crafts have played a key role in helping to define Canadian craft.

The Canadian Handicrafts Guild (founded in 1905) was instrumental in establishing commercial outlets for Aboriginal crafts. Examples of Guild exhibitions throughout the twentieth century consistently demonstrate its dedication to marketing baskets, beadwork, snowshoes, leatherwork, and other examples of First Nations craft. McMaster notes that the Guild, an organization composed of middle and upper class white women, was politically rebellious through these efforts, which contravened sections of the Indian Act: "Clearly the government wanted to abolish tribal costume and custom, preferring instead to show the products of an assimilated or 'civilized' Indian. The Guild, on the other hand, was interested in the reestablishment of the ancient arts and crafts."[72] Such controversial crafts were considered unsuitable as public emblems for the Canadian government; however, they were ideal as tourist souvenirs.

This distinction is essential to understanding how Aboriginal crafts have become incorporated into major Canadian buildings today. Ruth B. Phillips, in her book *Trading Identities*, traces how "the reassessment of the touristic and of commoditization has been an essential step in the establishment of a contemporary Native fine art practice."[73] Today's Aboriginal artists are keenly aware of ethnographic representations of historical craft objects, and their art is often a response to this categorization. As Robert Davidson, a leading Haida artist featured prominently in architectural spaces like the Vancouver International Airport observes: "Part of my struggle has been getting [Northwest Coast] art out of the curio stage."[74] The static stereotypes of Aboriginal crafts have been perpetuated by museums, which provide "reconstructions of continuous, linear and integrated historical narratives."[75] Unlike museums, public buildings and spaces can only display craft objects in interrupted narratives that are most often presented without the benefit of didactic panels or other learning aids. Sometimes the meaning of public craft objects referencing Aboriginal art or culture is obscured by the constant passage of people, surrounding structural changes, the careless treatment of the art (leaning vending machines, benches placed in front), or vandalism. Cultural appropriation is another potential source of tension. An interesting case in point is Murray's sculpture "Haida," which, as previously discussed, aroused great protest. Murray's bright blue, flat-planed sculpture was intended as a metaphor for its title, as were many of his other works from the 1970s, such as "Tundra," (1972), "Agulapak" (1974), and "Wasahaban" (1978). Murray was born in Vancouver and educated at the Regina College School of Art. His artistic influences were artists from the avant-garde New York art scene like Barnett Newman and David Smith, and so his relationship to Canada's Aboriginal community was largely textual, based in his choice of titles and his desire to convey natural themes through minimalist, geometric forms.

The late 1960s and early 1970s provided pivotal moments in the discussion of Aboriginal craft as political tools. Murray could easily employ a loaded title like "Haida" for his work because centuries of appropriation had enabled an unproblematized system of borrowing. However, the controversy over Murray's sculpture occurred simultaneously with growing debates over the relationship between Aboriginal artists and the Canadian fine art system that traditionally labelled their work as ethnographic curiosities. Just as the country had freely borrowed from the First Nations in promoting national symbols – from the name "Canada" to the canoe – stereotypes surrounding indigenous craft and art, in particular the concepts of nature and culture, became more entrenched.

Literary theorist Northrop Frye had a voice in the debates. His diagnosis was that to live in a country as large as Canada was to suffer from cultural and geographical isolation. In 1946 he had observed: "There is a feeling which seems ... Canadian ... a feeling of the melancholy of a thinly-settled country under a bleak, northern sky, of the terrible isolation of the creative mind in such a country."[76] Frye built his distinctly Canadian theories around the assumption that place served a primary role in determining national culture, leading to a sensibility not of "Who am I?" but of "Where is here?"[77] By the 1960s Frye recognized the importance of the Aboriginal community in his discussions of space and place: "Clearly [Native culture] forms a tradition which should be at the headwaters of our own and should be absorbed into our traditions."[78]

It is evident from this quotation that a lingering colonial attitude remained that non-Native culture was dominant. Richard Cavell's postcolonial reading of Frye's spatial metaphors for Canada brings the following interpretation: "The enterprise of colonialism has a fundamentally spatial aspect: the seizing of territories, the mapping of sites, the framing of landscapes, the construction of buildings, the displacement of peoples."[79] Given the violence of this history, the unapologetic borrowing of Aboriginal crafts by non-Native artists must have been perceived as a seemingly minor infraction during this time period, if it was apparent at all. As Phillips argues: "Non-Aboriginal artists have viewed indigenous arts as legitimate sources of inspiration. Until the late twentieth century, they tended to validate their borrowings of Aboriginal motifs and forms both as acts of homage to Aboriginal artistic traditions and as legitimate successors to them. Few non-Natives expected Aboriginal cultures to survive the competition of the cosmopolitan and technologically superior arts of the West."[80] For Aboriginal craftspeople and artists, however, this appropriation was becoming increasingly problematic.

"Indians of Canada" Pavilion at Expo '67

In the period leading up to Montreal's World Fair, Expo '67, the Canadian government's generous cultural funding (which included the Department of Public Works's one-percent art program) led to the decision to create a separate "Indians of Canada" pavilion at Expo '67. This pavilion successfully incorporated the public's expectations for "Nativeness" (containing displays of objects like snowshoes) along with political statements about the conditions faced by Canada's First Nations. Crafts played a vital role within the architecture of the space, which was designed to represent a giant tepee, with totem poles carved by the Hunt Brothers of British Columbia at the entrance (fig. 5.7).[81] Given the popularity of miniature totem poles as souvenirs and as displays in ethnography museums, these giant carvings excited many guests, lulling them into a sense of comfort. Any complacency quickly evaporated, however, when they entered the pavilion and were greeted with one of the first – and most political – public messages about the treatment of Canada's First Nations: "You have stolen our native land, our culture, our soul … and yet our traditions deserved to be appreciated, and those derived from an age-old harmony with nature even merited being adopted by you."[82]

Fig. 5.7
Model of the "Indians of Canada Pavilion," Expo '67.

The "Indians of Canada" pavilion represented the first revisionist approach to a display of Aboriginal culture at an international exhibition and served as an important starting point for Native artists and craftspeople to renegotiate the expectations placed upon their craft objects. While the dramatic political statement made by the "Indians of Canada" pavilion was effective in opening up new debates around the assumptions and stereotypes surrounding Aboriginal cultural productions, it would take almost another decade before non-Native craftspeople, artists, and architect s started displaying genuine sensitivity toward these issues.

"Homage to Salish Weavers"

In 1977 Katharine Dickerson's enormous wall hanging "Homage to Salish Weavers"[83] was unveiled in the Surrey, British Columbia, Taxation Data Centre, one of the last federal buildings to benefit from the one-percent art program (fig. 5.8). Made of hand-spun, hand-dyed wool, Dickerson's weaving was remarkable in that it was created using the traditional Salish twining technique. Unlike Robert Murray's metaphorical "Haida," Dickerson's title referred directly to the manipulation of materials in the piece. In Coast Salish twining, two or three strands are twisted together to create a design that is similar on the front and back of the piece. This technique is similar to the twining technique used to create Salish baskets. Dickerson, who was raised in the United States and lived in New York City before moving to Vancouver Island in the early 1970s, felt an immediate affinity for Salish twining, which she describes as using ceremonially herself: "each time I create in this style I view it as part of a healing process."[84] When she was asked to create a piece for the Surrey taxation centre she chose this technique because she knew "Surrey was part of the Salish area, and this would be a subtle way to ram it [the poor treatment of Aboriginals] down the government's throat."[85]

Dickerson sought approval from her Salish friends to base her "Homage to Salish Weavers" on a piece of woven trading cloth from the early 1900s that is housed in the Royal British Columbia Museum. After receiving their approval she promised she would not personally profit from the commission, but dedicate the money she earned to teaching weaving students how to carry on the twining tradition.[86] As was the case with many craftspeople commissioned at the time, after paying taxes, supplies, and labour, Dickerson's professional income from this commission was reduced to nothing, and her

Fig. 5.8
Katharine Dickerson, "Homage to Salish Weavers" (3.1 x 12.2 m), hand-spun, hand-dyed wool in Salish twining technique, 1977–78. Surrey, British Columbia.

offer to teach students this ancient technique became a labour of love. It was also a political strategy that she employed as a form of passive protest against the federal and provincial governments. When the Surrey Taxation Centre was opened in 1978, Dickerson and her Salish friends were forbidden to enter the building to hold a ritual ceremony before the weaving was unveiled. Dickerson's involvement with the Salish community contributes a complex reading to her "Homage to Salish Weavers" project. On the one hand, she must be commended for highlighting both the political narrative surrounding the loss of indigenous techniques like Coast Salish twining and the tensions between Aboriginal and non-Aboriginal communities in the Lower Mainland of British Columbia;[87] on the other hand it could be argued that she romanticized her relevance to the Coast Salish and her role in saving the twining technique. Ironically, Dickerson's political statement was eclipsed by the popularity of "Homage to Salish Weavers," which was briefly removed from the Surrey Taxation Centre before employees protested and had it returned to its original place.[88]

Certainly there is a long history of non-Native peoples desiring communion with Aboriginal culture and society, and visual markers of "Indianness" like Salish weaving, totem poles, and teepees are easily read associative symbols. Canadian children are still indoctrinated into reading nature as belonging to a "wild," "Indian" context through their participation in summer camps. While Canadians like to believe that these Native stereotypes are eroding, one can still attend Buffalo Bill's "Wild West" show at EuroDisney outside Paris, where families don chiefs' headdresses and, while eating a dinner of cornbread and chili, are divided into famous "Indian tribes" to battle the cowboys. One well-known example of a white woman who over-romanticized her "Native" role was Mary S. Edgar, who in 1922 became "Ogimaqua," director of a summer camp for girls in Ontario.[89] Such summer camps relied upon architectural ornamentation – such as totem poles outside the dining hall and carved headdresses over the cabins – to cue their campers to their new "native" status.[90] An intense level of cultural association and appropriation of this sort was widespread during the late nineteenth and early twentieth centuries, but it "was not a matter of respecting the experiences of racial minorities … 'going Native' had little to do with honouring or even accurately portraying Aboriginal tradition, but much to do with seeking a balm for the non-Native experience of modernity."[91]

For many Aboriginal craftspeople and artists this meaningless appropriation was a source of constant frustration, as the tourist market homogenized complex craft styles and techniques from diverse First Nations as uniformly "Indian." And this market has in turn affected the production of Native crafts. When Ojibway Chief Dalton Jacobs and Councillor Clifford Whetung opened "Ojibwacraft" in 1966, for instance, they began producing craft objects that fed into these preconceived stereotypes, such as traditional birch bark and porcupine quill boxes decorated with Canada's maple leaf and carved totem poles featuring a mix of West Coast, Plains, and Great Lakes imagery. When questioned about the authenticity of these totem poles, Whetung argued they were what the public demanded: "White people associate totem poles with Indians and seem to expect us to make them, so our people have obliged."[92]

Totem Poles

While many symbols of Canada have drawn upon Native themes, the totem pole became, and remains, central. It has been employed in miniature as an easily portable souvenir, and adds dramatic appeal to outside and inside built spaces. Robert Davidson must be credited with recontextualizing totem poles as cultural symbols within Haida culture. In 1966 Davidson, the great-grandson of Haida carver Charles Edenshaw, spent eighteen months apprenticing with Bill Reid, perfecting the craft skills he began cultivating at age thirteen when he carved his first totem pole miniature.[93] When Davidson first arrived in Vancouver in 1965 he gave public demonstrations of totem pole carving at the Eaton's department store,[94] but he soon altered his view of totem poles;

rather than being souvenirs they became political statements. It is interesting that Davidson entered the Vancouver School of Art in 1967, the same year that the "Indians of Canada" pavilion at Expo '67 used the Hunt Brothers' totem poles to make its dramatic political statement about the situation of Canada's Aboriginal peoples.

Davidson was two years into his studies when he made a strong contribution to the growing political awareness of Native craft cultures by carving a great totem pole for Old Masset, a village on Haida Gwaii. The raising of this totem was accompanied by traditional ceremonies, including a potlatch.[95] Other totem pole commissions soon followed, most notably a ten-foot totem pole for the City of Montreal in 1970, which was placed on the Expo '67 site, and a ten-foot totem pole presented as a gift from the people of Canada to Dublin, Ireland, at the 1970 conference of the World Crafts Council.[96] Davidson was flown to Dublin to "carve a totem pole, demonstrating the skills of the Canadian Indians in wood carving."[97] As political as Davidson was becoming in regard to totem poles, the international craft community still perceived these objects through entrenched colonial constructions of "Indianness." Following Davidson's participation as part of the Canadian delegation of the World Crafts Council organizers, Canada's organizer Mary Eileen Hogg received a letter of thanks from the Irish World Crafts Council representative, along with a newspaper clipping about the totem pole, which had been put up next to the Canadian black bear pit in the Zoological Gardens. Hogg was clearly outraged on behalf of the artist. She reported to her fellow Canadian representatives: "Any of you who would like to read [the clipping] are welcome to read it but the last paragraph starts off in such a way that I have not even been able to send a copy to the carver of the totem pole: The Red Indians of North America are far from savage and most of them stay on their reservations."[98] The placement of Davidson's totem pole beside the black bear pit at the Dublin Zoological Gardens reinforces major questions about the use of totem poles as ethnographic curiosities rather than art objects.

Today these exceptional objects are largely accepted as works of art; however centuries of colonization and the removal of totem poles from Canada to museums of ethnography and anthropology in Europe and beyond put contemporary examples in an awkward position. That is where the skill of artists like Davidson becomes important, for he is able to take traditional motifs and make subtle variations that render them culturally relevant to

Fig. 5.9
Robert Davidson, "The Three Watchmen,"
grouping of totem poles, one 15.2 m high and
two 9.7 m high, 1984. College Park, Toronto.

today's Aboriginal and non-Aboriginal viewers. In 1984 Davidson's "The Three Watchmen," a grouping of totem poles, one 15.2 metres and two 9.7 metres high, was raised in downtown Toronto at College Park in the Maclean-Hunter building (fig. 5.9). The juxtaposition of the traditional Haida motifs of these totem poles and the glass and steel mall-like space of the Maclean-Hunter building is striking. The surprise at finding the earthy materials and traditional images of Davidson's totem poles in downtown Toronto serves as a reminder that even today the sense that totem poles belong in certain spaces, such as Vancouver's Stanley Park, or outside the Canadian Museum of Civilization in Gatineau, Quebec, is fully entrenched. That is the power of "The Three Watchmen" – they shake viewers out of their complacent urban tasks and transport them to different geographical and cultural realms. It is fitting that these totem poles have been raised in an atrium space, as Kalman describes atriums as popular Canadian architectural devices: "Architects and planners have searched for ways to cope with the cold Canadian winter. One solution has been the development of the atrium – a high internal skylight space of the kind that emerged in buildings designed by a number of (mostly Toronto) firms during the 1970s."[99]

Juxtaposing the naturally lit atrium space of the Maclean Hunter building with the natural materials of Davidson's "The Three Watchmen" makes for a strangely symbiotic relationship. Given that the majority of the Department of Public Works's one-percent program art commissions sought regional or even national neutrality through abstraction and an absence of culturally specific motifs in a desire to indoctrinate the Canadian public into a more refined taste in art, there is a certain irony in how successfully "The Three Watchman" engages the public by breaking these contemporary art rules. This is not to say that Davidson is not a sophisticated contemporary artist who is aware of how to manipulate his materials and images to transport viewers beyond themselves. As Judith Ostrowitz describes it in her book *Privileging the Past*, Davidson's ability to re-imagine Haida culture through the creation of motifs and crests for non-Native clients results in exceptional art based on "poetic modifications."[100] "The Three Watchmen" incorporates an image of the Raven bringing a house to the Haida people; but whereas Haida totem poles place the three watchmen at the top of the pole, Davidson put them at the bottom of the poles for the Maclean-Hunter building, and he altered the traditional placement of the figures by positioning them back-to-back.[101] As Davidson himself explains: "The purpose of my art is to express the contemporary life and meaning of my ancestral culture, that of the Haida people of Haida Gwaii [Queen Charlotte Islands]. From the time I raised the first totem in this century in my home village of Masset, I have been committed to the use of cultural knowledge in order to celebrate the present as well as the past. As a bicultural Haida-Canadian artist, I draw upon my own experience of life to give personal and collective meaning to my work. 'The challenge is to create images that we can all relate to,' I mentioned when discussing my first major commission for a public location, 'The Three Watchmen,' a three-totem pole sculpture at the Maclean Hunter building in Toronto."[102]

Vancouver International Airport

Davidson was one of over twenty Aboriginal artists commissioned to create artworks for the Vancouver International Airport public artworks program, which was initiated prior to the launch of the new International Terminal in 1996. The terminal was designed by Vancouver-based Patkau Architects, internationally known for structures that are "[based] on principles of modern architecture and simultaneously inspired by the traditional landscape of the Canadian North West Coast."[103] There is nothing new in using Canadian airport terminals to make declarations of regional and national identity. In an essay entitled "Public Art: The Airports," Bernard Flaman outlines the federal government's 1964 airport art project, which injected modern art as a national statement into the Gander, Winnipeg, Toronto, and Vancouver airports as a "record of the collective cultural aspirations of a nation and a visual representation of a country searching for a place on the world stage."[104] Ironically, the 1996 Vancouver International Airport terminal superseded the 1960s efforts of the federal government with a new vision that is much more literal than its predecessor: "to create spaces that were inspired by the natural landscape of Canada, but brilliantly reinterpreted in the modernist idiom."[105]

Today's Vancouver International Airport has turned to First Nations artists to comfort visitors by providing an aesthetically pleasing, politically safe statement embedded in the sights, sounds, and smells that typify the West Coast landscape. And it works. This terminal is an exceptional space that provides international travellers, upon their arrival in Vancouver, with the excitement of being surrounded with Native art. It could be argued that this endeavour simply perpetuates stereotypes of "Indianness," "British Columbia," or "Canada," but the YVR Art Foundation has worked hard to ensure that its highlighting of Aboriginal art presents "a holistic approach" and acknowledges a "unique sense of place" that comes "alive in its spectacular display of Northwest Coast native art."[106] One cannot help feeling some level of cynicism toward the project, given that the Vancouver International Airport occupies land under dispute through land claims settlements but, rather than concealing the political realities of the situation, the YVR Art Foundation dealt with it by creating a "Musqueam Welcome Area" which first greets arriving travellers. The Musqueam, one of the Coast Salish nations, are represented by pieces all fashioned by Coast Salish women artists.

As international passengers enter the area, they are greeted by Susan A. Point's "Flight," which consists of two tall carved red cedar panels with sand-blasted glass circular panels (1993). They provide a regal entry to a stairwell and two escalators leading up to a carving six-metres in diameter (1994) that represents the world's largest Coast Salish spindle whorl (fig. 5.10). This element of "Flight" hangs centred in a waterfall wall of natural stone with plants at the base. Together, the three components of "Flight" operate as a dramatic statement to visitors, and the architectural elements of stairs, escalators, and waterfall walls (there is an additional cascading waterfall effect between the stairs and escalators) complete the impression. Patkau Architects lowered the ceiling panels over "Flight" to create a more intimate space and further draw the attention of the viewer. The long expanses of mezzanine walls finished with warm natural wood panels also help focus attention on Point's work.

Finally, the traveller is greeted by a strong statement on Musqueam independence suspended above and to the left of the lowered ceiling panels in the form of two weavings entitled "Out of the Silence." Completed in panels by Helen Callbreath, Gina Grant, Krista Point, Debra Sparrow, and Robyn Sparrow, these long striking weavings display bold geometric patterns with subtle motifs of flying birds and animal eyes in reds, oranges, black, and white. As a subtext to Point's aesthetically beautiful and welcoming "Flight" and the accompanying "Out of Silence" weavings comes a political statement – the reassertion of Coast Salish ownership over the spindle whorl and traditional weaving, which Dickerson had affirmed in her 1977 "Homage to Salish Weavers."

The overall effect of the soaring heights and light-filled, glass-walled architecture of the Vancouver International Airport in combination with the warmth and site-specificity of the Coast Salish art is tremendous. With the inclusion of water features and diorama-like settings that integrate trees, rocks, and wooden elements, a complete sensory experience surrounds new arrivals to Vancouver. But can these visitors grasp the loaded political subtext of some of the pieces? The answer would, of course, depend on an individual's background knowledge, but the high number of Aboriginal art works might initiate some questions from visitors unaware of the complex history of the relationship between Aboriginal and settler cultures in British Columbia and Canada. The concurrence of Native cultural symbols and global capitalist enterprises functioning within the space of the airport creates interest and provokes thought. Most notable among such works are Roy

Fig. 5.10
Susan Point, "Spindle Whorl" from "Flight," cedar installation, 1993. Vancouver International Airport.

Henry Vickers's two Raven House Posts, three-metre red cedar carvings that flank a Starbucks coffee shop. The most famous juxtaposition of capitalism and a piece in the Vancouver airport is seen in Bill Reid's "The Spirit of Haida Gwaii: The Jade Canoe," a monumental bronze sculpture that "holds centre court in the International Terminal Building, drawing thousands of people a day."[107] It serves as a symbol of Canada not only at the airport but also as it is depicted on twenty-dollar bills, which tourists acquire as a reminders of the piece (fig. 5.11).[108]

An international airport certainly is an excellent space for introducing the world to Northwest Coast art, but does it provide opportunities for visitors to question any political statements that these artists may have been making in their work? Or is this a built environment designed expressly for moving people quickly from place to place, leaving them only a fleeting impression of local culture? Given the success of the YVR Art Foundation's initiative, and the continued emphasis on Aboriginal culture through the Vancouver 2010

Fig. 5.11
Bill Reid, "The Spirit of the Haida Gwaii: The Jade Canoe," bronze with green patina, 1994.
Vancouver International Airport.

Winter Olympics, these larger questions of identity and political power remain unanswered. What is clear is that despite postcolonial theories intended to dispel assumptions that "Canadian culture is somehow a function of place, be it defined as 'landscape,' 'geography,' 'archipelago,' or 'North,'"[109] these stereotypes continue to grow stronger rather than weaker, and public art commissions play a central role in conveying this message. The feelings of displacement and alienation that are at the centre of the ongoing land-claim disputes between First Nations and the federal and provincial governments become sugar-coated for visitors when public art provides a welcoming, non-political message, even when this is an accidental reading due to a lack of information. On the other hand, a certain pride and power are expressed by the reintroduction of visual symbols and craft techniques that were once threatened during the Reservation Period. As Bill Reid wrote in his poem "The Jade Canoe," which is displayed alongside his sculpture at the airport: "A culture will be remembered for its warriors, philosophers, artists, heroes and heroines of all callings, but in order to survive it needs survivors. And here is our professional survivor … it is he who builds on the rubble and once more gets the whole thing going."[110]

Arthur Erickson's Museum of Anthropology

When considering the use of First Nations crafts as public symbols of Canadian identity within architecture, a seminal and enduring example is Arthur Erickson's Museum of Anthropology, opened in May 1976 at the University of British Columbia in Vancouver. While Northwest Coast Native carvings, totem poles, and weavings may seem out of context in downtown Toronto malls or international airports, Erickson's museum building perched on cliffs overlooking the Strait of Georgia surrounded by dense forest was one of the first architectural attempts to thoughtfully reconcile a sense of place for Aboriginal culture with contemporary architecture (fig. 5.12). Joan M. Vastokas, a recognized expert in the field of First Nations art, was so enamoured of Erickson's final building that she wrote a lead article on its triumphs in *artscanada* magazine. She described Erickson as "one of the few architects working today to understand the function and meaning of architecture as an art of environmental context and of cultural expression."[111] None of the reviews at the time critiqued Erickson's "outsider" role as a non-Native architect, praising him instead for his cultural and environmental sensitivity.[112]

Although composed of steel, glass, and concrete, the museum building was designed with its specific landscape in mind, and Erickson worked with landscape architect Kenneth Morris to suggest the atmosphere of a traditional Northwest Coast Native village.[113] Totem poles placed outside the museum were essential to achieving the character of a village site, and the ambience created by the building is reminiscent of a ceremonial house. Aboriginal crafts were vital, from the welcoming totem poles and monumental carved wooden doors by Ksan craftsmen from Hazelton, British Columbia,

to the objects housed inside. Post and beam supports lead the visitor inside the museum, and in combination with the carvings created an effect Vastokas described as having "mythological and cosmological significance."[114] Not only did Erickson collaborate with the Museum of Anthropology's collection in determining the design of the gallery spaces but he worked closely with contemporary First Nations artists, creating thoughtful spaces like a niche under a domed skylight built to highlight Bill Reid's monumental sculpture depicting "Raven Discovering Mankind in a Clamshell."[115] Vastokas concluded her review by praising Erickson's thoughtful approach to the Northwest Coast cultures that his building was designed to showcase, calling him a "cultural relativist" who was able to "design within a particular cultural context rather than imposing his own cultural or personal preconceptions upon a given task."[116]

Considering the imposition of colonial architecture upon Canada's landscape throughout the nineteenth and twentieth centuries, Vastokas's description was apt; however, a strong anthropological and ethnographic approach was inherent in the project. The representation of Aboriginal cultures still complied with preconceived expectations, and the sense that they should conform to a glass, concrete, and steel building prevailed. What was important about Erickson's museum was that it did not stop at the anthropological. It continues to showcase its objects as art pieces rather than simply ethnographic curiosities, and in 1976 this was a dramatic change in approach. In a review of the fiftieth anniversary of the Museum of Anthropology, Saloni Mathur calls Erickson's design "honest, gentle and humane" and points out that his close collaboration with contemporary Aboriginal artists "was exceptional for the way it blurred these boundaries [between fine art and ethnography] by emphasizing the visual qualities of Northwest Coast artefacts."[117]

Despite Erickson's success with the Museum of Anthropology a gap between the objects belonging to First Nations artists and the buildings designed by non-Native architects remained. With the selection of Douglas Cardinal as the chief architect of Ottawa's Museum of Civilization this gap began to close. Cardinal's native (Métis) ancestry is of significance, although the Museum of Civilization has been careful to downplay this as a factor in the choice of Cardinal: "It seems appropriate that a museum housing collections of Indian artefacts of national importance should be designed by someone with roots in Canada's Native culture, although this was not a factor in the selection decision."[118] Cardinal's undulating design for the museum was revolutionary, both in its shape and his use of computer-aided design, and these factors, combined with his Native status, led to "some eyebrows [being] raised in the architectural community."[119] Cardinal has been outspoken about his lack of interest in International Style standardized architecture, describing his education at the School of Architecture at the University of British Columbia as being embedded in these ideals: "You were supposed to be interested in early Le Corbusier and the Bauhaus School [but] that left me cold."[120] As Kalman argues, Cardinal's expressionistic designs for the Canadian Museum of Civilization "brought Prairie expressionism to Central Canada amidst a great deal of fanfare,"[121] but it also marked an important moment: the creation of a truly Aboriginal-positive space like Cardinal's Museum of Civilization had finally united the outstanding First Nations crafts and designs with architecture.

From the imposition of a legislated one-percent art program for federal buildings to the strong presence of Aboriginal craft in national architecture, craftspeople have been called upon to help define spaces as being "Canadian." As Anderson argues in *Imagined Communities*, the creation of cultural signifiers requires imagination and a shared desire to sustain them. The success of Aboriginal crafts in architectural spaces like the "Indians of Canada" pavilion at Expo '67, the Vancouver International Airport, and the University of British Columbia's Museum of Anthropology is ironic, for these objects operate as symbols of the power of perseverance in the face of oppression, while they are at the same time appropriated by settler culture. The relative failure of the Department of Public Works's one-percent federal art program is equally ironic. This narrative makes it clear that mandated monuments will meet resistance, and attempts to neutralize regional identities and political tensions through abstracted, neutral forms often generate negative responses. While the Allied Arts were supported throughout the late twentieth century in Canada, it is still too early to determine which craft objects will stand the test of time to become truly national monuments.

CONCLUSION

Well before this self-professed age of interdisciplinarity or, as craft theorist Glenn Adamson terms it, "postdisciplinarity,"[1] craft artists like Merton Chambers were boldly employing whatever means necessary to complete their artistic vision. The postwar period witnessed exciting overlaps between craft and architecture as they broke free of traditional expectations of the artisan as stonemason, carpenter, or stained glass artist and moved toward a perception of the craftsperson as artist. This was not a seamless transition, and debate continues today over the role of the craftsperson in contemporary architecture and art. While a postdisciplinary vision makes room for any artist to employ craft materials and techniques, the concept of a professional craftsperson still includes skill and the perfection of finished objects as fundamental qualities. It is my hope that the thematic structure of this book has enabled an understanding of the shifts within these broad areas relating to the identity of craft in architecture.

Materiality is central to any artistic discipline, and it may be argued that it is imperative to the survival of craft. It takes years of training in each craft material to master its skill sets, scientific intricacies, and aesthetic heritage. Even young interdisciplinary artists wishing to borrow elements from specific crafts find themselves frustrated by the level of knowledge required to understand the most basic principles behind clay, glass, textiles, metal, or wood. Financial investment in teaching craft at the post-secondary level is high, as ceramic studios require expensive kilns, and studios for textile, jewellery, wood, glass and metal demand not only pricey equipment but often costly materials as well. Unfortunately, in Canada a growing number of craft programs are being replaced by vaguely titled substitutes that suggest "material practice" without a commitment to a specific material. At the same time, architecture continues to require specific craft materials such as ceramics and textiles for components within buildings. It will be interesting to see how new interdisciplinary broad-based material arts programs interface with architecture and new technologies in the future. It is safe to say that any historical divide that positions the crafts as being tightly focused on particular sets of materials and fine arts as emphasizing site-specificity and a broader conceptualization of materials is becoming overruled.

The evolving pedagogical boundaries between art and craft will influence their presence as part of public built space, thus opening up exciting possibilities for the way craft materials engage with architecture. The twentieth-century emphasis on craft objects that stood as independent artworks, as espoused by the studio craft movement and formal post-secondary craft programs, has begun to run counter to the interdisciplinary concerns of undergraduate and graduate students – and in a different direction than fine art programs – in regard to shared materials and spaciality, and is leading craft further away from a goal of integration within architecture. In the twenty-first century the boundaries between art, craft, design, performance, installation, and new media are blurring: as a result craft is at a pivotal point that might allow it to move away from the traditional constraints of a single medium, and toward a fuller relationship with architecture.

As a consequence of the stereotypes surrounding certain craft materials and their associations with domesticity, form and scale became essential subjects for this book. Issues of utility, and gendered readings of traditional forms such as quilts are at odds with the desire for large-scale forms that can create a sense of awe and metaphysical reflection within built spaces. By integrating new materials such as fibre optics with traditional ones like woven wool and linen, craftspeople such as Mariette Rousseau-Vermette, Michelaine Beauchemin, and Charlotte Lindgren have succeeded in overcoming oppressive expectations around the crafts and have become internationally renowned Canadian public textile artists. Nevertheless, set principles related to craft forms still exist. Textiles are most often thought of as mere wall hangings, curtains, and upholstery fabrics; and worries still surface about the maintenance of monumental textile sculptures (witness Lindgren's reminder that textiles are easy to clean – all they require is a good beating with a broom).

Fig. 6.1
Greg Payce, "SSSSSSSSSSSSSSSS" (1.9 x 4.5 m), bronze, 2003. Calgary International Airport.

Ceramics are habitually read as wall murals and tiles, and are considered too delicate to exist as freestanding sculptures; Alberta ceramic artist Greg Payce was forced to substitute cast bronze for his well-known positive/negative space vase series when working with the Calgary International Airport (fig. 6.1).[2] Glass is pigeonholed into lighting or occasionally wall art (and very rarely as embedded wall elements), and wood and metal continue to be read as ideal for ornamenting and supporting walls, windows, and doors. Of course there are pragmatic reasons for these long-standing associations between craft materials and precise architectural uses, but these expectations are nevertheless limiting when craft artists wish to push beyond them and into the sculptural realm.

Ornament was another dominant theme in the preparation for this book. When I contacted administrators of hospitals, airports, universities, and cities regarding their public craft commissions, they frequently expressed confusion over the term architectural craft. After I clarified the materials and forms involved, they often replied that those things existed as decorations. This conflation between craft and ornament is loaded. Not only does it reference the Eurocentric assumption that refined, simplified ornament is progressive and civilized, whereas over-ornamentation is "primitive," but it calls up gendered labels around the feminine and decoration. This association with femininity and domesticity is particularly important in relation to public art and monuments.

Adrienne L. Burk looks at the history: "The forms of urban monuments common today largely arose at the end of the Middle Ages. Moving away from sepulchral forms into more public decorative sculpture during the Renaissance and baroque periods, by late nineteenth century Europe, 'the creating of public monuments became an artistic, political and social domain in its own right.'"[3] These periods, Burk continues, coincided with the rise of European colonization, and "closely allied to this were the scopic regimes of linear perspective and the naturalization of a kind of omniscient (and masculinist) 'gaze.'"[4] Therefore, monuments and public art were, and one could argue remain, aligned with iconic images, and ideas of masculinity associated with particular artistic materials such as bronze or stone, not quilting or weaving. Craft materials were perceived as falling well outside the monumental ideal, operating as decorative accessories rather than artistic statements. Feminist theorist Llewellyn Negrin concludes that even feminist attempts to overturn the stereotypes around ornament by rehabilitating it as an artistic tool have failed, as they "ultimately perpetuate … rather than undermine … stereotypical associations of the feminine with the sensuous, the superficial and the irrational."[5] According to this assertion, it could be argued that Canadian craftspeople like Jordi Bonet, who took the idea of ornament beyond the margins of modernist thought, from annoying addendum to being central to a building's aesthetic function, were particularly rebellious.

Given the Canadian focus of this book, the question of identity played an important role in shaping the research. Although it is difficult to provide proof or firm evidence to support this claim, it must be noted that regional differences shape the aesthetics of public art across the country. As architectural historian Harold Kalman has argued, regional architectural styles exist and they must be acknowledged in the search for a broader Canadian identity. For architecture and the crafts, this acknowledgment is often a result of the programming of art colleges and universities in specific areas, the representation of local jurors on selection committees, or the approach taken by architects employed to create high profile public buildings in each province. Despite the difficulties of identifying national and regional aesthetics, at every level pride in these unique aesthetics remains pronounced. From public art collections in smaller universities, hospitals, and airports to the larger projects commissioned by federal government's one-percent art program, it is often stated that the respective public art works help in defining not only their architectural spaces but the communities that use them.

As a consequence of Canada's multiculturalism, this issue has become even more tangled and complex. Not only are the vast majority of craftspeople who complete public commissions of European background but their objects most often reference widely accepted Western artistic ideas and influences; think, for example, of the unquestioned perpetuation of the Gothic Revival style in the carvings of Canada's Parliament Buildings. However, a strikingly high level of appropriation of Aboriginal images and craft traditions is found among efforts to express "Canadian" identity. This use of Aboriginal imagery is most pronounced at the Vancouver International Airport, where remarkable wooden carvings, Salish weavings, and totem poles greet visitors from around the world and confirm that they have arrived in Canada. The insertion of craft commissions as statements on identity is rarely decided upon by architects themselves; their presence is most often determined by committee or jury, suggesting yet another disparity between the vision of the craftsperson and the conceptualization of the architect whose space the objects will complete.

Although Canadian architectural historians have searched for a cohesive national identity through architecture, it has not been readily available. Certainly the Allied Arts shared, and continue to share, many regional similarities, from the West Coast style and Prairie Regionalism through the moderated vision of the International Style expressed in Central Canada. What is emerging in the twenty-first century is a lexicon of "great" works of architecture that incorporate craft in their vision. Consider, for example, the BC Electric Building with B.C. Binning's porcelain mural, Massey College with architect Ron Thom's own furniture and lighting designs and John Reeve's ceramic lamps and vases, and the Sturdy Stone Centre with its celebration of Saskatchewan ceramic murals and sculptures. These buildings and craft works make an interesting statement about the power of the modernist vision of pared-down ornamentation and the continued emphasis on excellence in craftsmanship. These are demonstrations of what Kalman argues – that Canadian architects never fully embraced the International Style, and they made modern architecture uniquely their own by adapting this style to regional materials and motifs. It could therefore be said that Canada was well positioned to enter the postmodern era in architecture and craft. Whereas European and American architects have been dismissed for embracing historical pastiche in the late 1980s and 1990s, Canadian architects like Brian MacKay-Lyons continued to look to the regional vernacular for clues on craftsmanship and ornamentation. This is not to say that Canada was immune from postmodern parodies in architecture and craft, but these were modulated through a long history of deconstructing the dogmas of modernism.

The continued relevance of this history is a gift in the age of anti-post-modern architecture. In August 2010 *Vanity Fair* magazine published an article by Matt Tyrnauer entitled "Architecture in the Age of Gehry." The article begins by emphasizing that Gehry was Canadian-born, and then, in summarizing the state of contemporary architecture, states that it is dependent on craft. Gehry confirms this dependence, complaining about the poor craftsmanship he had to put up with early in his career: "Some of the buildings I was given to do at that time had very low budgets, and I could not get the craftsmanship I was trained to have. I saw the hammer marks on the wood."[6] This is coincident with the idea that the postmodern return to decoration is not synonymous merely with a return to good craftsmanship. Tyrnauer writes: "A major subplot in this survey is the strong support for minimalism and the forceful rejection of Postmodernism," and goes on to state that postmodernist architects "had become nothing more than highly paid exterior decorators."[7] Here we have an exciting way of thinking about craft in architecture that bodes well for the future: it is essential to good buildings but not to be conflated with ornamentation.

From my countless on-site visits to large-scale public (secular) craft works, interviews with craftspeople and architects, and archival research, gaps between the fields of craft and architecture became clear. Following the Second World War, and continuing still today, many craftspeople have felt maligned by architecture and frustrated by the lack of opportunity to work within that sphere. Accompanying this aggravation is a sense that post-secondary craft education in Canada has never provided students with the knowledge to successfully apply for work with architects or within large-scale building projects. It is almost impossible to find courses that train students to prepare professional maquettes, to understand the intricacies of budgeting for enormous projects, or to grasp the multiple levels of professionals – ranging from architects and engineers to clients and interior designers – who will have an influence on their original vision. In turn, craftspeople have often perpetuated stereotypes of the architect as lacking interest in the craftsmanship behind processes and materials, and single-handedly responsible for creating cold, stark modernist spaces. Clearly, despite the promise of an increasingly interdisciplinary world, the realms of craft and architecture

Fig. 6.2
Neil Forrest, "Hiving Mesh" (5.0 x 3.5 x 1.0 m), porcelain, stainless steel fittings, Lucite, wire, 1999–2002.

remain somewhat at odds. But this gap is not due to purposeful animosity; it is the result of a lack of opportunity to collaborate. When architects and craftspeople find each other, the results are inspiring.

In 1999 the ceramic artist Neil Forrest and architect Philip Beesley began working together on Forrest's installation "Hiving Mesh" at Saint Mary's University Art Gallery in Halifax. Composed of almost a thousand wires and ceramic pieces and requiring careful engineering in the form of three interconnected suspended screens of hexagonal geometric supports, "Hiving Mesh" as Forrest describes it is a "detached ceramic ornament that responds to the spaces of contemporary architecture" (fig. 6.2). Beesley wrote the introduction to Forrest's exhibition catalogue, where he praised the ability of fired porcelain clay and glass paste to create "an interlinked matrix of hundreds of small ceramic objects, densely compressed fragments resembling plant bulbs and body organs."[8] To Beesley, the success of Forrest's work is a consequence of his ability to rethink traditional definitions of architectural ceramics, moving away from the fixed, or static form of ornamentation, to "a refreshed ornament expressing a new kind of architectural space."[9] Forrest was inspired to create "Hiving Mesh" after finding gnarled, deformed natural foliage on his walks near his rural Nova Scotia home. He pondered the implications of growth and cellular expansion in relation to ceramics and architectural space, and the subject continues to form the basis of much of his recent work. For Beesley, an architect, sculptor, and exhibition and graphic designer, Forrest's approach paralleled his own interest in the connection between architecture and organic forms.

Beesley is an exceptional Canadian architect in that he has actively associated himself with the contemporary craft scene. Between 1992 and 1994 he collaborated with the York Quay Gallery at Toronto's Harbourfront Centre to create "Designed by Commission," a craft collaboration. This was followed by his exhibition designs for the Gardiner Ceramic Museum and the Textile Museum of Canada. Beesley brings challenging ideas to craftspeople through his presentations at workshops and at conferences like the National Council on Education for the Ceramic Arts (NCECA). His publications feature ideas related to a variety of craft disciplines, and he relates them to developments within architecture. In his 2006 book *Responsive Architectures: Subtle Technologies* Beesley writes about the need for inter-relationship and emphasizes biology and the "interconnectedness in molecular detail."[10] By looking at the fundamental lessons offered by organic forms, architecture can be related to craft, which has always relied upon the transformation of raw materials into solid three-dimensional objects. Furthermore, the flexibility of interconnectedness offers architects an important metaphor for future conditions: "A wave of new industrial processes is transforming building design and construction. The next generation of architecture will be able to sense, change and transform itself."[11] And the crafts play a central role in these future developments. According to Beesley, textiles are "at the core of a revolution in architecture. Soft textile foundations are fundamentally changing the way we think about our built environment. Textile-based building concepts range from flexible skeletons and meshwork skins to structures that move and respond to their occupants."[12] Like Gottfried Semper before him, Beesley returns to ancient historical precedents to express the importance of textiles within architecture: "the first building materials to emerge were not masonry, but woven."[13] However, Beesley's vision of the role of textiles in future architecture stresses craft in the service of architecture:

"every fiber has an integral role in maintaining structure, each as important as its neighbor."[14]

At the start of the new millennium there is a certain irony in returning to previous traditions that place the materials and processes of the artisan as subservient to architecture. During the postwar period, the studio craft movement struggled mightily to free craft from this hierarchical idea, foregrounding craft as art and the craftsperson as individualistic artist. How will Beesley's ideas work, given the context of contemporary craft? The answer is to be found in his collaborations with Neil Forrest, which continued during the 2007 conference for Acadia (Association of Computer-Aided Design in Architecture) held at Forrest's teaching institution, NSCAD University. This conference emphasized the use of computers and new technologies in architecture, planning, and building science, highlighting technology's potential to fill the traditional role of the artisan in the detailed work of producing large-scale textile, ceramic, wood, and metal structures. In return, these new possibilities allow craftspeople to continue fulfilling the role of artist in relation to architecture. The enormous textile skins for buildings might involve craftspeople at the concept stage, but they would be designed and manufactured through Building Information Modeling (BIM), rapid prototyping, Computer-Aided Design (CAD) and Computer-Aided Manufacture (CAM). The use of these software and computer programs allows craftspeople working as artists the freedom to create individual, one-of-a-kind statements on the concepts behind architecture and craft, like Forrest's "Hiving Mesh." What this new perspective changes, in a positive manner, is the collaborative role played by craftspeople. Their expertise in materials and their understanding of the fundamental properties of textiles, for example, will become increasingly important as architects reconsider their interconnectedness with traditional materials in the context of new technologies and innovative industries. These possibilities allow us to foresee exciting future directions for architectural craft.

Still, the utopian vision of craft and architecture reuniting through new technologies has many hurdles to overcome. Over the past decade computers have been celebrated as the future for architecture and craft, but a backlash is developing, and it is centred on the idea that both architects and craftspeople must engage with their hands. The celebrated Swiss architect Jacques Herzog (who along with Pierre de Meuron was responsible for the "Bird's Nest" stadium built for the 2008 Beijing Olympics) strikes a cautionary note about technology: "Computers cannot do anything without the assistance of the human brain. I always give the same example: When you go into old cathedrals, they are extremely physical, and they follow the laws of craftsmanship, but they transport something we cannot explain, which is what makes great buildings, and that hasn't changed at all."[15] Most pressing is the issue of access – of craftspeople to architects, and new technologies and education to craft in relation to architecture. Interacting with expensive software systems and equipment during undergraduate or graduate studies is one thing; but gaining access to these necessary tools in the development of architectural craft is quite another matter when the average annual income of a Canadian craftsperson falls near the poverty line.[16] Another factor is the continued lack of support for uniting craftspeople and architects. Starting in the mid-1960s Anita Aarons envisioned a future in which these groups would be easily connected via published guides to the work of outstanding architectural craftspeople that would land on the desks of all Canadian architects through the Royal Architectural Institute of Canada. Her "Allied Arts" catalogues of 1966 and 1968 represented an attempt to do this, but archival records show that poor sales and negative reviews of the catalogues prevented this idea from coming to fruition.

Today the Internet allows architects and craftspeople to quickly find information on each other: however, professional guidelines are still necessary, and sadly lacking. This becomes most obvious when one examines the risk factors involved in craftspeople taking on large-scale commissions. First, only a select handful of craftspeople tend to be networked on these opportunities. These are often makers who have formal levels of post-secondary education and have made professional contacts within architecture and interior design, or have served as jurors for major craft exhibitions and prizes. Second, few craftspeople possess the training in creating professional architectural maquettes that properly express their creative vision. Textile artists Mariette Rousseau-Vermette and Carole Sabiston both noted that committees and juries for major architectural commissions judge craftspeople's submissions not only on their artistic merit and budgets, but on their successful presentation at the initial stages. Third, craftspeople tend to underestimate the value of their labour and materials in their bid to win the commission. This undervaluation becomes an enormous problem as the work progresses, and as changes to material, redesigning, the hiring of additional staff to help with the execution of the work, and increased installation costs through the need to hire unionized labour within specific building sites fall under the artist's own budget.

Finally, the moral rights of the artist remain a murky legal area. Many craftspeople still do not insist on having a clause regarding their moral rights written into architectural contracts. As a result, the fate of a piece of public art when the winds of change affect the style of a building frequently becomes a source of controversy. Unless a craftsperson has considered the future of his or her piece during the contractual phase, a long, drawn-out legal battle may ensue when a piece is removed, altered, or destroyed. Toronto lawyer and art advocate Aaron Milrad has written extensively on the risks associated with public artworks in his books *The Art World: Law, Business and Practice in Canada* (1980) and *Artful Ownership: Art Law, Valuation and Commerce in the United States, Canada and Mexico* (2000). As indicated by Milrad, craftspeople put themselves in tenuous legal situations in relation to copyright, taxation, insurance, liability, and reproduction rights when they sign any contract for a public work. Yet few craftspeople are well versed in how to approach the legalities surrounding architectural commissions. As the research for this book showed, it is very common for large-scale public works simply to disappear. On numerous occasions, directions to craft pieces led to blank walls, to elevators, to plywood covering devices or to altered, smaller versions of works. When property managers and on-site security guards were questioned about the location of commissioned works, most stated that they did not know their whereabouts. Others openly confessed to avoiding the issue of the moral rights of the artist during renovations by allowing pieces to remain on-site – albeit hidden – and building around or hiding them.

The ease with which a craftsperson's public art object can disappear is lessening, thanks to explosions of indignation on blogs, websites and on-line photo journals that pay homage to, and document, outstanding examples of Canadian architectural craft. Most extensive are sites such as Benoît Clairoux's exceptional "Works of Art in the Montreal Metro," where he provides a well-researched history and overview accompanied by images of the works, including Fredéric Back's stained glass at the Place-des-Arts metro, Jean-Paul Mousseau's ceramic circles at the Peel metro, and Jordi Bonet's "Citius, Altius, Fortius," concrete mural at the Pie-IX metro.[17] Montreal's metro system and Toronto's subway system garner many on-line reviews, and the Toronto Transit Commission's official website features an article by Eli McIlveen, "Art on the TTC," which provides an overview with images.[18] While McIlveen's article exists on the official website, interest in Toronto's subway art ranges from hip, edgy reviews like David Topping's article "69 Days on the TTC" at the *Torontoist*, to the sale of "Toronto subway buttons" featuring the ceramic tile art of various stations.[19] Serious attempts to draw attention to the issue of anonymous public craft objects can also be found on-line, in articles such as *Fibre Quarterly*'s "Who Made That? A Question about Public (Textile) Art in Canada."[20] Many cities, provinces, universities, and corporations responsible for commissioning public art and craft have gone on-line with their holdings, making the works not only easier to research and find but harder to remove during renovations or reconstruction. Sites like the City of Vancouver's "Public Art" contain extensive listings of commissions, installations, artists' policies and forthcoming calls for competitions.[21]

Vancouver is also home to trendy public art installations, such as the 2009 "Blanket Bus," a Vancouver transit bus covered in colourful afghans that made reference to the popular DIY (do-it-yourself) movement. Created by the artist's collective Instant Coffee, the "Blanket Bus" was part of a project entitled "88 Blocks: Art on Main," which continues to bring thoughtful, fun public art and craft projects into the public realm while maintaining a strong on-line presence. Vancouver's deputy mayor, Heather Deal, attributes the success of the "Blanket Bus" to its ability to animate public spaces.[22] The positive response to the "Blanket Bus" emphasized the grandmotherly and domestic nature of afghans, again reinforcing the gendered idea that textiles have the ability to bring comfort and softness to impersonal public spaces, even if they are simply suggested by their images being driven past viewers on crowded urban streets. The effusion of formal and informal websites that explore the many facets of public architectural craft bodes well for raising awareness of the visual and written traces of these artworks, and hopefully will offset some of the loss caused by their removal and destruction.

But on-line attempts to draw attention to architectural craft are not sufficient on their own. As the field of craft history, theory, and critical writing continues to widen and strengthen, practioners and theoreticians need to examine the implications of craft's intersections with architecture. Overlaps and interdisciplinary experiments are referred to occasionally, as in Glenn Adamson's book *Thinking through Craft,* and in a range of disciplinary journals, for example, Olga Zorzi Pugliese's article "Beautifying the City: 1960s Artistic Mosaics by Italian Canadians in Toronto" in *Quaderni d'Italianistica;*[23] however, sustained investigation into architectural craft is necessary.

I have written this book in the hope that its considerations of the larger issues of materiality, scale, form, ornament, and identity in relation to Canadian craft will open up discussion of these ideas in relation to postwar developments in other nations. The thoughts developed here are reflections on the state of contemporary craft as it developed in parallel with, and often away from, architecture. In order to circumvent damaging stereotypes of craft as belonging to the realm of kitschy, naïve art, as suggested by the proliferation over the past decade of fibreglass whales, cows, lobsters, and moose decorated in mosaics, felting, and beads in cities across North America, sophisticated theoretical discussion of the implications of craft within built environments is vital. In this book I have endeavoured to offer an overview of Canadian developments within architectural craft; however, with things changing so rapidly in the realm of new technologies, craft, and architecture, it is just the start. Many exciting developments lie ahead.

Royal Architectural Institute of Canada
Allied Arts Award Recipients
(Award suspended in 1995, reinstituted as a biennial award in 2005)

Year	Name	Category
2009	Paul Raff	Architect/Visual Artist
2007	Warren Carther Artist	Architectural Glass
2005	James Dow Philip Gabriel	Photographer Lighting Designer
1995	Cornelia Hahn Oberlander	Landscape Architect
1994	William Ronald Reid	Maker of Things
1992	Mary Filer	Design – Stained Glass
1991	Av Isaacs	Art Dealer and Activist
1989	Michael Snow	Sculptor

Year	Name	Category
1987	Joe Fafard	Sculptor
1986	Michael Hayden	Sculptor in Light
1985	David Alexander Colville	Artist
1984	Katie Ohe	Sculptor
1983	Alfred Pellan	Artist
1982	Henry Kalen	Architectural Photographer
1981	Harold Town	Artist
1980	Roy Leadbeater	Sculptor
1979	Nubuo Kubota	Sculptor
1978	Gordon Smith	Artist
1977	Robert Gray Murray	Sculptor
1976	Micheline Beauchemin	Tapestry Designer
1975	Thomas Forrestall	Artist
1974	Ed Drahanchuk	Potter-Designer
1973	Charles Daudelin	Sculptor
1972	Vancouver Art Kiosk	Committee and Art City Group
1971	Ron Baird	Sculptor
1970	Tony Tascona	Painter

Year	Name	Category
1969	Ted Bieler	Sculptor
1968	Eli Bornstein	Artist
1967	Gerald Trottier	Painter/Sculptor
1966	Ernestine Tahedl	Artist-designer Stained Glass
1965	Jordi Bonet	Sculptor/Muralist
1964	Claude Roussel	Sculptor
1963	Cleeve Horne	Painter and Sculptor
1962	B.C. Binning	Painter and Muralist
1961	Sylvia Daoust	Sculptor
1960	Leo Mol	Sculptor
1959	Alexander S. Carter	Heraldic Decoration
1958	Louis Archambault	Sculptor
1957	Alan B. Beddoc	Artist
1957	Yvonne Williams	Design-Stained Glass
1956	Lionel A.J. Thomas	Artist
1955	Donald C. MacKay	Painter and Muralist
1954	Howard Dunnington-Grubb	Landscape Architect
1953	Armand Filion	Sculptor

NOTES

ABBREVIATIONS USED
AO Archives of Ontario
DPW Department of Public Works
NSCAD Nova Scotia School of Art and Design
RAIC Royal Architectural Institute of Canada

CHAPTER ONE

1 Anita Aarons, "The Integrators," *Architecture Canada*, ser. 495, vol. 43, no. 12 (December 1966), 22.

2 W. Lee Rensselaer, *Ut Pictura Poesis: The Humanistic Theory of Painting*, 1.

3 George P. Landow, "Ruskin and the tradition of ut pictura poesis," on Victorian Web, http://www.victorianweb.org/authors/ruskin/atheories/1.1.html (accessed 15 February 2009).

4 Johann Wolfgang von Goethe, "Art and Handicraft," (1797) in Isabelle Frank, *The Theory of Decorative Art: An Anthology of European and American Writings 1750–1940*, 150.

5 Joan Evans, "Introduction" to John Ruskin, *The Lamp of Beauty: Writings on Art*, vii.

6 Ruskin even went as far as establishing his own medieval fiefdom, the Guild of St George, to oppose the industrial conditions of late nineteenth-century London.

7 Evans, "Introduction," xiii.

8 John Ruskin, "Preface," *A Joy for Ever*, viii.

9 John Ruskin, "Modern Manufacture and Design, Lecture III," in Frank, *The Theory of Decorative Art*, 47.

10 Ibid., 47.

11 See Fiona MacCarthy, "Art for the People: William Morris, Burne-Jones and the Politics of Art," *Journal of Stained Glass*, vol. 31 (2007), 53–65; Charles Harvey and Jon Press, "The Quest for a Life of Purpose: Morris before the Firm, 1834–1861," in Harvey and Press, *William Morris: Design and Enterprise in Victorian Britain*; and Martin Harrison, "Church Decoration and Stained Glass," in Linda Parry, ed., *William Morris*.

12 William Morris, "The Arts and Crafts of To-day" (1889), in Frank, *The Theory of Decorative Art*, 64.

13 Ashlar is an ancient type of stone work, used as an alternative to brick.

14 Morris, "The Arts and Crafts of To-day," 65.

15 Barry Downs, quoted in Harold Kalman, *A Concise History of Canadian Architecture*, 553.

16 John Ruskin, *Collected Works*, xxii, 9, quoted in Nikolaus Pevsner, *The Sources of Modern Architecture and Design*, 20.

17 Pevsner, *The Sources*, 20.

18 Ruskin's *The Lamp of Beauty* was on the reading list of the Victoria College of Art (now NSCAD University) when it was established in 1887, and influential architects like Montreal's Edward and W.S. Maxwell owned Ruskin's *Modern Painters* (see the Maxwell Brothers' library holdings at http://cac.mcgill.ca). Robarts Rare Book Library at the University of Toronto has one of the world's leading collections of original publications by William Morris and his Kelmscott Press. See Anita Grants, *Selectivity, Interpretation and Application: The Influence of John Ruskin in Canada*.

19 Mary N. Woods, *From Craft to Profession: The Practice of Architecture in Nineteenth-Century America*, 4.

20 Ibid., 4.

21 Ibid., 5.

22 Ibid., 7.

23 See Peter Davey, *Arts and Crafts Architecture*; Sheila Kirk, *Philip Webb: Pioneer of Arts and Crafts Architecture*; and Ray Watkinson, "Church Decoration and Stained Glass," in Linda Parry, ed., *William Morris*.

24 See Sandra Alfoldy, *Crafting Identity: The Development of Professional Fine Craft* 12–14 and Elliott A. Krause, *Death of the Guilds: Professions, States, and the Advance of Capitalism*.

25 Toni Fountain, "Doing Business with Artists in 1991," in *The Guild 6: The Designer's Source of Artists and Artisans*, 5. Today the author uses the name Toni Sikes.

26 Jack Lenor Larsen, "The Personalization of Crafts," in *The Guild 6*, 106.

27 Ibid.

28 Calgary Allied Art Foundation, http://www.caafonline.org/collect.html (accessed 18 February 2009).

29 RAIC, "The Architect Looks at Public Relations," April 1960 booklet, p. 5, LAC, RAIC fonds, MG 28, I239, vol. 18, file 18.1.

30 Memo from RAIC Executive Offices, "Next Award of Allied Arts Medal," 15 December 1953. LAC, RAIC fonds, MG 28, I239, vol. 19, file 3.

31 Ibid.

32 RAIC Press Release No. 53-104 "Architects helping the Allied Arts," (20 April 1953). LAC, RAIC fonds, MG 28, I239, vol. 19, file 3. The jury members for the granting of the commission were: R. Schofield Morris, president of the RAIC; Robert W. Pilot, president of the Royal Canadian Academy; Pierre Normandeau, president of the Sculptors' Society of Canada; the sculptor Sylvia Daoust (who won the RAIC Allied Arts award in 1961); and the architect J. Roxburgh Smith.

33 Ibid. Julien Hébert was awarded $1,000.00 for his winning design.

34 RAIC minutes, 19 January 1953. LAC, RAIC fonds, MG 28, I239, vol. 19, file 3. The medal was manufactured by Lamond and Sons Limited, Manufacturing Jewellers, came individually boxed in a blue velvet case, and was valued at $25.00.

35 R. Schofield Morris, letter to Armand Filion, 7 April 1953. LAC, RAIC fonds, MG 28, I239, vol. 19, file 3.

36 Memo from RAIC Executive Offices, "Next Award of Allied Arts Medal," 15 December 1953. LAC, RAIC fonds, MG 28, I239, vol. 19, file 3.

37 RAIC Press Release No. 54–205, "Allied

Arts Medal," 28 April 1954. LAC, RAIC fonds, MG 28, I239, vol. 19, file 3.

38 Minutes of Executive Committee Meeting 14 February 1959, p. 3. LAC, RAIC fonds, MG 28, I239, vol. 19, file 3.

39 Bruce Brown, President, RAIC to Fred Price, Executive Director, RAIC 25 November 1964. LAC, RAIC fonds, MG 28, 139, vol. 19, file 19.5.

40 George W. Lord, Alberta Association of Architects, letter to R. Schofield Morris, president, RAIC, 11 March 1953. LAC, RAIC fonds, MG 28, I239, vol. 19, file 3.

41 Clifford Wiens, president, Saskatchewan Association of Architects, letter to Maurice Holdham, Executive Secretary, RAIC, 27 January 1971. LAC, RAIC fonds, MG 28, I239, vol. 19, file 19.5.

42 Gerald Trottier, letter to Mr Fowler, RAIC, 23 March 1967. LAC, RAIC fonds, MG 28, I239, vol. 19, file 19.5.

43 Rachel Gotlieb, *Thor Hansen: Crafting a Canadian Style*, 1.

44 Ibid.

45 Thor Hansen, "Hand-Wrought Happiness: An Address by Thor Hansen, Art Director, Public Relations Department, The British American Oil Company Limited," 1956, 8. AO, box C26, M111, file 3.

46 Ibid., 15.

47 Gotlieb, *Thor Hansen*, 6.

48 Thor Hansen at Huronia Museum, http://huroniamuseumtest.wordpress.com/tag/thor-hansen/ (accessed 25 February 2009).

49 Ibid.

50 Gotlieb, *Thor Hansen*, 2.

51 Thor Hansen, "B-A's Canadiana Program: An Address by Thor Hansen," 16 June 1958. AO, box C26, M111, file 3.

52 Ibid.

53 Gotlieb, *Thor Hansen*, 3.

54 Ibid., 3.

55 Ibid., 4.

56 Thor Hansen, "B-A's Canadiana Program," 3.

57 Ibid., 5.

58 Ibid., 6.

59 Ibid., 4.

60 "Rich Colors Tell of Canada as Business Firm Turns to Art," *Vancouver Sun*, 18 June 1954. AO, box C26, M111, file 3.

61 Kalman, *A Concise History of Canadian Architecture*, 555.

62 Gotlieb, *Thor Hansen*, 9.

63 "Mural in the Foyer of the new British American Oil Office," *Canadian Art*, vol. 18, no. 1 (Jan/Feb 1961), 56.

64 Lawren Harris, "What the Public Wants," *Canadian Art*, vol. 12, no. 1 (autumn 1954), 9.

65 Ibid., 10.

66 Ibid., 12–13.

67 Midland Ontario's Huronia Museum has collected many Thor Hansen pieces and features a Thor Hansen Room.

68 Penny Sparke, "Introduction," Susie McKellar and Penny Sparke, eds., *Interior Design and Identity*, 2.

69 Ibid., 2.

70 Joan Harland and Ruth Stirk, *The History of Interior Decoration/Design at the University of Manitoba 1938–1997* (unpublished manuscript). University of Manitoba, School of Architecture Library.

71 Ibid., iii. For a history of the education of women as architects in Canada see Annmarie Adams and Peta Tancred, *Designing Women: Gender and the Architectural Profession* (Toronto: University of Toronto Press, 2000).

72 Harland and Stirk, *The History of Interior Decoration*, v.

73 Kalman, *A Concise History of Canadian Architecture*, 567.

74 Ibid., v.

75 Ibid., 17. In the academic year 1943/44 twenty-one students were registered, with forty-one the following year. The first male student enrolled in 1945, and by 1949 twelve men were students in the program.

76 Ibid., 23. The photographs measured 12″ x 18″.

77 Ray Ellenwood, *Egregore: The Montreal Automatist Movement*, 6.

78 Ibid.

79 Jean-Marie Gauvreau, *Nos intérieurs de demain*.

80 Sandra Alfoldy, "Eleanor Milne: The Making of an Artist in Canada," Virtual Museum of Canada.

81 Eleanor Milne, personal interview, Ottawa, Ontario, 19 November 1998.

82 Alfoldy, "Eleanor Milne."

83 "Adieu: Not Au Revoir," *Noosa News*, 4 January 2000, 2.

84 Sandra Alfoldy, "The Metaphysics of Craft: Anita Aarons's Crafts for Architecture," in Sandra Alfoldy and Janice Helland, eds., *Craft, Space and Interior Design, 1855–2005*, 192.

85 Anita Aarons, "The Dual Nature of Commissioned Work," *Journal* RAIC, ser. 473, vol. 42, no. 2 (February 1965), 13.

86 Ibid., 14.

87 Ibid., 14.

88 "Introduction," *Allied Arts Catalogue*, vol. 1, nos. 1–48 (October 1966).

89 Ibid.

90 Anita Aarons, "Art and the 58th RAIC Assembly," *Journal* RAIC, ser. 478, vol. 42, no. 7 (July 1965), 48.

91 E. Kimball, "The Company of Young Craftsmen," *SW Magazine*, 1 July 1967. AO, Ontario Crafts Council, Archives of Canadian Craft, MU5771, box 26, EH2-EJ.

92 Ibid.

93 Alfoldy, "The metaphysics of craft," 190.

94 Anita Aarons, "Time Factors in Commissioned Work," *Journal* RAIC, ser. 474, vol. 42, no. 3 (March 1965), 24.

95 Anita Aarons, "Signs, Signals, Symbols and Tradition," *Journal* RAIC, ser. 475, vol. 42, no. 4 (April 1965), 40.

96 Clement Greenberg, "The Status of Clay," in Garth Clark, ed., *Ceramic Millennium*, 4.

97 Bruce Metcalf, "Replacing the Myth of Modernism," in Sandra Alfoldy ed., *Neocraft: Modernity and the Crafts*, 5.

98 Sandra Alfoldy and Janice Helland "Introduction," in Sandra Alfoldy and Janice Helland, eds., *Craft, Space and Interior Design*, 2.

99 Larsen, "The Personalization of Crafts," in *The Guild 6*, 106.

100 Kalman, *A Concise History of Canadian Architecture*, 570–1.

CHAPTER TWO

1 Theodor W. Adorno, "Functionalism Today," in Neil Leach, ed., *Rethinking Architecture: A Reader in Cultural Theory*, 12.

2 While a range of makers have always shared craft materials, recent publications such as Joseph Magliaro and Shu Hungs, *By Hand: The Use of Craft in Contemporary Art* argue that this trend has increased in recent years.

3 "Gottfried Semper" in *The Dictionary of Modern Design* (Oxford: Oxford University Press, 2005), http://www.answers.com/topic/gottfried-semper (accessed 31 March 2009).

4 Gottfried Semper, "The Theory of Technique: Introduction to Style in the Technical and Tectonic Arts," in Isabelle Frank, *The Theory of the Decorative Arts: An Anthology of European and American Writings, 1750–1940*, 221.

5 Ibid., 223.

6 Ibid., 224–5.

7 Jonathan A. Hale, "Gottfried Semper's Primitive Hut as an Act of Self-Creation," *Architectural Research Quarterly* (2005) vol. 9, no. 1, 45–9.

8 Adolf Loos, "Ornament and Crime," in Bernie Miller and Melony Ward, eds., *Crime and Ornament: The Arts and Popular Culture in the Shadow of Adolf Loos*, 8.

9 Adorno, "Functionalism Today," 12.

10 Ibid., 13.

11 Ibid., 14.

12 Anita Aarons, "Art and Architecture," *Journal RAIC*, ser. 472, vol. 42, no. 1 (January 1965), 56.

13 Adorno, "Functionalism Today," 14–15.

14 Anita Aarons, "Montreal … Achievement and Faith," *Journal RAIC*, ser. 480, vol. 42, no. 9 (September 1965), 16.

15 Jacques de Roussan, *Jordi Bonet*, 6–7.

16 Guy Robert, *Jordi Bonet*, 11.

17 Ibid., 109.

18 Ibid.

19 Ibid., 111.

20 Anita Aarons, "Art and the 58th RAIC Assembly," *Journal RAIC*, ser. 478, vol. 42, no. 7 (July 1965), 48.

21 Ibid.

22 *Toronto Star* (21 December 1968) quoted in H.G. Levitch, "Art at Queen's Park," brochure, 1968.

23 Janet Wright, *Crown Assets: The Architecture of the Department of Public Works 1867–1967*, 5.

24 "Art at Queen's Park," Archives of Ontario, on-line exhibition, http://www.archives.gov.on.ca/english/on-line-exhibits/art-qp/index.aspx (accessed 2 December 2010).

25 Ibid.

26 Arnold Edinborough, "Office Art, Canadian-Style: It Helps Keep Civil Servants Civil," *The Financial Post* (13 February 1971), 18.

27 Sadly, Jordi Bonet's smaller commissions are not always accorded the same level of respect as his large-scale murals. In 2001 the police station on Gottigen Street in Halifax, Nova Scotia, removed and destroyed its headquarters sign, which had been designed and executed by Bonet in the early 1970s.

28 Peter Collins, *Concrete: The Vision of a New Architecture*, second edition, 21.

29 Jean-Auguste Lebrun, quoted in Collins, *Concrete*, 25.

30 Collins, *Concrete*, 101.

31 Ibid., 123.

32 Ibid. Collins discusses Frank Lloyd Wright's textile block houses as another manifestation of craft impulses in concrete architecture.

33 Royal Alberta Museum, "On-the-Grounds," self-guided tour brochure, 2004.

34 Martin Heidegger, "Building, Dwelling, Thinking," in Leach, *Rethinking Architecture*, 120.

35 Ibid., 121.

36 Hans-Georg Gadamer, "The Ontological Foundation of the Occasional and the Decorative," in Leach, *Rethinking Architecture*, 135.

37 Glenn Adamson, *Thinking through Craft*, 95.

38 Gloria Hickey, "Introduction," in Gloria Hickey, ed., *Common Ground: Contemporary Craft: Architecture and the Decorative Arts*, 16.

39 Ibid.

40 Myriam Blais, "The Meaning of Techniques and Materials," in Hickey, ed., *Common Ground*, 47.

41 Ibid., 49.

42 Ibid., 50.

43 Lutz Haufschild, "Inspired Light, Space Inspired Thoughts about Light in Architecture," in Hickey, ed., *Common Ground*, 66.

44 Ibid., 66.

45 Ibid.

46 Rita Beiks, Vancouver International Airport Authority, personal interview, Vancouver, British Columbia 9 June 2004.

47 Haufschild, "Inspired Light," 71.

48 Bernard Flaman, "Public Art and Canadian Cultural Policy: The Airports," in Annie Gérin and James S. McLean, eds., *Public Art in Canada*, 75.

49 Ibid.

50 Ibid., 80, 91.

51 Charlotte Lindgren, personal interview, Halifax, Nova Scotia, 5 May 2004.

52 Mariette Rousseau-Vermette, personal interview, Ste. Adèle, Quebec, 29 April 2005.

53 Ibid.

54 Ibid.

55 Ibid.

56 Ibid.

57 Robin Muller, personal interview, 28 September 2010, Halifax, Nova Scotia.

58 Susan Surette, email interview, 14 July 2010.

59 See Lucy Lippard, Marie Fleming, et al., *Joyce Wieland* (Toronto: Art Gallery of Ontario, 1987) and John O'Brian, "Anthem lip-sync (Joyce Wieland's signature is inseparable from her art)," *Journal of Canadian Art History*, vol. 21, no. 1–2 (2000), 140–51.

60 Annie Gérin, "Introduction," Annie Gérin and James S. McLean, eds., *Public Art in Canada*, 5.

61 Lydia Matthews, "Homespun Ideas: Reinterpreting Craft in Contemporary Culture," in *Practice Makes Perfect: Bay Area Conceptual Craft*, exhibition catalogue (San Francisco: Southern Exposure, 2005) as quoted in Warren Selig and Mi-Kyoung Lee, "Materiality and Meaning: A Re-examination of Fiber and Material Studies in Contemporary Art and Culture," press release, February 2008.

62 These "truths" are taken from John Ruskin's *The Lamp of Beauty: Writings on Art*.

63 A. Welby Pugin, "On Metalwork" (1841), in Isabelle Frank, *The Theory of the Decorative Arts: An Anthology of European and American Writings, 1750–1940*, 35.

64 William Morris, "The Revival of Handicraft" (1888), in Isabelle Frank, *The Theory of the Decorative Arts: An Anthology of European and American Writings, 1750–1940*, 171.

65 Tom Crook, "Craft and the Dialogics of Modernity: The Arts and Crafts Movement in Late-Victorian and Edwardian England," *Journal of Modern Craft*, vol. 2, no. 1 (March 2009), 17–18.

66 Lisa Pace Vetter, *"Women's Work" as Political Art: Weaving and Dialectical Politics in Homer, Aristophanes and Plato*, ix.

67 Ibid., 2.

68 Sigmund Freud, "Lecture 33: Femininity" (1933), in *New Introductory Lectures on Psychoanalysis: The Complete Psychological Works of Sigmund Freud*, 140.

69 Le Corbusier, "The Decorative Arts of Today" (1925), in Frank, *Theory of Decorative Art*, 216.

70 John Ruskin, "The Lamp of Beauty" (1849) in Isabelle Frank, *The Theory of the Decorative Arts: An Anthology of European and American Writings, 1750–1940*, 44.

71 Brian MacKay-Lyons, personal interview, Halifax, Nova Scotia, 23 August 2004.

72 Ibid.

73 Ibid.

74 See Sandra Alfoldy, "Suzanne Swannie: Shifting Ground," exhibition catalogue, MSVU Art Gallery, 23 October–12 December 2004.

75 Brian MacKay-Lyons, personal interview, Halifax, Nova Scotia, 23 August 2004.

76 Richard Sennet, *The Craftsman*, 1.

77 Pierre Bourdieu (Randal Johnson, ed.), *The Field of Cultural Production*, 43.

78 See Bruce Metcalf, "Replacing the Myth of Modernism," in Sandra Alfoldy, ed., *Neocraft: Modernity and the Crafts*, 4–32. It should be noted that while Vasari privileged painters and sculptors in his writings, he also acknowledged the importance of sculptors who worked in clay, notably Luca Della Robia, and sculptors who dealt with architectural decorations, such as Lorenzo Ghiberti.

79 See Mike Press, "Handmade Futures: The Emerging Role of Craft Knowledge in Our Digital Culture," in Alfoldy, ed., *Neocraft*, 249–66.

80 Kiki Smith, quoted in Shu Hung and Joseph Magliaro, eds., *By Hand: The Use of Craft in Contemporary Culture*, 140.

81 Martin Heidegger, "The Thing," in Albert Hofstadter (trans.), *Poetry, Language, Thought*, 167.

82 Richard Osborne and Borin Van Loon, *Introducing Sociology*, 61.

83 Shane Gannon, "The Popularity of Max Weber's 'The Protestant Work Ethic and the Spirit of Capitalism': An Analysis of Historical Trends and Scholarship," on *Gateway: An Academic Journal on the Web* (winter 2002). http:grad.usask.ca/gateway/shanegannon_WeberPopularity.html (accessed 6 August 2008).

84 Gottfried Semper, "Introduction to Style in the Technical and Tectonic Arts" (1860), in Frank, *Theory of Decorative Art*, 223.

85 Frank Lloyd Wright, "The Art and Craft of the Machine" (1901), in Frank, *Theory of Decorative Art*, 207.

86 Anni Albers, "The Weaving Workshop," in Herbert Bayer, Walter Gropius, et al., eds., *Bauhaus 1919–1928*, 141.

87 John Roberts, *The Intangibilities of Form: Skill and Deskilling in Art After the Readymade*, 2.

88 Warren Selig, quoted in Vicki Halpern and Diane Douglas, eds., *Choosing Craft: A History Told by Artists*, 91.

89 See the work of Glenn Adamson, Garth Clark, Arthur Coleman Danto, and Warren Selig.

90 Roberts, *The Intangibilities of Form*, 3.

91 Sandra Alfoldy and Rachel Gotlieb, *On the Table: 100 Years of Functional Ceramics in Canada*, 100.

92 Jack Sures, phone interview, 8 June 2004.

93 See Stuart Hall, *Representation: Cultural Representations and Signifying Practices*.

94 Jane Lind, *Joyce Wieland*, 237.

95 Unfortunately, Library and Archives Canada has listed the Department of Public Works (Public Works Canada) Federal Art Programs documents as restricted, so specific names, dates and quotations may not be used here. However, these records can be found at the National Archives of Canada, Ottawa, under Public Works Canada, "Fine Art," accession number 4440, RG 11.

CHAPTER THREE

1 Arthur Danto, "Visionary Ceramics," in *American Ceramics*, vol. 15, no. 2 (October 2007), 26.

2 See Thomas Gordon Smith, ed., *Vitruvius on Architecture*, Liisa Kanerva, *Between Science and Drawings: Renaissance Architects on Vitruvius's Educational Ideas*

(Helsinki: Finnish Academy of Science and Letters, 2006), and Indra Kagis McEwen, *Vitruvius: Writing the Body of Architecture* (Cambridge, Massachusetts: MIT Press, 2003).

3 Le Corbusier, *Le Modulor and Other Buildings and Projects, 1944–1945*, 3.

4 Although it must be noted that Le Corbusier formulated complicated mathematical equations for "Le Modulor," they were flexible. "Le Modulor" was based on the navel height of a male figure, and was segmented according to the Golden Ratio.

5 Judi Loach, "Le Corbusier and the Creative Use of Mathematics," *British Journal for the History of Science*, vol. 31, no. 109 (June 1998), 185. The emphasis on aesthetics in relation to mathematics was not only a Western conceit. Japanese architect Ikebe Kiyoshi worked from the 1940s to the 1970s employing his theory of the module. Kiyoshi described the resulting buildings as living evidence that "Beauty is Mathematics." See Izumi Kuroishi, "Mathematics for/from Society: The Role of the Module in Modernizing Japanese Architectural Production," *Nexus Network Journal*, vol. 11, no. 2 (July 2009), 201–16.

6 Le Corbusier, "The Decorative Art of Today," in Isabelle Frank, ed., *The Theory of Decorative Art: An Anthology of European and American Writings 1750–1940*, 214.

7 Ibid., 213.

8 Twentieth-century craft studios, like those of today, were classified by size. In order to allow a craftsperson to retain control over all aspects of design and production, studios are assumed to be the domain of one to three craftspeople (usually a single maker or a partnership). Once an increased number of apprentices or employees is achieved, fundamental shifts occur in the

way craft objects are produced, creating another classification of craft production studio. For a breakdown of the sizes of craft studios in relation to output see Bert Pereboom, "Profile and Development Strategy for Craft in Canada" (2003) and "Study of the Crafts Sector in Canada" (2001) available at http://www.canadian-craftsfederation.ca/html/advocate_ccf.html (accessed 3 October 2009).

9 Leopold Kohr, *The Breakdown of Nations*, ix.

10 Leopold Kohr, *The Overdeveloped Nations: The Diseconomies of Scale*, 29.

11 Howard Risatti, *A Theory of Craft: Function and Aesthetic Expression*, 29–40.

12 Ibid., 33.

13 Ibid.

14 Ibid., 34.

15 John Ruskin, "Modern Manufacture and Design: Lecture III" (1859), in Isabelle Frank, ed., *The Theory of Decorative Art: An Anthology of European and American Writings 1750–1940*, 48.

16 Risatti, *A Theory of Craft*, 35.

17 Ibid.

18 Martin Heidegger, "Building, Dwelling, Thinking," in Neil Leach, ed., *Rethinking Architecture: A Reader in Cultural Theory*, 100.

19 Ibid., 102.

20 Many excellent materialist feminist and design theories have been written concerning the domestic role of craft following the industrial revolution. Among them are Judy Attfield and Pat Kirkham, eds., *A View from the Interior: Feminism, Women and Design* (London: Women's Press, 1989); Rozsika Parker, *The Subversive Stitch* (London: Women's Press, 1984); Rozsika Parker and Griselda Pollock, *Old Mistresses: Women, Art and Ideology* (New York: Pantheon, 1982); Christopher Reed,

ed., *Not at Home: The Suppression of Domesticity in Modern Art and Architecture* (London: Thames and Hudson, 1996); and Adrian Forty, *Objects of Desire: Design and Society since 1750* (New York: Thames and Hudson, 1992).

21 Information taken from the bronze plaque located at Barbara Paterson's sculpture "Famous Five" in Olympic Square, Calgary, Alberta, 18 July 2009.

22 F5F – Famous Five Foundation website, http://www.famous5.ca/frames_education_monuments.htm (accessed 10 August 2009). The famous five were Nellie McClung, Louise McKinney, Henrietta Muir Edwards, Irene Parlby, and Emily Murphy. The sculpture was unveiled in Calgary on October 18, 1999, exactly seventy years after the "Persons' Case," and in 2000 one was unveiled in Ottawa on Parliament Hill.

23 Danto, "Visionary Ceramics," 23.

24 Ibid., 38.

25 Huguette Bouchard-Bonet, *Jordi Bonet*, 12.

26 Ibid.

27 Ibid., 6.

28 Ibid., 13.

29 Ibid.

30 Ibid., 14.

31 Ibid.

32 Ibid.

33 Guy Robert, *Jordi Bonet*, 11.

34 Robert Fulford, "Some Hard Truths about Public Art," *Toronto Daily Star* (7 February 1967), 5.

35 Ibid.

36 Ibid.

37 Janet Wright, *Crown Assets: The Architecture of the Department of Public Works, 1867–1967*, 263.

38 Ibid., 2.

39 Anita Aarons, "Commissioning Public Art – Who? How?" in *Architecture Canada*,

ser. 517, vol. 45, no. 10 (October 1968), 31.

40 Ibid., 31.

41 Ibid.

42 Lionel Thomas, letter to Mr A.E. Webb, 16 August 1965. Royal BC Museum British Columbia Archives, GR 999, DPW, box 1, file 5, Advisory Committee on Applied Arts, BC Museum and Archives Minutes and Memos, 1965.

43 A.E. Webb, letter to Lionel Thomas, 8 July 1965. Royal BC Museum British Columbia Archives, GR 999, DPW, box 1, file 5, Advisory Committee on Applied Arts, BC Museum and Archives Minutes and Memos, 1965.

44 Lionel Thomas, letter to F. Peter, 22 December 1965. Royal BC Museum British Columbia Archives, GR 999, DPW, box 1, file 5, Advisory Committee on Applied Arts, BC Museum and Archives Minutes and Memos, 1965.

45 A.E. Webb, letter to Mr P.P. Ochs, 4 June 1968. Royal BC Museum British Columbia Archives, GR999, DPW, box 1, file 5, Advisory Committee on Applied Arts, BC Museum and Archives Minutes and Memos, 1965.

46 Ibid.

47 Ibid.

48 "Museum Sculptor on Strike," *The Daily Colonist* (28 May 1968). Royal BC Museum British Columbia Archives, GR 999, DPW, box 1, file 9, Advisory Committee on Applied Arts, BC Museum and Archives Misc. Correspondence and Memos re: Nootka Whalers Sculpture, 1967–1969.

49 "Art in Public Buildings," *Craftsman/ L'Artisan*, vol. 5, no. 2 (1972), 20.

50 Ibid.

51 Ibid.

52 Elizabeth Kimball, "The Company of Young Craftsmen," *SW Magazine* (1 July

1969). Archives of Ontario, MV 5771 (F1157) box 26, Binder: Ontario Craftsmen and Craft Development September 1965 to November 1968.

53 "Terms of Reference for an Advisory Committee on Fine Art Works for New Building Projects by the Department of Public Works," 10 April 1968, 3. National Archives of Canada, Government Organizations: Public Works, 1967–1973, MG 28, I222, vol. 16.

54 "The Standard Form of Agreement Between the Department of Public Works and Artists," National Archives of Canada, Government Organizations: Public Works, 1967–1973, MG 28, I222, vol. 16. Article 1, "The Artist's Services," clearly states: "The Artist will supply all materials and perform all services necessary to produce the Artwork and its installation." Furthermore: "Any deterioration or failure of the Artwork within a period of ten years after final acceptance will be repaired, replaced or otherwise made good by the Artist immediately on notification of and to the complete satisfaction of the Department."

55 Jack Sures, telephone interview, 29 July 2004.

56 Ibid.

57 Ibid.

58 Ibid.

59 "Sturdy Stone Centre," booklet, Government Services Saskatchewan, n.d. University of Regina Archives, Jack Sures fonds, 99-38, box 6, file 48.

60 Jack Sures, personal interview, 3 November 2010, Regina, Saskatchewan.

61 Ibid.

62 Nobuo Kubota, letter to Mrs Donaghue, DPW, 11 June 1978. LAC, DPW, MG 28, I222, file 4440-C105/5.

63 "Focus on Carole Sabiston," *Craftsman/ L'Artisan*, vol. 6, no. 2 (1973), 2.

64 Carole Sabiston, personal interview, 7 June 2004, Victoria, British Columbia.

65 Ibid.

66 Ibid.

67 Ibid.

68 Ibid.

69 Annie Gérin, "Introduction," Annie Gérin and James McLean, eds., *Public Art in Canada: Critical Perspectives*, 8.

70 James Adams, "Haydn Llewellyn Davies," *Globe and Mail*, 4 April 2008: R5.

71 Ibid.

72 Ibid.

73 Ibid.

74 Ibid.

75 See http://haydndaviessculptor.ca/destruction.html (accessed 30 October 2009).

76 James Adams, "Sculptor's Family Decries Dismantling of Wood Piece," *Globe and Mail*, found on Homage2Homage website, http://haydndaviessculptor.ca/destruction.html (accessed 30 October 2009).

77 Guiliana Bruno, *Public Intimacy: Architecture and the Visual Arts*, 3.

78 Sabiston, personal interview, 7 June 2004.

79 Mariette Rousseau-Vermette, personal interview, Ste Adèle, Quebec, 29 April 2005.

80 Personal interview with anonymous BC Liquor Store employee, Creston, British Columbia, 2 August 2009.

81 Public observation at the Macdonald Block, Bay and Wellesley streets, 14 May 2005, Toronto, Ontario.

82 Public observation at the Credit Union main building, 10 June 2004, Vancouver, British Columbia.

83 Jane Lind, *Gathie Falk* (Vancouver and Toronto: Douglas & McIntyre, 1989), 12.

84 Art Perry, "Gathie Falk and Richard Prince," *Vanguard*, vol. 8, no. 9 (November 1979). The Centre for Contemporary Canadian Craft, The Canadian Art Database: Canadian Writers' Files:

http://ccca.finearts.yorku.ca/c/writing/p/per ry/perr003t.html (accessed 2 November 2009).

85 Fulford, "Some Hard Truths," 8.

86 Glenn Adamson, *Thinking through Craft*, 93.

87 Ibid., 100.

88 Ibid.

89 Ibid., 101.

90 Ibid., 66.

91 See Sandra Alfoldy, "Moncrieff Williamson, Maritime Regionalism, and the Dream of a National Craft Museum," *Journal of Canadian Art History*, vol. 28 (2007), 39–52.

92 "Expo a Storehouse of World's Treasure," *Montreal Star*, 28 April 1967. Prince Edward Island Archives, Moncreiff Williamson Fonds, RG 44, S.2, box 25, Canadian Guild of Crafts file.

93 Dorothy Todd Henaut, "1967–The Moment of Truth for Canadian Crafts," *artscanada*, vol. 24, no. 104 (January 1967), 20–2.

94 Lee Plested, *From Our Land: The Expo '67 Canadian Craft Collection*, 8.

95 Ibid., 14.

96 Harold Kalman, *A Concise History of Canadian Architecture*, 585.

97 Anita Aarons, "The Artists and Expo," *Architecture Canada*, ser. 501, vol. 44, no. 6 (June 1967), 17.

98 Ibid., 19.

99 Rousseau-Vermette, personal interview, Ste Adèle, Quebec, 29 April 2005.

100 Kalman, *A Concise History*, 582.

101 See Rose-Marie Arbour, "Arts visuels et espace public: l'apport de deux femmes artistes dans les années 60 au Québec, Micheline Beauchemin et Marcelle Ferron," (1989), http://classiques.uqac.ca/con tem porains/arbour_rose_marie/arts_visuels_et_ espace_public/arts_visuels_et_espace_ public.pdf (accessed 12 November 2009).

102 Helen Duffy, "Fibre Art in Canada," in *Canada Mikrokosma: An Exhibition of Contemporary Canadian Tapestries*, 1982, 13.

103 Ibid.

104 Ibid.

105 Rousseau-Vermette, personal interview, Ste-Adèle, Quebec, 29 April 2005.

106 Carole Collet, "The Next Textile Revolution," in Sarah Bonnemaison and Christine Macy, eds., *Responsive Textile Environments*, 15.

107 Sarah Bonnemaison and Christine Macy, "Responsive Textile Environments," in Bonnemaison and Macy, eds., *Responsive Textile Environments*, 7.

108 Robin Muller, personal interview, 12 June 2009.

109 "Concert Hall by Arthur Erickson," *Concrete Quarterly*, vol. 137 (April–June 1983), 16–19.

110 Rousseau-Vermette, personal interview, Ste Adèle, Quebec, 29 April 2005. It is unfortunate that Rousseau-Vermette's careful collaboration with the architectural team did not prevent the destruction of her ceiling in 2005.

111 Ibid.

112 "Woven in Worb: Gottfried Semper's Odd Theories about Textiles and Building are Imaginatively Reinterpreted in Stainless Steel," *Architectural Review* (August 2004): http://findarticles.com/p/articles/mi_ m3575/is_1290_216/ai_n6186274/?tag=co ntent;col1 (accessed 15 November 2009).

113 Adamson, *Thinking through Craft*, 65–6.

CHAPTER FOUR

1 Jennifer Bloomer, quoted in Patricia Morton, "The Social and the Poetic: Feminist Practices in Architecture, 1970–2000," in Amelia Jones, ed., *The Feminism and Visual Culture Reader*, 279.

2 See W. Rogatnick, Ian M. Thom, and Adele Weder, *B.C. Binning*, and the University of British Columbia Archives, Belkin Art Gallery fonds, box 11, ser. 13.6–6.2, Acquisitions and Correspondence, 1935–1977.

3 Harold Kalman, *A Concise History of Canadian Architecture*, 535.

4 Ibid., 542.

5 Ibid., 570–1.

6 Karin Cope, "Becoming Animal, Becoming Others in Art and Literature," public lecture, NSCAD University, 28 January 2010.

7 E.H. Gombrich, *The Sense of Order: A Study in the Psychology of Decorative Art*, 3.

8 Ibid., 5.

9 Janet Wright, *Crown Assets: The Architecture of the Department of Public* Works, 5.

10 Ibid., 17.

11 Glenn Adamson, *Thinking through Craft*, 139.

12 James Trilling, *The Language of Ornament*, 10.

13 This chapter also conflates these terms, although art historians like Debra Schafter and Jean-Claude Bonne have distinguished the subtle differences between them.

14 Isabelle Frank, "Gombrich, Perception and the Ordering of Ornament," paper delivered at the College Art Association conference, 11 February 2010.

15 Gombrich, *The Sense of Order*, 17.

16 Brent C. Brolin, *Architectural Ornament: Banishment and Return*, 189.

17 Anita Aarons, "The Dual Nature of Commisioned Work," ser. 473, *Journal RAIC*, vol. 42, no. 2 (February 1965), 13. For more on the work of Anita Aarons see Sandra Alfoldy, "The Metaphysics of Craft: Anita Aarons' 'Craft for Architecture,'" in Sandra Alfoldy and Janice Helland, eds., *Craft, Space and Interior Design 1855–*

2005 (Aldershot: Ashgate Publishing Limited, 2008), 189–205.

18 See *Journal RAIC*, ser. 475 no. 4, April 1965.

19 Anita Aarons, "Signs, Signals, Symbols and Traditions," *Journal RAIC*, ser. 475, vol. 42, no. 4 (April 1965), 38.

20 Ibid., 38.

21 Ibid., 39.

22 Anita Aarons, "Post War Trip – Old and New World," *Journal RAIC*, ser. 479, vol. 42, no. 10 (October 1965), 24.

23 Anita Aarons, "Across Canada Round Up," *Architecture Canada*, ser. 506, vol. 44, no. 11 (November 1967), 21.

24 Anita Aarons, "Canadian Handicrafts and the Architect," *Journal RAIC*, ser. 476, vol. 42, no. 5 (May 1965), 19.

25 Owen Jones, *The Grammar of Ornament*, 31.

26 John Ruskin, "Modern Manufacture and Design: Lecture III" (1859), in Isabelle Frank, ed., *The Theory of Decorative Art: An Anthology of European and American Writings 1750–1940*, 51.

27 John Ruskin, *On Art and Life*, 5.

28 Ibid., 2.

29 Adolf Loos, "Ornament and Crime" (1908), in Isabelle Frank, ed., *The Theory of Decorative Art: An Anthology of European and American Writings 1750–1940*, 288.

30 Ibid., 290.

31 Ibid., 293.

32 Ibid.

33 Ibid., 291.

34 The South Kensington Museum in London (as of 1899 the V&A Museum) was established in 1857 as a teaching institution to inform designers, architects, craftspeople, and the general public of the principles of good design and good ornament.

35 Donald Buchanan, "Design in Industry – A

Misnomer," *Canadian Art* (summer 1945), quoted in Joy Parr, *Domestic Goods: The Material, The Moral and the Economic in the Postwar Years*, 48.

36 Humphrey Carver, "Home-Made Thoughts on Handicrafts," *Canadian Forum*, March 1940, 386–7 (LAC, RG 20-601) quoted in Parr, *Domestic Goods*, 44.

37 Parr, *Domestic Goods*, 43.

38 Ellen Easton McLeod, *In Good Hands: The Women of the Canadian Handicrafts Guild*, 272.

39 Parr, *Domestic Goods*, 43.

40 Alena M. Buis, "The Practical Side of Decorating: Paul-Émile Borduas at the École du meuble," in Metro Borduas, www.metroborduas.concordia.ca/html/papersok/alena.htm (accessed 17 February 2010).

41 Ibid.

42 Gloria Lesser, *École du meuble 1930–1950: Interior Design and Decorative Art*, 10.

43 Buis, "The Practical Side of Decorating."

44 Ibid.

45 See Michel van Schendel, "Refus Global, or the Formula and History," *Yale French Studies*, no. 65 (1983), 53–73 and François-Marc Gagnon, *Refus Global*.

46 Buis, "The Practical Side of Decorating." The other artists who espoused this belief were Stanley Cosgrove, Robert La Palme, and Alfred Pellan.

47 Elissa Auther, "The Decorative, Abstraction, and the Hierarchy of Art and Craft in the Art Criticism of Clement Greenberg," *Oxford Art Journal*, vol. 27, no. 3 (2004), 340.

48 Ibid., 340.

49 Ibid., 344.

50 William Morris, "The Arts and Crafts of To-day"(1889), in Isabelle Frank, ed. *The Theory of Decorative Art*, 63–4.

51 Auther, "The Decorative, Abstraction and the Hierarchy of Art and Craft," 347.

52 Kalman, *A Concise History*, 612.

53 Ibid., 355.

54 Adamson, *Thinking through Craft*, 139.

55 See Harold Kalman, *A History of Canadian Architecture* and Janet Wright, *Crown Assets: The Architecture of the Department of Public Works, 1867–1997*.

56 See Sandra Alfoldy, *R. Eleanor Milne: The Making of an Artist in Canada*, Canada's Digital Collections, 1999 http://epe.lac-bac.gc.ca/100/205/301/ic/cdc/milne/prevs-culpt.html and Frederick J. Way, "She Carves our History," *Star Weekly Toronto* (29 May 1965), 33. When Eleanor Milne retired as Dominion Sculptor in 1993, Maurice Joanisse, who began as Milne's assistant in 1971, took over the position as Public Works and Government Services Canada Federal Sculptor.

57 Eleanor Milne, personal interview, Ottawa, Ontario, 29 October 1998.

58 Christine Boyanoski, *Loring and Wyle, Sculptors' Legacy*.

59 Eleanor Milne, personal interview, Ottawa, 1 October 1998.

60 Ibid.

61 Eleanor Milne, personal interview, Ottawa, 19 November 1998.

62 Eleanor Milne, personal interview, Ottawa, 1 October 1998, quoted in Alfoldy, "R. Eleanor Milne: The Making of an Artist in Canada."

63 Gombrich, *The Sense of Order*, 18.

64 Trilling, *The Language of Ornament*, 6.

65 Ibid., 10.

66 Ibid.

67 Loos, "Ornament and Crime," 291.

68 Walter Gropius, "Manifesto of the Staatliche Bauhaus in Weimar," (1919) in Isabelle Frank, ed., *The Theory of Decorative Art*. 83.

69 Alexander Dorner, "The Background of the Bauhaus," in Herbert Bayer, Walter Gropius, and Ise Gropius, eds., *Bauhaus 1919–28*, 10.

70 Sigrid Wortmann Weltge, *Women's Work: Textile Art from the Bauhaus*, 10.

71 Alfred H. Barr, "Preface," in Herbert Bayer, Walter Gropius, and Ise Gropius, eds., *Bauhaus 1919–1928*, 6.

72 Kalman, *A Concise History*, 536.

73 Percy Nobbs, quoted in Kalman, *A Concise History*, 536.

74 Ibid., 570.

75 Ian Johnston, personal interview, 9 July 2004, Nelson, British Columbia.

76 Ibid.

77 Ian Johnston, "Leftover and Under," http://www.ianjohnstonstudio.com/work/leftover-and-under/text/ (accessed 5 March 2010).

78 Ibid.

79 Phyllis Lambert, *Mies in America*, 419.

80 According to *fibre quarterly* the following textile artists have work on display in the Toronto-Dominion Centre buildings: Tamara Jaworska "Quartet Modern" (First Canadian Place, King St West); Sofia Dlugopolska, "Infinity"; Jacqueline Liscott, "Untitled"; Maria Ciechornska, "Untitled"; Paulette-Marie Sauvé, "Iridescent Marsh/Marais Irise (Canadian Pacific Tower); Kaija Sanelma Harris, "Sun Ascending"; and Joanna Staniskis "Untitled."

81 "Who Made That: A Question about Public (Textile) Art in Canada?" *fibre quarterly*, vol. 3, no. 1 (winter 2007), http://www.velvethighway.com/winter07/whoMADEit.html

82 John Vollmer, "Tamara Jaworska Tapestries – Tapisseries," as quoted on http://www.velvethighway.com/winter07/whoMADEit.html

83 Kalman, *A Concise History*, 557.

84 Ruth Chambers, "Artist Statement: Ruth Chambers 2010."

85 Amy Gogarty, "'A Bell Rings Out' – Recollection, Architecture, and Ceramics at the End of Modernity," in *Mobile Structures: Dialogues Between Ceramics and Architecture in Canadian Art* (Regina: MacKenzie Art Gallery, 2007), 46.

86 Ibid.

87 Chambers, "Artist Statement."

88 Kenneth Frampton, *Patkau Architects*, 9.

89 Ibid., 10.

90 Chambers, "Artist Statement."

91 Ruth Chambers, personal interview, 5 November 2010, Regina, Saskatchewan.

92 Information provided during a public tour of Frank Lloyd Wright's Oak Park house and studio, Oak Park, Illinois, February 2010.

93 Robert Venturi, *Complexity and Contradiction in Architecture*, 17.

94 Ibid., 17.

95 Kalman, *A Concise History*, 599.

96 John C. Parkin, quoted in Kalman, *A Concise History*, 599.

97 Rachel Gotlieb, "Suzanne Swannie and Danish Modernism in Canada," in *Danish Modern: Suzanne Swannie Textil*, 4.

98 Suzanne Swannie, personal interview, 29 August 2004, Halifax, Nova Scotia.

99 Gotlieb, "Suzanne Swannie," 5.

CHAPTER FIVE

1 Benedict Anderson, *Imagined Communities*, 6.

2 Deborah Tiwari, "Canada Remembers Stone Carving Nears Completion," *Ensemble* (August/September 1995), 15.

3 Harold Kalman, *A Concise History of Canadian Architecture*, vii.

4 Annie Gérin, "Introduction" to Annie Gérin and James S. McLean, eds., *Public Art in Canada: Critical Perspectives*, 7.

5 Timothy J. Stanley, "Creating the 'Space' for Civic Dialogue," *Phi Delta Kappan*, vol. 85, no. 1 (spring 2003), 38.

6 John Ruskin, *The History of Venice: Written for the Help of the Few Travellers who Still Care for her Monuments*, v.

7 Kalman, *A Concise History*, 535.

8 Porter House and Bobak House are just two examples of the influence of 1940s and 1950s Vancouver's houses on the development of West Coast Regionalism. Irena Anne Zenewyck identifies three characteristics for these contemporary homes that are synonymous with West Coast Regionalism: first, "the wide overhang extending from a flat roof as the most prominent feature," second, "the extensive use of glass," and third, "the functional and aesthetic employment of local building materials, wood in particular." Allan Collier argues that the popularization of these West Coast design initiatives was a result of the 1949 exhibition "Design in Living" (Vancouver Art Gallery) and the 1952 exhibition "Design for Living" (Ottawa), the latter of which was sponsored in part by the B.C. lumber industry. See Irene Anne Zenewych, *Regionalism in the Face of Universality: West Coast Modernism as Architectural Landscape*, (MA thesis, Department of Geography, Simon Fraser University, 1989), 48–9 and Allan Collier, "Design in Western Canada," in Robert Stacey, ed., *Achieving the Modern: Canadian Abstract Painting and Design in the 1950s* (Winnipeg: Winnipeg Art Gallery, 1993), 109.

9 John Woodworth, "The Graeme Kings Built a Modern Room Behind a Traditional Georgian," *Western Homes and Living* (August/September 1950), 22–3; quoted in Sherry McKay, "The Object of Living: Western Homes and Living," in Alan C. Elder and Ian M. Thom, *A Modern Life: Art and Design in British Columbia 1945–1960* (Vancouver: Vancouver Art Gallery and Arsenal Pulp Press, 2004), 154.

10 See Rachelle Chinnery, "Significant Material: Ceramics of British Columbia 1945–1960," in Alan C. Elder and Ian M. Thom, *A Modern Life: Art and Design in British Columbia 1945–1960)*, 81–90.

11 Suilio Venchiarutti, architect, quoted in Joy Parr, *Domestic Goods: The Material, the Moral and the Economic in the Postwar Years*, 186.

12 Massey College History, http://www.utoronto.ca/Massey/history/html (accessed 19 June 2009).

13 Personal interview and tour of Massey College by the visitor, the Hon. H.N.R. Jackman, 6 June 2006.

14 Sandra Alfoldy and Rachel Gotlieb, *On the Table: 100 Years of Functional Ceramics in Canada*, 57.

15 Gail Crawford, *Studio Ceramics in Canada*, 232.

16 Kalman, *A Concise History*, 571.

17 Ibid.

18 Anita Aarons, "The Dual Nature of Commissioned Work," *Journal RAIC*, ser. 473, vol. 42, no. 2 (February 1965), 13.

19 In 2004 Eli Bornstein's striking wall mural for the Winnipeg airport was rendered anonymous by the placement of a pop-dispensing machine over the title/artist plaque – just one of many instances of artworks being used as walls for the placement of commercial vending machines, this researcher discovered.

20 Eli Bornstein, "Foreword," *The Structurist*, no. 2 (1961–62), 2.

21 "Public Relations Objectives of RAIC," 30 August 1959. LAC, RAIC, MG 28 1239, vol. 18.

22 "The Architect Looks at Public Relations:

A Guide for Provincial and Chapter Relations Committee Chairmen Prepared by the Royal Architectural Institute of Canada," April 1960. LAC, RAIC, MG 28 1239, vol. 18.

23 "Public Relations Objectives of RAIC," 30 August 1959. LAC, RAIC, MG 28 1239, vol. 18.

24 "The Royal Architectural Institute of Canada – the RAIC Today," rough draft of paper. LAC, RAIC, MG 28 1239, vol. 18.

25 Robert A. Diotte, Senior Departmental Assistant to MG, letter to Mr Lloyd Crouse, MP, 18 August 1980. LAC, Public Works Canada, Fine Art, RG 11, 4440-06813, vol. 4, box 83.

26 Dominik Polson, "Fine Art Proposal, Transport Canada Training Institute, Cornwall, Ontario, 1977," 2. LAC, Public Works Canada, Fine Art, RG 11, 4440-C105/5, box 78.

27 Janet Wright, *Crown Assets: The Architecture of the Department of Public Works 1867–1967*, 263.

28 Ibid., 263.

29 The Public Works Canada files at Library and Archives Canada are restricted documents, so I am unable to specify any monetary amounts spent on individual commissions nor am I able to include any inflammatory statements by individual architects or artists involved in the program. Within the archival holdings are several letters and memos from and to architects indicating their displeasure with the selection process for artists, and their views that their region (and sometimes Canada as a whole) was lacking in professional artists to fulfil commissions for buildings. These documents can be found many places, including the following files: LAC, Public Works Canada, Fine Art, RG 11, 4440-

A3711-1, Fine Art, Alma, Quebec; 4440-A55/1 Fine Art, Antigonish, Nova Scotia; 4440-D22/1-1 Don Mills Ontario; 4440-H2/5-1 Hamilton, Ontario; 4440-G9/1 Giquet, Newfoundland.

30 Paul Roberton, "Federal Buildings Galleries, of a Sort," *Edmonton Journal*, 27 May 1974. LAC, Public Works Canada, Fine Art, RG 11, 4440-H70/1 DPW Press Clipping.

31 Arthur Laing, minister of Public Works, letter to Allan MacEachen, president of the Privy Council, Ottawa 9 April 1971. LAC, Public Works Canada, Fine Art, RG 11, 4440-A55/1 Fine Art, Antigonish, Nova Scotia Government of Canada Building.

32 The other members of the original committee were: Mira Godard, director of the Agnes Lefort Gallery, Montreal; Nancy Robertson, director of the Norman Mackenzie Art Gallery, Regina; Richard Simmins, Vancouver art consultant, former director of Exhibition Extension Service for the National Gallery of Canada; and Stuart Allen Smith, director of the Beaverbrook Art Gallery, Fredericton, New Brunswick. See Anita Aarons, "Commissioning Public Art – Who? How?" *Architecture Canada*, ser. 517, vol. 45, no. 10 (October 1968), 31.

33 Ibid., 31.

34 Anita Aarons, "Art and Architecture," *Journal RAIC*, ser. 472, vol. 42, no. 1 (January 1965), 55.

35 See the problems surrounding the commissioning of a textile wall hanging for the Halifax RCMP headquarters. LAC, Public Works Canada, Fine Art, RG 11, 4440-H4/16-2, Halifax, Nova Scotia, RCMP Headquarters Building.

36 Roberton, "Federal Buildings Galleries."

37 Alan Gregson, letter to Mr J.A.H. Makay,

Minister of Public Works, 13 September 1977. LAC, Public Works Canada, Fine Art, RG 11, 4440-H64/1.

38 Kay Kritzwiser, "Ottawa Showplace for Stunning Art but Many Works Provoke Hostility," *Globe and Mail*, Entertainment and Travel section, (24 November 1973), 15.

39 Ibid.

40 Robin Laurence, Ian M. Thom, et al., *Gathie Falk*, 45.

41 See LAC, Public Works Canada, Fine Art, RG 11, 4440-D22/1-1 and LAC, Public Works Canada, Fine Art, RG 11, 4440-01/43-1, box 83, vol. 4.

42 "Editorial: It Looks Great on the Outside," *The Listowel Banner*, 24 February 1977. LAC, Public Works Canada, Fine Art, RG 11, 4440-L7/1-1.

43 Letter Re: Federal Building at Antigonish, Nova Scotia, 4 March 1971. LAC, Public Works Canada, Fine Art, RG 11, 4440-A55/1.

44 James Nelson, "Ottawa is Seething," *The Whig Standard*, 29 September 1973.

45 Wayne Howell, "If it's Inoffensive, it's Got to be Great Canadian Art," *Toronto Star*, 5 October 1973.

46 "Background on Haida," LAC, Public Works Canada, Fine Art, RG 11, 4440-01/43-14, box 83, file no. 602-717-2.

47 Ferem Real Estate, Rocky Mountain House, Alberta, letter to Public Works Minister, name illegible, no date provided. LAC, Public Works Canada, Fine Art, RG 11, 4440-01/43-14, box 83, file no. 602-717-2.

48 Kay Kritzwiser, "Ottawa Showplace for Stunning Art, 15.

49 Robert Murray, letter to Mr K.C. Stanley, director, Resources, Design, Construction, Department of Public Works, 13 March 1974. LAC, Public Works Canada, Fine Art, RG 11, 4440-01/43-1, Lester B. Pearson Building, vol. 4.

50 Robert Epp, personal interview, Winnipeg, Manitoba, 14 May 2004.

51 Ibid.

52 RPS Cultural Property Inventory, "No. 1 Northern," 1998. File viewed in Public Works Canada offices, Halifax, Nova Scotia, 21 July 2003.

53 Dr N. Stolow, letter to H.G. Cole, 5 October 1973. LAC, Public Works Canada, Fine Art, RG 11, 4440-01/43-1, vol. 3.

54 Gathie Falk, letter to Mr W. Durdin, director of Central Services Division, Department of External Affairs, 28 November 1973. LAC, Public Works Canada, Fine Art, RG 11, 4440-01/43-1, vol. 3.

55 Robert Murray, letter to Mr K.C. Stanley, director, Resources, Design, Construction, Department of Public Works, 13 March 1974. LAC, Public Works Canada, Fine Art, RG 11, 4440-01/43-1, Lester B. Pearson Building, vol. 4.

56 Roberton, "Federal Buildings Galleries."

57 Wright, *Crown Assets*, 263.

58 L.G. Sincennes, department assistant, letter to Mrs Pat Gee, 18 April 1974, LAC, Public Works Canada, Fine Art, RG 11, 4440-S165/1-1.

59 Mrs Virginia Anderson, letter to the Honourable Jean-Eudes Dube [sic] Minister of Public Works, 8 January 1974. LAC, Public Works Canada, Fine Art, RG 11, box 83, 4440-01/43-1.

60 "Dubé Turns Opinion Hunter on Sculpture," *Ottawa Citizen*, 1 March 1974.

61 Memo, 5 May 1976, from Fine Art Liaison Officer Pacific Region to M. Pinney, chief, Fine Art Program. LAC, Public Works Canada, Fine Art, RG 11, 4440-C63/1.

62 Joseph Sleep, letter to Advisory Committee, Clementsport Post Office, n.d. LAC, Public

Works Canada, Fine Art, RG 11, file 4440-C117/1.

63 Letter from Paul Hébert to Public Works Canada Regional Office, Halifax, 13 September 1977. LAC, Public Works Canada, Fine Art, RG 11, file 4440-C117/1.

64 Guy Hérin-Lajoie letter to K.C. Stanley, 23 October 1970. LAC, Public Works Canada, Fine Art, RG 11, 4440-F36/1-1.

65 Benedict Anderson, *Imagined Communities*, 11.

66 Ibid., 12.

67 Robert Ellis, *Official Descriptive and Illustrated Catalogue of the Great Exhibition of the Works of Industry of All Nations*, vol. 2, 958.

68 Ibid., 970.

69 Ibid., 957.

70 Gerald R. McMaster, "Tenuous Lines of Descent: Indian Arts and Crafts of the Reservation Period," *Canadian Journal of Native Studies*, vol. 9, no. 2 (1989), 206.

71 Kalman, *A Concise History*, 630, 628.

72 Ibid., 213. See also Ellen Easton McLeod, *In Good Hands: The Women of the Canadian Handicrafts Guild*.

73 Ruth B. Phillips, *Trading Identities: The Souvenir in Native North American Art from the Northeast, 1700–1900*, 279.

74 Ibid., 279.

75 Ibid., 69.

76 Northrop Frye, "The Narrative Tradition in English Canadian Poetry" (1946), in Branko Gorjup, ed., *Northrop Frye, Mythologizing Canada: Essays on the Canadian Literary Imagination*, 38.

77 Richard Cavell, "Where is Frye? Or, Theorizing Postcolonial Space," *Essays on Canadian Writing*, issue 56 (fall 1995), 110.

78 Northrop Frye, quoted in Cavell, "Where is Frye?" 111.

79 Ibid., 110.

80 Ruth Phillips, "'New and Yet Old': Aboriginality and Appropriation in Canadian Ceramics," in Sandra Alfoldy and Rachel Gotlieb, eds., *On the Table: 100 Years of Functional Ceramics in Canada*, 64.

81 "Indians Spend Expo Cash to Tell of Poor Deal," *Globe and Mail*, 7 April 1967, 3.

82 *The Memorial Album of the First Category Universal and International Exhibition Held in Montreal from 27 April to 29 October 1967*, 118.

83 Dickerson's "Homage to Salish Weavers" measures 3.1 m x 12.2 m.

84 Katharine Dickerson, public lecture, NSCAD University, Halifax, Nova Scotia, 11 March 2005.

85 Katharine Dickerson, personal interview, Halifax, Nova Scotia, 7 March 2005.

86 Ibid.

87 British Columbia is dealing with an enormous number of land claim settlements that raise contentious issues left over from the process of colonization. See Renisa Mawani, "Legalities of Nature: Law, Empire, and Wilderness Landscapes in Canada," *Social Identities*, vol. 13, no. 6 (November 2007), 715–34.

88 Katharine Dickerson, personal interview, Halifax, Nova Scotia, 7 March 2005.

89 Sharon Wall, "Totem Poles, Teepees, and Traditions: 'Playing Indian' at Ontario Summer Camps, 1920–1955," *Canadian Historical Review*, vol. 86, no. 3 (2005), 513.

90 In Germany "going Native" remains big business. In 1994 I had the opportunity to visit an "Indian Village" outside Munich, where German tourists paid large sums of money to dress up as Native dancers, eat bannock, and sleep in teepees.

91 Ibid., 514.

92 Harvey Currell, "Indian Craftsmen are Skilled Carvers," *The Telegram*, 23 November 1966, 34.

93 David R. Newhouse, Cora J. Voyager, and Dan Beavon, *Hidden in Plain Sight: Contributions of Aboriginal Peoples to Canadian Identity and Culture*, 137.

94 Hilary Stewart, *Robert Davidson: Haida Printmaker*, 11.

95 Ibid., 11.

96 Hilary Stewart, *Looking at Totem Poles*, 150.

97 Aileen Osborn Webb, letter to Prime Minister Pierre Elliott Trudeau, 2 March 1970. LAC, Canadian Crafts Council/World Crafts Council, MG 28 1274, vol. 34.

98 *Canadian Craft Council 1974 Report*, 14–15. LAC, Canadian Crafts Council/ World Crafts Council, MG 28 1274, vol. 34.

99 Kalman, *A Concise History*, 595.

100 Judith Ostrowitz, *Privileging the Past: Reconstructing History in Northwest Coast Art* (Vancouver: UBC Press, 1999), 148.

101 Ibid., 148.

102 "Robert Davidson," http://www.nativeonline.com/davidson.htm (accessed 20 June 2009).

103 Kenneth Frampton, *Patkau Architects*, 7.

104 Bernard Flaman, "Public Art: The Airports," in Annie Gérin and James S. McLean, eds., *Public Art in Canada: Critical Perspectives*, 90–1.

105 Ibid., 91.

106 Rita Beiks, ed., *Land, Sea, Sky: Art at YVR*, i–ii.

107 Ibid., 8.

108 During my time touring and researching the Vancouver International Airport, I spoke with tourists at the "Spirit of Haida Gwaii" seating area, who informed me that they were purchasing twenty-dollar bills to bring home as their souvenirs.

109 Cavell, "Where is Frye?" 110.

110 Bill Reid, "The Jade Canoe: A Poem," in Rita Beiks, ed., *Land, Sea, Sky: Art at YVR*, 11.

111 Joan M. Vastokas, "Architecture as Cultural Expression," *artscanada*, issue 208/209 (October/November 1976), 1.

112 It was not until the celebration of the fiftieth anniversary of the Museum of Anthropology in 1999 that subtle critiques about Erickson's non-Native status began to surface. See Saloni Mathur, "Redefining the Ethnographic Object: An Anthropology Museum Turns Fifty," *American Anthropologist*, vol. 102, no. 3 (September 2000), 593–7.

113 Vastokas, "Architecture as Cultural Expression," 3.

114 Ibid., 3.

115 Reid's "Raven Discovering Mankind in a Clamshell" is over 2 metres high.

116 Vastokas, "Architecture as Cultural Expression" 14.

117 Mathur, "Redefining the Ethnographic Object," 594.

118 "Written in Stone: An Architectural Tour of the Canadian Museum of Civilization: Douglas Cardinal," http://www.civilization.ca/cmc/about-the-museum/building-and-galleries/written-in-stone/full-tour/douglas-cardinal (accessed 1 July 2009).

119 Ibid.

120 Douglas Cardinal, quoted in Kalman, *A Concise History*, 578.

121 Ibid., 580.

CONCLUSION

1 Glenn Adamson, "Affective Objects: The Reinvention of Craft," lecture, NSCAD University, 4 December 2010.

2 Greg Payce, public lecture, NSCAD University, 2 March 2004.

3 Adrienne L. Burk, "Beneath and Before: Continuums of Publicness in Public Art," *Social and Cultural Geography*, vol. 7, no. 6 (December 2006), 950.

4 Ibid.

5 Llewellyn Negrin, "Ornament and the Feminine," *Feminist Theory*, vol. 7, no. 2 (2006), 219.

6 Matt Tyrnauer, "Architecture in the Age of Gehry," *Vanity Fair*, no. 600 (August 2010), 161.

7 Ibid., 165.

8 Philip Beesley, "Hiving Mesh," in *Hiving Mesh*, 2.

9 Ibid.

10 Philip Beesley et al. eds., *Responsive Architectures: Subtle Technologies*, 3.

11 Ibid., 6.

12 Philip Beesley and Sean Hanna, "Lighter: A Transformed Architecture," in Matilda McQuaid, ed., *Extreme Textiles: Designing for High Performance*, 103.

13 Ibid., 107.

14 Ibid., 109.

15 Matt Tyrnauer, "Architecture in the Age of Gehry," *Vanity Fair*, no. 600 (August 2010), 167.

16 According to the Canadian Crafts Federation's "Profile and Development Strategy for Craft in Canada" (2003), the average annual income for a Canadian craftsperson was $17,500. The Canadian Council on Social Development reports that the 2001 poverty line for urban Canadians was $18,841. See Peartree Solutions for Canadian Crafts Federation, "Profile and Development Strategy for Craft in Canada," 2003, 21, and the Canadian Council on Social Development, http://www.ccsd.ca/factsheets/fs_licol.htm (accessed 2 April 2010).

17 Benoît Clairoux (translated by Matthew McLauchlin), "Works of Art in the Montreal Metro," http://www.metrodemontreal.com/history/art/index.html

18 Eli McIlveen, "Art on the TTC," Transit Toronto, http://transit.toronto.on.ca/spare/0008.shtml

19 See "Spacing – Toronto Subway Buttons," at http://spacing.ca/buttons.htm and David Topping, "69 Days on the TTC," Torontoist, http://torontoist.com/2006/09/69.php

20 "Who Made That: A Question about Public (Textile) Art in Canada," *Fibre Quarterly*, vol. 3, no. 1 (Winter 2007). http://www.velvethighway.com/winter07/whoMADEit.html

21 See City of Vancouver "Public Art," http://vancouver.ca/commsvcs/cultural/publicart/index.htm

22 88 Blocks – Art on Main, http://buzzer.translink.ca/index.php/2009/01/main-street-public-art-program-has-its-official-launch/

23 See Olga Zorzi Pugliese, "Beautifying the City: 1960s Artistic Mosaics by Italian Canadians in Toronto," *Quaderni d'Italianistica*, vol. 27, no. 1 (2007), 93–114.

BIBLIOGRAPHY

Aarons, Anita. *"Across Canada Round Up."* *Architecture Canada*, ser. 506, vol. 44, no. 11 (November 1967).
– "Art and Architecture." *Journal RAIC*, ser. 472, vol. 42, no. 1 (January, 1965).
– "Art and the 58th RAIC Assembly." *Journal RAIC*, ser. 478, vol. 42, no. 7 (July 1965).
– "Canadian Handcrafts and the Architect." *Journal RAIC*, ser. 476, vol. 42, no. 5 (May 1965).
– "Commissioning Public Art – Who? How?" *Architecture Canada*, ser. 517, vol. 45, no. 10 (October 1968).
– "Montreal … Achievement and Faith." *Journal RAIC*, ser. 480, vol. 42, no. 9 (September 1965).
– "Post War Trip – Old and New World." *Journal RAIC*, ser. 479, vol. 42, no. 10 (October 1965).
– "Signs, Signals, Symbols and Tradition." *Journal RAIC*, ser. 475, vol. 42, no. 4 (April 1965), 40.
– "The Artists and Expo." *Architecture Canada*, ser. 501, vol. 44, no. 6 (June 1967).
– "The Dual Nature of Commissioned Work." *Journal RAIC*, ser. 473, vol. 42, no. 2 (February 1965).

– "The Integrators," *Architecture Canada*, ser. 495, vol. 43, no. 12 (December 1966).
– "Time Factors in Commissioned Work." *Journal RAIC*, ser. 474, vol. 42, no. 3 (March 1965), 24.
Adams, James. "Haydn Llewellyn Davies." *Globe and Mail*, 4 April 2008.
– "Sculptor's Family Decries Dismantling of Wood Piece." *Globe and Mail*, found on Homage2Homage website, http://haydn-daviessculptor.ca/destruction.html (accessed 30 October 2009).
Adamson, Glenn. *Thinking through Craft.* Oxford and New York: Berg, 2007.
– "Affective Objects: Design and the Re-Invention of Craft." Public Lecture, NSCAD University, Halifax, Nova Scotia (3 December 2010).
– "Adieu: Not Au Revoir." *Noosa News*, 4 January 2000, 2.
Adorno, Theodor W. "Functionalism Today." In Neil Leach, ed. *Rethinking Architecture: A Reader in Cultural Theory.* London and New York: Routledge, 1997.
Albers, Anni. "The Weaving Workshop." Herbert Bayer, Walter Gropius, et al., eds. *Bauhaus 1919–1928.* New York: Museum of Modern Art, 1938.

Alfoldy, Sandra. *Crafting Identity: The Development of Professional Fine Craft.* Montreal and Kingston: McGill-Queen's University Press, 2005.

– "Eleanor Milne: The Making of an Artist in Canada." Virtual Museum of Canada. http://epe.lac-bac.gc.ca/100/205/301/ic/cdc/milne/essay.html (accessed 26 February 2009).

– "Struggles for Recognition: Canada's Textile Pioneers." In Melanie Egan et al, eds. *Crafting New Traditions: Canadian Innovators and Influences.* Gatineau: Canadian Museum of Civilization and Harbourfront Centre, 2008.

– "The Metaphysics of Craft: Anita Aarons's Crafts for Architecture." In Sandra Alfoldy and Janice Helland, eds. *Craft, Space and Interior Design, 1855–2005.* Hampshire and Burlington: Ashgate, 2008.

– "Suzanne Swannie: Shifting Ground." Exhibition catalogue. MSVU Art Gallery, 23 October–12 December 2004.

Alfoldy, Sandra and Rachel Gotlieb, eds. *On the Table: 100 Years of Functional Ceramics in Canada.* Toronto: Gardiner Museum, 2007.

Anderson, Benedict. *Imagined Communities.* London and New York: Verso, 1983, 1991.

Anderson-Dolcini, Catherine. *One-Percent for Whom? Canada's Public Works Fine Art Programme, 1964–1978: Its Rise and Demise.* MA thesis, Carleton University, 2000.

Anderson, Mrs Virginia. Letter to the Honourable Jean-Eudes Dube [sic], 8 January 1974. LAC, Public Works Canada, Fine Art, RG 11, Box 83, 4440-01/43-1.

"The Architect Looks at Public Relations: A Guide for Provincial and Chapter Relations Committee Chairmen prepared by the Royal Architectural Institute of Canada," April 1960. LAC, RAIC, MG 28, 1239, vol. 18.

Anonymous. Letter Re: Federal Building at Antigonish, Nova Scotia, 4 March 1971. LAC, Public Works Canada, Fine Art, RG 11, 4440-A55/1.

"Art in Public Buildings." *Craftsman/L'Artisan,* vol. 5, no. 2 (1972).

Auther, Elissa. "The Decorative, Abstraction, and the Hierarchy of Art and Craft in the Art Criticism of Clement Greenberg." *Oxford Art Journal,* vol. 27, no. 3 (2004).

"Background on Haida." LAC, Public Works Canada, Fine Art, RG 11, 4440-01/43-14, box 83, file no. 602-717-2.

Barr, Alfred H. "Preface." Herbert Bayer, Walter Gropius, and Ise Gropius, eds. *Bauhaus 1919–1928.* New York: Museum of Modern Art, 1938, 1975.

Beesley, Philip. "Hiving Mesh." In *Hiving Mesh.* Halifax: Saint Mary's University Art Gallery, 2000.

– et al., eds. *Responsive Architectures: Subtle Technologies.* Toronto: Riverside Architectural Press, 2006.

– and Sean Hanna. "Lighter: A Transformed Architecture." In Matilda McQuaid, ed. *Extreme Textiles: Designing for High Performance.* New York: Princeton Architectural Press, 2005.

Beiks, Rita, ed. *Land, Sea, Sky: Art at YVR.* Vancouver: YVR Art Foundation, 2003.

– Personal interview. Vancouver, British Columbia 9 June 2004.

Blais, Myriam. "The Meaning of Techniques and Materials." In Gloria Hickey, ed. *Common Ground: Contemporary Craft, Architecture and the Decorative Arts.* Hull: Canadian Museum of Civilization, 1999.

Bornstein, Eli. "Foreword." *The Structurist,* vol. 1, no. 2 (1961–62).

Bouchard-Bonet, Huguette. *Jordi Bonet.* Montreal: Éditions Marcel Broquet, 1986.

Bourdieu, Pierre. *The Field of Cultural Production.* Randal Johnson, ed. New York: Columbia University Press, 1993.

Boyanoski, Christine. *Loring and Wyle, Sculptors' Legacy.* Toronto: Art Gallery of Toronto, 1987.

Brolin, Brent C. *Architectural Ornament: Banishment and Return*. New York and London: W.W. Norton, 2000.

Brown, Bruce. Letter to Fred Price, 25 November 1964. LAC, RAIC fonds, MG 28, 139, vol. 19, file 19.5.

Bruno, Guiliana. *Public Intimacy: Architecture and the Visual Arts*. Cambridge, Massachusetts: MIT Press, 2007.

Buchanan, Donald. "Design in Industry – A Misnomer." *Canadian Art*, vol. 2, no. 5 (summer 1945).

Buis, Alena M. "The Practical Side of Decorating: Paul-Émile Borduas at the École du Meuble." *Metro Borduas*, www.metroborduas. concordia.ca/html/papersok/alena.htm (accessed 17 February 2010).

Burk, Adrienne L. "Beneath and Before: Continuums of Publicness in Public Art." *Social and Cultural Geography*, vol. 7, no. 6 (December 2006).

Calgary Allied Art Foundation. http://www.caafonline.org/collect.html (accessed 18 February 2009).

Canadian Craft Council 1974 Report. LAC, Canadian Crafts Council/World Crafts Council, MG 28I274, vol. 34.

Carver, Humphrey Carver. "Home-Made Thoughts on Handicrafts." *Canadian Forum* (March 1940).

Cavell, Richard. "Where is Frye? Or, Theorizing Postcolonial Space." *Essays on Canadian Writing*, issue 56 (fall 1995).

Charles, Susan. "Fine Craft Art." In Mary E. Black Gallery. *Land, Sea and Memory: Laurie Swim*. Halifax: Mary E. Black Gallery, 23 July–4 September 2010.

Chinnery, Rachelle. "Significant Material: Ceramics of British Columbia 1945–1960." Alan C. Elder and Ian M. Thom, eds. *A Modern Life: Art and Design in British Columbia 1945–1960*. Vancouver: Vancouver Art Gallery and Arsenal Pulp Press, 2004.

City of Vancouver. "Public Art." http://vancouver.ca/commsvcs/cultural/ publicart/index.htm

Clairoux, Benoît (translated by Matthew McLauchlin). "Works of Art in the Montreal Metro." http://www.metrodemontreal.com/ history/art/index.html

Collet, Carole. "The Next Textile Revolution." In Sarah Bonnemaison and Christine Macy, eds. *Responsive Textile Environments*. Halifax: TUNS Press, 2007.

Collier, Allan. "Design in Western Canada." In Robert Stacey, ed. *Achieving the Modern: Canadian Abstract Painting and Design in the 1950s*. Winnipeg: Winnipeg Art Gallery, 1993.

Collins, Peter. *Concrete: The Vision of a New Architecture*. Montreal and Kingston: McGill-Queen's University Press, 2004.

"Concert Hall by Arthur Erickson." *Concrete Quarterly*, vol. 137 (April–June 1983).

Cope, Karin. "Becoming Animal, Becoming Others in Art and Literature." Public lecture, NSCAD University, 28 January 2010.

Crawford, Gail. *Studio Ceramics in Canada*. Fredericton: Goose Lane Editions in association with the Gardiner Museum, 2005.

Crook, Tom. "Craft and the Dialogics of Modernity: The Arts and Crafts Movement in Late-Victorian and Edwardian England." *The Journal of Modern Craft*, vol. 2, no. 1 (March 2009).

Currell, Harvey. "Indian Craftsmen are Skilled Carvers." *The Telegram* (23 November 1966).

Danto, Arthur. "Visionary Ceramics." *American Ceramics*, vol. 15, no. 2 (October 2007).

Davey, Peter. *Arts and Crafts Architecture*. London: Phaidon, 1997.

De Roussan, Jacques. *Jordi Bonet*. LaPrairie, Quebec: Éditions Marcel Broquet, 1986.

Dickerson, Katharine. Personal interview, Halifax, Nova Scotia, 7 March 2005.

– Public lecture, NSCAD University, Halifax, Nova Scotia, 11 March 2005.

Diotte, Robert A. Letter to Mr Lloyd Crouse, MP. 18 August 1980. LAC, Public Works Canada, Fine Art, RG 11, 4440-06813, vol. 4, box 83.

Dorner, Alexander. "The Background of the Bauhaus." Herbert Bayer, Walter Gropius, and Ise Gropius eds. *Bauhaus 1919-1928*. New York: Museum of Modern Art, 1938, 1975.

"Dubé Turns Opinion Hunter on Sculpture." *Ottawa Citizen* (1 March 1974).

Duffy, Helen. "Fibre Art in Canada." *Canada Mikrokosma: An Exhibition of Contemporary Canadian Tapestries*. Agnes Etherington Art Centre and the Barbican Centre for the Arts and Conferences, 1982.

Edinborough, Arnold. "Office Art, Canadian-style: It Helps Keep Civil ServantsCivil." *The Financial Post* (13 February 1971).

"Editorial: It Looks Great on the Outside." *The Listowel Banner* (24 February 1977). LAC, Public Works Canada, Fine Art, RG 11, 4440-L7/1-1.

"88 Blocks – Art on Main." http://buzzer.translink.ca/index.php/2009/01/main-street-public-art-program-has-its-official-launch/

Ellenwood, Ray. *Egregore: The Montreal Automatist Movement*. Montreal: Exile Editions, 1992.

Ellis, Robert. Official Descriptive and Illustrated Catalogue of the Great Exhibition of the Works of Industry of All Nations, vol. 2. London: William Clowes and Sons, 1851.

Epp, Carole. Musing About Mud. Blog Spot (19 October 2007). http://musingaboutmud.blogspot.com/2007_10_01_archive.html (accessed 16 February 2009).

Epp, Robert. Personal interview, Winnipeg, Manitoba, 14 May 2004.

Evans, Joan. "Introduction." John Ruskin. *The Lamp of Beauty: Writings on Art*. London: Phaidon, 1959, 1995.

"Expo a Storehouse of World's Treasure." *The Montreal Star*, 28 April 1967. Prince Edward Island Archives, Moncreiff Williamson Fonds, RG 44, S.2, box 25, Canadian Guild of Crafts file.

Falk, Gathie. Letter to Mr W. Durdin, Director of Central Services Division, Department of External Affairs, 28 November 1973. LAC, Public Works Canada, Fine Art, RG 11, 4440-01/43-1, vol. 3.

Ferem Real Estate. Letter to Public Works Minister, no date. LAC, Public Works Canada, Fine Art, RG 11, 4440-01/43-14, box 83, file no. 602-717-2.

Flaman, Bernard. "Public Art and Canadian Cultural Policy: The Airports." In Annie Gérin and James S. McLean, eds., *Public Art in Canada*. Toronto: University of Toronto Press, 2009.

F5F – Famous Five Foundation website. http://www.famous5.ca/frames_education_monuments.htm.

"Focus on Carole Sabiston." *Craftsman/L'Artisan*, vol. 6, no. 2 (1973).

Forrest, Neil. "Hiving Mesh." In Sandra Alfoldy ed. *Neocraft: Modernity and the Crafts*. Halifax: NSCAD University Press, 2007.

Fountain, Toni. "Doing Business with Artists in 1991." *The Guild 6: The Designer's Source of Artists and Artisans*. Madison, Wisconsin: Kraus Sikes Inc., 1991.

Frampton, Kenneth. *Patkau Architects*. New York: Monacelli Press, 2006.

Frank, Isabelle. "Gombrich, Perception and the Ordering of Ornament." Paper delivered at the College Art Association conference, 11 February 2010.

– ed. *The Theory of Decorative Art: An Anthology of European and American Writings 1750–1940*. New Haven, London: Yale University Press for the Bard Graduate Center for Studies in the Decorative Arts, 2000.

Freud, Sigmund. "Lecture 33: Femininity." *New Introductory Lectures on Psychoanalysis: The Complete Psychological Works of Sigmund Freud*. New York: W.W. Norton and Co, 1990.

Frye, Northrop. "The Narrative Tradition in English Canadian Poetry." Branko Gorjup, ed. *Northrop Frye, Mythologizing Canada: Essays on the Canadian Literary Imagination*. New York, Ottawa, Toronto: Legas, 1996.

Fulford, Robert. "Some Hard Truths about Public Art." *Toronto Daily Star*, 7 February 1967.

Gadamer, Hans-Georg. "The Ontological Foundation of the Occasional and the Decorative." Neil Leach, ed. *Rethinking Architecture*. London and New York: Routledge, 1997.

Gagnon, Francois-Marc. *Refus Global*. Montreal: Montreal Museum of Fine Arts and Art Gallery of Ontario, 1988.

Gannon, Shane. "The Popularity of Max Weber's 'The Protestant Work Ethic and the Spirit of Capitalism': An Analysis of Historical Trends and Scholarship." *Gateway: An Academic Journal on the Web* (winter 2002). http:grad.usask.ca/gateway/shanegannon_WeberPopularity.html (accessed 6 August 2008).

Gauvreau, Jean-Marie. *Nos intérieurs de demain*. Montreal: Librairie d'Action canadienne-française, 1929.

Gérin, Annie and James S. McLean, eds. *Public Art in Canada*. Toronto: University of Toronto Press, 2009.

Gombrich, E.H. *The Sense of Order: A Study in the Psychology of Decorative Art*. Ithaca, New York: Cornell University Press, 1979.

Gotlieb, Rachel. "Suzanne Swannie and Danish Modernism in Canada." In *Danish Modern: Suzanne Swannie Textil*. Halifax, Mount Saint Vincent University Art Gallery, 2008.

– *Thor Hansen: Crafting a Canadian Style*. Toronto: Textile Museum of Canada, 2005.

Greenberg, Clement. "The Status of Clay." Garth Clark, ed. *Ceramic Millennium*. Halifax, NSCAD Press, 2006.

Grants, Anita. *Selectivity, Interpretation and Application: The Influence of John Ruskin in Canada*. Concordia University, Doctoral Dissertation, 2006.

Gregson, Alan. Letter to Mr J.A.H. Makay, 13 September 1977. LAC, Public Works Canada, Fine Art, RG 11, 4440-H64/1.

Gregor, Helen Frances, "Tapestry in Canada." *The Rotarian* (April 1983), 41.

Gropius, Walter. "Manifesto of the Staatliche Bauhaus in Weimar." In Isabelle Frank. *The Theory of Decorative Art: An Anthology of European and American Writings 1750–1940*.

Hale, Jonathan. "Gottfried Semper's Primitive Hut as an Act of Self-Creation." *Architectural Research Quarterly*, vol. 9, no. 1 (2005), 45–9.

Hall, Stuart. *Representation: Cultural Representations and Signifying Practices*. London: Sage Publications and the Open University, 1997.

Hansen, Thor. "B-A's Canadiana Program: An Address by Thor Hansen." AO, box C26, MIII, file 3.

– "Hand-Wrought Happiness: An Address by Thor Hansen, Art Director, Public Relations Department, The British American Oil Company Limited." AO, box C26, MIII, file 3.

Harland, Joan and Ruth Stirk. *The History of Interior Decoration/Design at the University of Manitoba 1938-1997* (unpublished manuscript). Winnipeg: University of Manitoba, School of Architecture Library, 1998.

Harris, Lawren. "What the Public Wants." *Canadian Art*, vol. 12, no. 1 (autumn 1954), 9.

Harrison, Martin. "Church Decoration and Stained Glass." In Linda Parry, ed. *William Morris*. London: V&A Publications, 1996.

Harvey, Charles and Jon Press. "The Quest for a Life of Purpose: Morris before the Firm,

1834–1861." In Charles Harvey and Jon Press, eds. *William Morris: Design and Enterprise in Victorian Britain.* Manchester: Manchester University Press, 1991.

Haufschild, Lutz. "Inspired Light, Space Inspired Thoughts about Light in Architecture." Gloria Hickey, ed. *Common Ground: Contemporary Craft, Architecture and the Decorative Arts.* Hull: Canadian Museum of Civilization, 1999.

Hébert, Paul. Letter to Public Works Canada Regional Office, Halifax, 13 September 1977. LAC, Public Works Canada, Fine Art, RG 11, file 4440-C117/1.

Heidegger, Martin. "Building, Dwelling, Thinking." In Neil Leach, ed. *Rethinking Architecture.* London and New York: Routledge, 1997.

– "The Thing." Albert Hofstadter, trans. *Poetry, Language, Thought.* New York: Harper and Row Publishers, 1971.

Henaut, Dorothy Todd. "1967 – The Moment of Truth for Canadian Crafts." *Artscanada,* vol. 24, no. 104 (January 1967).

Hérin-Lajoie, Guy. Letter to K.C. Stanley, 23 October 1970. LAC, Public Works Canada, Fine Art, RG 11, 4440-F36/1-1.

Hickey, Gloria. "Introduction." Gloria Hickey ed. *Common Ground: Contemporary Craft, Architecture and the Decorative Arts.* Hull: Canadian Museum of Civilization, 1999.

Howell, Wayne Howell. "If It's Inoffensive, It's Got to Be Great Canadian Art." *Toronto Star* (5 October 1973).

Hung, Shu and Joseph Magliaro eds. *By Hand: The Use of Craft in Contemporary Culture.* New York: Princeton Architectural Press, 2007.

"Indians Spend Expo Cash to Tell of Poor Deal." *Globe and Mail* (7 April 1967).

Irwin, Kathleen and Rory MacDonald. *Sighting/citing/siting.* Regina: Canadian Plains Research Center, 2009.

Johnston, Ian. Personal interview. Nelson, British Columbia 9 July 2004.

Jones, Amelia, ed. *The Feminism and Visual Culture Reader.* London, New York: Routledge, 2001.

Jones, Owen. *The Grammar of Ornament.* New York: DK Publishing, 2001.

Kalman, Harold. *A History of Canadian Architecture.* Toronto: Oxford University Press, 1994.

– *A Concise History of Canadian Architecture.* Toronto: Oxford University Press, 2000.

Kimball, Elizabeth. "The Company of Young Craftsmen." *SW Magazine* (1 July 1967). AO, Ontario Crafts Council, Archives of Canadian Craft, MU5771, box 26, EH2-EJ.

Kirk, Sheila. *Philip Webb: Pioneer of Arts and Crafts Architecture.* Chichester: Wiley-Academy, 2005.

Kohr, Leopold. *The Breakdown of Nations.* New York: Rinehart and Co. Inc., 1957.

– *The Overdeveloped Nations: The Diseconomies of Scale.* New York: Schocken Books, 1978.

Krause, Elliott A. *Death of the Guilds: Professions, States, and the Advance of Capitalism.* New Haven and London: Yale University Press, 1996.

Kritzwiser, Kay. "Ottawa Showplace for Stunning Art but Many Work Provoke Hostility." *Globe and Mail* (24 November 1973).

Kubota, Nobuo. Letter to Mrs Donaghue, 11 June 1978. LAC, Department of Public Works, MG 28, I222, file 4440-C105/5.

Laing, Arthur. Letter to Allan MacEachen, 9 April 1971. LAC, Public Works Canada, Fine Art, RG 11, 4440-A55/1 Fine Art, Antigonish, Nova Scotia Government of Canada Building.

Lambert, Phyllis. *Mies in America.* Montreal, New York: Canadian Centre for Architecture and Whitney Museum of Art, Harry N. Abrams Publisher, 2001.

Lambton, Gunda. *Stealing the Show: Seven*

Women Artists in Canadian Public Art. Montreal and Kingston: McGill-Queen's University Press, 1994.

Landow, George P. "Ruskin and the tradition of ut pictura poesis." *Victorian Web*. http://www.victorianweb.org/authors/ruskin/a theories/1.1.html (accessed 15 February 2009).

Larsen, Jack Lenor. "The Personalization of Crafts." *The Guild 6: The Designer's Source of Artists and Artisans*. Madison, Wisconsin: Kraus Sikes Inc., 1991.

Laurence, Robin and Ian M. Thom, eds. *Gathie Falk*. Toronto: Douglas & McIntyre, 2000.

Le Corbusier. "The Decorative Arts of Today." In Isabelle Frank. *The Theory of Decorative Art: An Anthology of European and American Writings 1750–1940.*

– *Le Modulor and Other Buildings and Projects, 1944–1945*. New York, Paris: Fondation Le Corbusier, 1983.

Lerner, Loren R. and Mary F. Williamson. *Art and Architecture in Canada: A Bibliography and Guide to Literature*. Toronto: University of Toronto Press, 1991.

Lesser, Gloria. *École du Meuble 1930–1950: Interior Design and Decorative Art*. Montreal: Montreal Museum of Decorative Art, 1989.

Levitch, H.G. "Art at Queen's Park." Brochure (1968).

Lind, Jane. *Joyce Wieland*. Halifax, Toronto: James Lorimer and Co., 2001.

Lindgren, Charlotte. Personal interview. Halifax, Nova Scotia, 5 May 2004.

Loach, Judi. "Le Corbusier and the Creative Use of Mathematics." *The British Journal for the History of Science*, vol. 31, no. 109 (June 1998).

Loos, Adolf. "Ornament and Crime." In Bernie Miller and Melony Ward, eds. *Crime and Ornament: The Arts and Popular Culture in the Shadow of Adolf Loos*. Toronto: YYZ Books, 2006.

Lord, George W. Letter to R. Schofield Morris,

11 March 1953. LAC, RAIC fonds, MG 28, 1239, vol. 19, file 3.

MacCarthy, Fiona. "Art for the People: William Morris, Burne-Jones and the Politics of Art." *Journal of Stained Glass*, vol. 31 (2007), 53–65.

MacDonald, Rory. Telephone Interview. 18 February 2009.

MacKay-Lyons, Brian. Personal interview. Halifax, Nova Scotia, 23 August 2004.

Massey College History. http://www.utoronto.ca/Massey/history/html (accessed 19 June 2009).

Mathur, Saloni. "Redefining the Ethnographic Object: An Anthropology Museum Turns Fifty." *American Anthropologist*, vol. 102, no. 3 (September 2000).

Matthews, Lydia. "Homespun Ideas: Reinterpreting Craft in Contemporary Culture." *Practice Makes Perfect: Bay Area Conceptual Craft*. San Francisco: Southern Exposure, 2005.

McIlveen, Eli. "Art on the TTC." Transit Toronto, http://transit.toronto.on.ca/spare/0008.shtml

McKay, Sherry. "The Object of Living: *Western Homes and Living*." Alan C. Elder and Ian M. Thom, eds. *A Modern Life: Art and Design in British Columbia 1945–1960*. Vancouver: Vancouver Art Gallery and Arsenal Pulp Press, 2004.

McMaster, Gerald R. "Tenuous Lines of Descent: Indian Arts and Crafts of the Reservation Period." *Canadian Journal of Native Studies*, vol. 9, no. 2 (1989).

McLeod, Ellen Easton. *In Good Hands: The Women of the Canadian Handicrafts Guild*. Montreal and Kingston: Carleton University Press by McGill-Queen's University Press, 1999.

Memo, 5 May 1976. Fine Art Liaison Officer Pacific Region to M. Pinney, Chief Fine Art Program. LAC, Public Works Canada, Fine Art, RG 11, 4440-C63/1.

Memo RAIC Executive Offices. "Next Award of Allied Arts Medal," 15 December 1953. LAC, RAIC fonds, MG 28, 1239, vol. 19, file 3.

The Memorial Album of the First Category Universal and International Exhibition Held in Montreal from 27 April to 29 October 1967. Toronto: Thomas Nelson and Sons, 1968.

Metcalf, Bruce. "Replacing the Myth of Modernism." Sandra Alfoldy, ed. *Neocraft: Modernity and the Crafts*. Halifax, NSCAD Press, 2007.

Milgram, Lynne. "Foreward." *Helen Frances Gregor: Textiles in Architecture*. Textile Museum of Canada, 7 April 1990–1 July 1990.

Milne, Eleanor. Personal interview, Ottawa, Ontario, 1 October 1998.

– Personal interview, Ottawa, 29 October 1998.

– Personal interview, Ottawa, 19 November 1998.

Minutes of Executive Committee Meeting (14 February 1959). LAC, RAIC fonds, MG 28, 1239, vol. 19, file 3.

Mitchell, W.J.T. "Utopia and Critique." In W.J.T. Mitchell, ed. *Art and the Public Sphere*. Chicago, London: University of Chicago Press, 1992.

Moore, Oliver. "Her Quilts are no Mere Patchwork." *Globe and Mail* (11 August 2010): R2.

Morris, R. Schofield. Letter to Armand Filion, 7 April 1953. LAC, RAIC fonds, MG 28, 1239, vol. 19, file 3.

Morris, William. "The Arts and Crafts of Today." In Isabelle Frank, ed. *The Theory of Decorative Art: An Anthology of European and American Writings 1750–1940*.

"The Revival of Handicraft." In Isabelle Frank, ed. *The Theory of the Decorative Arts: An Anthology of European and American Writings, 1750–1940*.

Morton, Patricia. "The Social and the Poetic: Feminist Practices in Architecture, 1997–2000." In Amelia Jones, ed. *The Feminism and Visual Culture Reader*. London, New York: Routledge, 2001.

Murray, Robert. Letter to Mr K.C. Stanley, 13 March 1974. LAC, Public Works Canada, Fine Art, RG 11, 4440-01/43-1, Lester B. Pearson Building, vol. 4.

"Museum Sculptor on Strike." *The Daily Colonist* (28 May 1968). Royal BC Museum British Columbia Archives, GR 999. Department of Public Works, box 1, file 9, Advisory Committee on Applied Arts, BC Museum and Archives Misc. Correspondence and Memos re: Nootka Whalers Sculpture, 1967–1969.

"Mural in the Foyer of the New British American Oil Office." *Canadian Art*, vol. 18, no. 1. (Jan./Feb. 1961): 56.

Negrin, Llewellyn Negrin. "Ornament and the Feminine." *Feminist Theory*, vol. 7, no. 2 (2006).

Nelson, James. "Ottawa is Seething." *The Whig Standard* (29 September 1973).

Newhouse, David R., Cora J. Voyager, and Dan Beavon. *Hidden in Plain Sight: Contributions of Aboriginal Peoples to Canadian Identity and Culture*. Toronto: University of Toronto Press, 2005.

Osborne, Richard and Borin Van Loon. *Introducing Sociology*. New York: Totem Books, 1999.

Ostrowitz, Judith. *Privileging the Past: Reconstructing History in Northwest Coast Art. Vancouver*. Vancouver: UBC Press, 1999.

Parr, Joy. *Domestic Goods: The Material, The Moral and the Economic in the Postwar Years*. Toronto, London: University of Toronto Press, 1999.

Payce, Greg. Public lecture, Visiting Artist Lecture Series, NSCAD University, 2 March 2004.

Pereboom, Bert. "Profile and Development Strategy for Craft in Canada." (2003) http://www.canadiancraftsfederation.ca/html/advocate_ccf.html (accessed 20 January, 2011)

Perry, Art. "Gathie Falk and Richard Prince." *Vanguard*, vol. 8, no. 9 (November 1979).

Pevsner, Nikolaus. *The Sources of Modern Architecture and Design*. London: Thames and Hudson, 1968, 1989.

Phillips, Ruth B. "'New and Yet Old': Aboriginality and Appropriation in Canadian Ceramics." In Sandra Alfoldy and Rachel Gotlieb, eds. *On the Table: 100 Years of Functional Ceramics in Canada*. Toronto: Gardiner Museum, 2007.

– *Trading Identities: The Souvenir in Native North American Art from the Northeast, 1700–1900*. Seattle, London, Montreal, and Kingston: University of Washington Press and McGill-Queen's University Press, 1998.

Plested, Lee. *From Our Land: The Expo '67 Canadian Craft Collection*. Charlottetown: Confederation Centre Art Gallery, 2004.

Polson, Dominik. "Fine Art Proposal, Transport Canada Training Institute, Cornwall, Ontario, 1977." LAC, Public Works Canada, Fine Art, RG 11, 4440-C105/5, box 78.

Press, Mike. "Handmade Futures: The Emerging Role of Craft Knowledge in Our Digital Culture." Sandra Alfoldy, ed. *Neocraft: Modernity and the Crafts*. Halifax: NSCAD Press, 2007.

"Public Relations Objectives of RAIC," 30 August 1959. LAC, RAIC, MG 28, 1239, vol. 18.

Pugin, A. Welby. "On Metalwork." In Isabelle Frank, ed. *The Theory of the Decorative Arts: An Anthology of European and American Writings, 1750–1940*.

Pugliese, Olga Zorzi. "Beautifying the City: 1960s Artistic Mosaics by Italian Canadians in Toronto." *Quaderni d'Italianistica*, vol. 28, no. 1 (2007).

Raven, Arlene. W.J.T. Mitchell, ed. *Art and the Public Sphere*. Chicago, London: University of Chicago Press, 1992.

Reed, Christopher, ed. *Not at Home: The Suppression of Domesticity in Modern Art and Architecture*. London: Thames and Hudson, 1996.

Reid, Bill (William Ronald). "The Jade Canoe: A Poem." Rita Beiks, ed. *Land, Sea, Sky: Art at YVR*. Vancouver: YVR Art Foundation, 2003.

Rensselaer, W. Lee. *Ut Pictura Poesis: The Humanistic Theory of Painting*. New York: Norton, 1967.

Risatti, Howard. *A Theory of Craft: Function and Aesthetic Expression*. Chapel Hill: University of North Carolina Press, 2007.

Robert, Guy. *Jordi Bonet*. Sainte-Adèle: Éditions du Songe, 1975.

Royal Architectural Institute of Canada. "The Architect Looks at Public Relations" (April 1960). LAC, RAIC fonds, MG 28, 1239, vol. 18, file 18.1.

RAIC Executive Offices Memo. "Next Award of Allied Arts Medal," 15 December 1953. LAC, RAIC fonds, MG 28, 1239, vol. 19, file 3.

RAIC minutes (19 January 1953). LAC, RAIC fonds, MG 28, 1239, vol. 19, file 3.

RAIC Press Release No. 53–104. "Architects Helping the Allied Arts." (20 April 1953). LAC, RAIC fonds, MG 28, 1239, vol. 19, file 3.

RAIC Press Release No. 54-205. "Allied Arts Medal." (28 April 1954). LAC, RAIC fonds, MG 28, 1239, vol. 19, file 3.

"Rich Colors Tell of Canada as Business Firm Turns to Art." *Vancouver Sun*, 18 June 1954. AO, box C26, M111, file 3.

Risatti, Howard. *A Theory of Craft: Function and Aesthetic Expression*. Chapel Hill: University of North Carolina Press, 2007.

"Robert Davidson." http://www.nativeonline.com/davidson.htm (accessed 20 June 2009).

Robert, Guy. *Jordi Bonet*. Sainte-Adèle: Éditions du Songe, 1975.

Robertson, Paul. "Federal Buildings Galleries, of a Sort." *Edmonton Journal* (27 May 1974).

LAC, Public Works Canada, Fine Art, RG 11, 4440-H70/I. DPW Press Clipping.

Roberts, John. *The Intangibilities of Form: Skill and Deskilling in Art After the Readymade.* London, New York: Verso, 2007.

Rogatnick, W., Ian M. Thom, and Adele Weder. *B.C. Binning.* Vancouver: Douglas & McIntyre, 2006.

Rousseau-Vermette, Mariette. Personal interview. Ste Adèle, Quebec, 29 April 2005.

RPS Cultural Property Inventory, "No. 1 Northern," 1998. File viewed in Public Works Canada offices, Halifax, Nova Scotia, 21 July 2003.

Ruskin, John. *A Joy for Ever.* London, New York: Routledge, 1994.

"Modern Manufacture and Design, Lecture III." In Isabelle Frank, ed. *The Theory of Decorative Art: An Anthology of European and American Writings 1750–1940.*

– *On Art and Life.* London: Penguin Books, 1853, 2004.

– *The History of Venice: Written for the Help of the Few Travellers Who Still Care for her Monuments.* Sunnyside, Kent: George Allen, 1877.

– *The Lamp of Beauty: Writings on Art.* London: Phaidon Press, 1995.

Sabiston, Carole. Personal interview, 7 June 2004. Victoria, British Columbia.

Selig, Warren. Quoted in Vicki Halpern and Diane Douglas, eds. *Choosing Craft: A History Told by Artists.* Raleigh: North Carolina University Press, 2009.

Semper, Gottfried. "Introduction to Style in the Technical and Tectonic Arts." In Isabelle Frank, *The Theory of the Decorative Arts: An Anthology of European and American Writings, 1750–1940.*

– "The Theory of Technique. Introduction to Style in the Technical and Tectonic Arts." In Isabelle Frank, *The Theory of the Decorative Arts: An Anthology of European and American Writings, 1750–1940.*

Sennett, Richard. *The Craftsman.* New Haven: Yale University Press, 2008.

Sincennes, L.G. Letter to Mrs Pat Gee, 18 April 1974. LAC, Public Works Canada, Fine Art, RG 11, 4440-S165/1-1.

Sleep, Joseph. Letter to Advisory Committee, Clementsport Post Office, no date. LAC, Public Works Canada, Fine Art, RG 11, file 4440-C117/1.

Smith, Thomas Gordon. *Vitruvius on Architecture.* New York: Monacelli Press, 2003.

"Spacing – Toronto Subway Buttons." at http://spacing.ca/buttons.htm

Sparke, Penny. "Introduction." Susie McKellar and Penny Sparke, eds. *Interior Design and Identity.* Manchester: Manchester University Press, 2004.

"The Standard Form of Agreement Between The Department of Public Works and Artists." LAC, Government Organizations: Public Works, 1967-1973, MG 28, I222, vol. 16.

Stanley, Timothy J. "Creating the 'Space' for Civic Dialogue." *Phi Delta Kappan*, vol. 85, no. 1 (spring 2003).

Stewart, Hilary. *Looking at Totem Poles.* Seattle: University of Washington Press, 2003.

– *Robert Davidson: Haida Printmaker.* Vancouver: Douglas & McIntyre, 1979.

Stowlow, Dr N. Letter to H.G. Cole, 5 October 1973. LAC, Public Works Canada, Fine Art, RG 11, 4440-01/43-1, vol. 3.

Sures, Jack. Telephone interview, 29 June 2004.

Swannie, Suzanne. Personal interview, 29 August 2004, Halifax, Nova Scotia.

"Terms of Reference for an Advisory Committee on Fine Art Works for New Building Projects by the Department of Public Works," (10 April 1968). LAC, Government Organizations: Public Works, 1967–1973, MG 28, I222, vol. 16.

"The Royal Architectural Institute of Canada: The RAIC Today," rough draft of paper. LAC, RAIC, MG 28 1239, vol. 18.

Thomas, Lionel. Letter to Mr A.E. Webb, 16 August 1965. Royal BC Museum British Columbia Archives, GR 999. Department of Public Works, box 1, file 5. Advisory Committee on Applied Arts, BC Museum and Archives Minutes and Memos, 1965.

– Letter to F. Peter, 22 December 1965. Royal BC Museum British Columbia Archives, GR 999. Department of Public Works, box 1, file 5. Advisory Committee on Applied Arts, BC Museum and Archives Minutes and Memos, 1965.

Tiwari, Deborah. "Canada Remembers Stone Carving Nears Completion." *Ensemble* (August/September 1995).

Topping, David. "69 Days on the TTC." *Torontoist*. http://torontoist.com/2006/09/69.php

Trilling, James Trilling. *The Language of Ornament*. London: Thames and Hudson, 2001.

Trottier, Gerald. Letter to Mr Fowler, 23 March 1967. LAC, RAIC fonds, MG 28, 1239, vol. 19, file 19.5.

Van Schendel, Michel. "Refus Global, or the Formula and History." *Yale French Studies*, no. 65 (1983).

Vastokas, Joan M. "Architecture as Cultural Expression." *Artscanada*, issue 208/209 (October/November 1976).

Venturi, Robert. *Complexity and Contradiction in Architecture*. New York: Museum of Modern Art, 1966, 1977.

Vetter, Lisa Pace. *"Women's Work" as Political Art: Weaving and Dialectical Politics in Homer, Aristophanes and Plato*. Lanham, Maryland: Lexington Books, 2005.

Vollmer, John E. "Helen Frances Gregor: Textiles in Architecture." *Helen Frances Gregor: Textiles in Architecture*. Textile Museum of Canada, 7 April 1990–1 July 1990.

– *Tamara Jaworska Tapestries – Tapisseries*. Oakville, Ontario: Royal Canadian Academy and Mosaic Press, 1982.

von Goethe, Johann Wolfgang. "Art and Handicraft." In Isabelle Frank, ed. *The Theory of Decorative Art: An Anthology of European and American Writings 1750–1940*.

Wall, Sharon. "Totem Poles, Teepees, and Traditions: 'Playing Indian' at Ontario Summer Camps, 1920–1955." *Canadian Historical Review*, vol. 86, no. 3 (2005).

Way, Frederick J. "She Carves our History." *Star Weekly Toronto* (29 May 1965).

Webb, A.E. Letter to Lionel Thomas, 8 July 1965. Royal BC Museum British Columbia Archives, GR 999. Department of Public Works, box 1, file 5, Advisory Committee on Applied Arts, BC Museum and Archives Minutes and Memos, 1965.

– Letter to Mr P.P. Ochs, 4 June 1968. Royal BC Museum British Columbia Archives, GR 999, Department of Public Works, box 1, file 5, Advisory Committee on Applied Arts, BC Museum and Archives Minutes and Memos, 1965.

Webb, Aileen Osborn. Letter to Prime Minister Pierre Elliott Trudeau, 2 March 1970. LAC, Canadian Crafts Council/World Crafts Council, MG 28, 1274, vol. 34.

Weltge, Sigrid Wortmann. *Women's Work: Textile Art from the Bauhaus*. London: Thames and Hudson, 1983.

"Who Made That? A Question about Public (Textile) Art in Canada." *fibre quarterly*, vol. 3, no. 1 (winter 2007). http://www.velvethighway.com/winter07/whoMADEit.html

Wiens, Clifford. Letter to Maurice Holdham, 27 January 1971. LAC, RAIC fonds, MG 28, 1239, vol. 19, file 19.5.

Woods, Mary. *From Craft to Profession: The*

Practice of Architecture in Nineteenth-Century America. Berkeley, Los Angeles: University of California Press, 1999.

"Woven in Worb: Gottfried Semper's Odd Theories about Textiles and Building are Imaginatively Reinterpreted in Stainless Steel." *Architectural Review* (August 2004). http://findarticles.com/p/articles/mi_m3575/is_1290_216/ai_n6186274/?tag=content;col1

Wright, Frank Lloyd. "The Art and Craft of the Machine." In Isabelle Frank, ed. *The Theory of Decorative Art: An Anthology of European and American Writings 1750–1940.*

Wright, Janet. *Crown Assets: The Architecture of the Department of Public Works, 1867–1997.* Toronto: University of Toronto Press, 1997.

"Written in Stone: An Architectural Tour of the Canadian Museum of Civilization: Douglas Cardinal." http://www.civilization.ca/cmc/about-the-museum/building-and-galleries/written-in-stone/full-tour/douglas-cardinal (accessed 1 July 2009).

Zenewyck, Irena Anne. *Regionalism in the Face of Universality: West Coast Modernism as Architectural Landscape.* MA thesis, Simon Fraser University, 1989.